Approaches
to the Oriental Classics

Approaches
to the Oriental Classics

ASIAN LITERATURE AND THOUGHT

IN GENERAL EDUCATION

Edited by Wm. Theodore de Bary

COLUMBIA UNIVERSITY PRESS

NEW YORK AND LONDON

Proceedings of a conference held at Columbia University, September 12 and 13, 1958.

The Conference on Oriental Classics was made possible by a grant from the Carnegie Corporation of New York. That Corporation is not, however, the author, owner, publisher, or proprietor of this publication, and is not to be understood as approving by virtue of its grant any of the statements made or views expressed therein.

Distribution of this volume has been aided by the Asia Society and the U. S. National Commission for UNESCO.

Contents

Preface

When the first Colloquium on Oriental Books was held at Columbia College in the fall of 1948, there was an extraordinary sense of expectation and enthusiasm among the select group of undergraduates and their instructors. For the students, who had already gained an appreciation of some major works in the Western tradition through the established humanities sequence, this offered a new vista of the range of human creativity in literature and thought, a new chance to exercise the critical faculties which had been strengthened and sharpened by contact with the giants of the West. For the instructors it was no less of an adventure. As teachers long associated with the Western humanities program, they were aware that this experiment climaxed years of faculty discussion, reaching back into the 1930s. They knew of the long-standing hope that through some such course as this general education in Columbia College could embrace the Oriental traditions as well as the Western. They realized, too, how many difficulties remained to be surmounted in practice if the experiment were to prove a success.

Today, ten years later, there are new students and new teachers, but still the same excitement and sense of adventure in approaching the Oriental classics. To the humanities teacher there will be nothing remarkable in this. Classics or great books, whether of the East or West, are by definition ever new. They would not be with us now had not men in each new age found them meaningful and challenging. But the Oriental classics have a special advantage not shared by the great books of the West. The latter may be ever-new but never novelties. They will always have to struggle against the prejudice that classics, though perhaps containing a kind of perennial wisdom, could hardly offer anything fresh or original. Yet this is exactly why many students are attracted to the master-pieces of Oriental literature and thought. They come from a world that has just assumed a new importance in their eyes, while yet retaining, in the minds of some, the kind of romantic appeal which the East has always exerted because it was strange and seemingly mysterious.

In point of fact, of course, many of the greatest works from the East cannot be considered novelties at all in the Western world. Several hundred years have passed since the introduction to Europe in the seventeenth and eighteenth centuries of basic texts from the Confucian and Hindu traditions, and much earlier even than this the great Arab philosophers were known and respected by scho-lastics like St. Thomas Aquinas. Though it has only been with the passage of time and the expenditure of much scholarly effort that a more adequate rendering and understanding of the texts has become possible, the mere fact that works like the *Analects,* the Lao Tzu, the Upanishads, and the *Bhagavad Gītā* have been translated and retranslated into Western languages so many times, is evidence enough of the attention given them well before our own time. Added to this is the importance attached to these books by some of the most influential thinkers and writers of the recent past—by philosophers like Leibnitz, Emerson, Schopenhauer, and Nietszche, by poets and playwrights like Wordsworth, Yeats, Pound, Eliot, and Claudel, and by novelists like Tolstoy, Joyce, Rolland, Huxley, and so on.

It can hardly be argued that the influence of Oriental models has been decisive with such spokesmen of the modern West, or that a familiarity with the originals has become indispensable to an understanding of these writers and their works. Nor should it be argued that the prime value of an introduction to the Oriental classics derives, not from our need to understand these works for what they are in themselves, but from a desire to recognize in contemporary literature obscure allusions to the secret knowledge and symbols of the East. What is demonstrated, however, by this long and serious concern for the important productions of the major Asian civilizations, is that novelty or strangeness need not be looked upon today as the main inducements to the Western reader in approaching them. Rather we have reached the point, on the higher levels of intellectual and literary achievement, where the so-called "Oriental" classics can no longer be considered exclusively the heritage of the East—where, though it may be premature to speak of a "world" tradition, we may at least claim now as in some sense our own what was formerly viewed as the peculiar property of others.

From the educational point of view, this recent development presents us with a new problem and a new need. The classics of the Oriental world may not require any introduction to the West in general, but their very presence amongst us raises a question as to what place they should have in the liberal education which American colleges attempt to provide each new generation. If we are still justified in referring to these books as "Oriental," it is because their provenance is such as to present special problems in interpretation for even the educated reader. Understandably, then, American colleges have been slow to undertake a task of instruction which ordinary prudence suggested would take years of pedagogic preparation. In the past decade, however, there have been signs of an intense desire and vigorous effort on the part of liberal arts colleges to get on with this task. As is pointed out in one of the papers included in these proceedings, there are now in this country over six hundred organizations devoted to stimulating interest in and spreading knowledge of Asia. A significant number of these are active on the level of undergraduate education. This, together with the spontaneous interest that has sprung up among students all over the country, has led to a demand for courses on Asian civilizations which compels serious attention on the part of college faculties and administrators.

In Columbia College we have attempted to meet this need through a course modeled on the first year of Western Humanities. It involves the reading and discussion, in colloquium form, of great works of literature, philosophy, and religion from the Near East, India, China, and Japan. In addition to canonical works like the Qur'ān, the Upanishads, Shankara, the *Analects,* and so on, we take up a variety of plays, poetry, novels, and some art forms for which there is no exact counterpart in Western literature. Parallel to this and complementary to it is another course in Oriental Civilizations, dealing with the history, institutions, and general culture of China, Japan, India, and Pakistan. The basic principle in the Oriental Humanities, as distinguished from the Civilizations course, is that these individual works are not considered primarily for their historical importance, but for their intrinsic value to men in any place or time. This is not to say that historical factors can be dispensed with in an understanding of such texts, or that we would not prefer our Humanities students to take the Civilizations course along with it or even beforehand if possible. But it does commit us to the idea that certain products of the human mind are worth understanding and assimilating for what they are in themselves, for the human values they give expression to.

A question may still be raised, however, whether it is possible for college students to read and grasp thirty or forty of these Oriental classics in one year. It is a question which arises not only among those of us who conduct the final examinations in this course when confronted with the disappointing performance of some of our students, but also among those who feel that the cultural context of these works, their original languages and ways of thought, are so radically different from our own that a full understanding of them cannot be gotten by even the best students without prolonged and intensive study.

Now, leaving aside the problem of whether anyone, even the most thorough specialist, can ever be said fully to have understood any of these works, we must certainly admit that it is possible by more intensive study to get a better grasp of these books than the student gets in the Humanities course. Still, this is no reason for denying the great majority of students, who cannot afford such intensive study, that measure of benefit which derives from reading them at least once. If they have inquiring minds at all, they are going to attempt this anyhow, and those who are concerned that students not misunderstand these works should certainly try to provide them with an opportunity to make that first reading of the texts both a more appreciative and a more critical one. At Columbia we try to do this by taking them up in a colloquium discussion guided by two instructors, one a specialist in the literature dealt with and the other, when possible, a teacher drawn from another discipline whose background would be in the Western Humanities. The function of the latter is both to help the student relate what he learns to relevant aspects of the Western tradition, and to insure that the discussion is maintained on a general level, so that the specialist does not drag the conversation off into bypaths most familiar to him personally. There is also the incidental advantage of this arrangement that it introduces some of the rest of the faculty, as well as the students, to these books for the first time.

The Oriental Humanities course is offered as an elective to juniors and seniors who have already completed the required general education course in the first two years. Believing that Oriental studies for undergraduates should represent an extension or fulfillment of the student's liberal education, rather than an exotic alternative to it, we think it important that he should have a good grounding in Western civilization and thought before attempting what must inevitably be stranger and more difficult to comprehend in the Oriental traditions. And, as I think we have found almost invariably to be true, the student who has thus achieved a certain maturity of mind and judgment, will actually be in a better position to appreciate what is most profound in the Orient. Confucius and Mencius will be all the more meaningful to the man who knows Plato and Aristotle. The mystics of Islam, Hinduism, and Buddhism will be even more significant to the man who has read St. Augustine and Dante.

In sponsoring the conference on Oriental Classics in General Education, the Committee on Oriental Studies of Columbia College hoped to share with others the experience it has thus gained in teaching the Oriental humanities, and to take stock of what it was doing in the light of the needs and experiences of others. To serve its wider purposes this cooperative endeavor had to be predicated on a recognition that the purposes and requirements of education vary greatly from college to college, as do the resources available for the task. It was only natural, then, that the focus of the conference should have been the books themselves, rather than any particular method by which they had been introduced to students, whether at Columbia or elsewhere. Our only presumption was that those participating in the conference were concerned with general education in some form, and with the Oriental classics as fitting subjects for study by the liberally educated. Accordingly, our main topics of discussion were formulated as:

1. Oriental classics and the teaching of the humanities—the relation of the Oriental traditions to the purposes of education in the West and the place of the Oriental humanities in the college curriculum.

2. Some great books of the Oriental traditions—representative works from among those to which American undergraduates should be introduced or which merit a place among the books which any educated person ought to read. Works from the Near East and India were taken up in one session; those from China

and Japan in another. The papers and discussion took up two main questions: why certain books deserve to be read, and how they can best be presented to a Western audience.

3. Approaches to the teaching of the Oriental humanities in American education, including the experience and the problems of non-Orientalists in presenting these books to undergraduates either through "great books" courses or through courses in particular disciplines, such as philosophy, comparative literature, and religion, etc.

Given this general framework, I think two developments in the conference could almost have been predicted. The first were good-natured but heartfelt protests that such-and-such a work, "the greatest thing of its kind" in such-and-such a tradition, was not included among those to be discussed in the conference papers. If Chinese and Japanese poetry could be so honored, why not Persian? If the Confucian *Analects,* why not Lao Tzu or Mencius? The answer (and I think it was fully appreciated in advance even by those who could not restrain their enthusiasm for their favorite books) is that we put forth here only a few examples which would suggest the range and variety of Oriental classics available. The full list of such texts read in the Oriental Humanities course at Columbia College is, of course, much longer, and even it lacks certain titles for which a strong case could be made if more time were available.[1]

The second development which could have been expected was the general split among the delegates (and an almost even one) between the professional Orientalists on the one hand, and on the other, the liberal arts teachers who had some experience of general education work, but no special knowledge of Asia. There were few indeed who combined both area specialization and a familiarity with the teaching of great books. It was, however, precisely this situation which provided the *raison d'être* of the conference—a need to bring

[1] Translations from the Oriental classics, as prepared for the Columbia College program, are listed at the end of this volume.

together scholars and teachers of diverse backgrounds and disciplinary preparation, who would be unlikely in meetings of their own professional groups to get together for the discussion of an educational problem so many-sided as this. Quite apart from the exchanges which were possible in the conference sessions themselves, undoubtedly one of the chief values of the meetings was the opportunity they provided for many teachers to consult personally and informally with specialists in certain fields concerning their own individual problems.

The difference in approach between the so-called "specialists" and "nonspecialists" was reflected in several of the questions most warmly debated in the formal sessions themselves, both among the panelists and in comments from the floor. In the first day's discussions a point of view strongly put forth by those representing linguistic and philological disciplines, and most ardently championed by Dr. Hahn of Hunter College, was that the teaching of these classics should never be entrusted to persons unacquainted with the language of the original; in fact, only a teacher strongly motivated enough to acquaint himself with the original text, and therefore ready to submit to the discipline of language study, should qualify. Against this it was contended, perhaps with the greatest gusto by Dr. Burch of Tufts University, that in the understanding and appreciation of many of these works, a wide variety of disciplines—not only academic, but psychological and religious—had relevance; consequently, by the strictest standards the linguist himself might fall as far short as anyone else in fully qualifying for the task.

Closely related to this point was the question raised concerning the appropriateness of attempting to deal with such a large number and variety of Oriental texts in a single course. Dr. Irani of City College was inclined to doubt that important philosophical works, such as those of the Indian tradition, could be adequately handled except in a course devoted specifically and exclusively to Indian philosophy. From a somewhat different point of view Dr. Van Buitenen of Chicago contended that such texts should always be taught in direct conjunction with material presenting the social and cultural context, that is, in a course dealing with each civilization as a whole. His colleague, Dr. Mahdi, countered that all too often in such cases attention became focused on the social and cultural peculiarities of each situation, while the universal values of the work were overlooked. It thus became evident that the handling of Oriental classics in a humanities program almost inevitably brought to the fore issues which underlay the very basis of general education, and which would be resolved by each individual more in terms of his educational philosophy as a whole than in terms which related specifically to Oriental subject matter.

An equally basic difference in approach arose over the matter of translation in the second day's discussions. Professor Keene of Columbia was quick to assert that strictly literal translation ends in being no translation at all, and that, while the translator has an obligation to establish the meaning of the original and render it faithfully, he must never lose sight of the prime need for putting the translation into readable English. Professor Boodberg, of the University of California at Berkeley, represented probably the position furthest removed from this in his attack on the kind of "linguistic or cultural imperialism" which insists on converting foreign terms and concepts into the nearest Western equivalents, however rough or distorted they may be, rather than facing up to the need for creative translation which would realize the full potentialities of the English language and enrich it with new expressions coined to express concepts from other traditions. In this view the work of genuine translation in the West has just barely been begun.

It was unlikely, of course, that such issues could be fully dealt with in any single conference, but that some reexamination and modification of points of view took place was quite evident as the discussions proceeded. The final session, which dealt with the problems of the non-Orientalist in approaching and teaching the Asian classics, served further to sift out of these discussions a few practical recommendations as to the most immediate steps which could be taken to aid the smaller liberal arts colleges in particular:

1. Encourage the training of teachers who combined specialization in Oriental studies with at least some introduction to the methods of general education.

2. Assist non-Orientalists with experience in general education to obtain some background in Oriental studies either through internships at the larger graduate centers or through summer institutes.

3. Stimulate the production of improved translations, preferably in inexpensive editions, and of background studies or teaching aids (in the humanities, especially materials dealing with the structure of the original languages, literary genres, and the techniques of philosophic exposition).

4. Arrange further conferences which would enable teachers to consult with specialists who could direct them to the right materials for further study.

In conclusion it should be noted that much of the success of the conference can be assigned to the notable spirit of good-will and cooperation which prevailed among the delegates. This encouraged the serious and outspoken expression of differences of opinion, while at the same time it helped to narrow the areas of disagreement through a clarification of ideas and a sympathetic understanding of them. In this connection some mention should also be made of the great contribution to these sessions by the respective chairmen, W. Norman Brown of Pennsylvania, Edwin O. Reischauer of Harvard, and Hugh Borton of Haverford. They guided the discussions with great skill and judgment, and with a keen eye to achieving positive results.

Lastly I should like to make public my thanks to colleagues on the conference committee whose attention to the arrangements for the sessions contributed so much to the efficient, pleasurable, and profitable use of everyone's time: John T. Meskill, Eileen J. Boecklen, Ainslee T. Embree, Ichiro Shirato, and Ted Takaya.

WM. THEODORE DE BARY

Columbia College, November, 1958

Conference on
Oriental Classics in General Education

HELD AT COLUMBIA UNIVERSITY
SEPTEMBER 12 AND 13, 1958

PROGRAM
Friday, September 12
9:30 a.m.
Subject: Oriental Classics and the Teaching of the Humanities
Chairman: James Gutmann, Columbia University
Opening Remarks
Wm. Theodore de Bary, Columbia University
Welcome
Jacques Barzun, Dean of the Faculties and Provost of Columbia University
Papers
Great Books—East and West
Mark Van Doren, Columbia University
Education in a Multicultural World
Thomas Berry, Far Eastern Institute, Seton Hall
Panel Discussion
Lyman Bryson, Columbia Broadcasting System
Moses Hadas, Columbia University
Barry Ulanov, Barnard College

2:00–5:00 p.m.
Subject: Some Great Books of the Oriental Traditions: The Middle East and India
Chairman: W. Norman Brown, University of Pennsylvania

Papers
> The Qur'an
>> Arthur Jeffery, Columbia University
> Ibn Khaldun
>> Muhsin Mahdi, University of Chicago
> The Upanishads
>> George Burch, Tufts University
> Indian and Greek Epics
>> Robert Antoine, Xavier College, Calcutta
> Shakuntala
>> John D. Mitchell, New York City

Panel Discussion
>> George Artola, Baltimore
>> K. D. Irani, City College of New York
>> Maan Madina, Columbia University
>> J. A. B. Van Buitenen, University of Chicago
>> Royal W. Weiler, Columbia University
>> R. Bayly Winder, Princeton University

6:30 p.m.

Dinner
> Guests of Honor
>> John G. Palfrey, Dean of Columbia College
>> The Honorable Mr. Ahmed Bokhári, Under-Secretary of the United Nations, Former Ambassador Extraordinary and Plenipotentiary of Pakistan to the United Nations

Address
> Books and World Education
>> The Honorable Mr. Ahmed Bokhári

8:00 p.m.

Film
> *Aoi No Uye* A Japanese Nō play

Saturday, September 13
9:30 a.m.
Subject: Some Great Books of the Oriental Traditions: China and Japan
Chairman: Edwin O. Reischauer, Harvard University

Papers
    The Analects of Confucius
        Herman L. Sinaiko, University of Chicago
    The Lotus Sutra
        Wing-tsit Chan, Dartmouth College
    The Chinese Novel
        Yi-tse Mei Feuerwerker, Cambridge, Mass.
    The Tale of Genji
        Donald Keene, Columbia University
    Chinese and Japanese Poetry
        Kenneth Rexroth, San Francisco
Panel Discussion
        Peter A. Boodberg, University of California
        James I. Crump Jr., University of Michigan
        Charles MacSherry, Smith College
        Y. P. Mei, State University of Iowa
        Harold Shadick, Cornell University
        Chi-chen Wang, Columbia University
        Hellmut Wilhelm, University of Washington

        2:00–5:00 p.m.
        Subject: Approaches to the Teaching of the Oriental Humanities
        Chairman: Hugh Borton, Haverford College
Papers
    Asian Literature in Comparative Courses: Some Practical Problems
        G. L. Anderson, New York University
    Oriental Humanities and the Non-Orientalist
        Arthur Danto, Columbia University
Panel Discussion
        George K. Brady, University of Kentucky
        Yu-kuang Chu, Skidmore College
        Walter Langlois, Boston College
        Clark Marlor, Adelphi College

PART ONE

Oriental Classics and
the Teaching of the Humanities

JACQUES BARZUN

Opening Remarks

Professor de Bary, Ladies and Gentlemen:

I am very glad that Professor de Bary, in welcoming you, referred to Columbia College and to my association with it as a teacher, because in adding to his greeting the welcome of the University, I should like to stress the particular interest that Columbia College has taken from the beginning in the movement which brings us together today. As you doubtless know, it was Columbia College which, after World War I, set up a course called "Contemporary Civilization in the West"—a result of the exchange of ideas and of persons which World War I brought about.

But it did not take World War II to stimulate in the College itself an interest in the contemporary and ancient civilizations of the East. It was in the early 1930s that the late J. J. Coss, who had been one of the molders of the original, Western Contemporary Civilization course, began to campaign for a parallel Eastern course. Indeed, he traveled through the East in order to know a little better what he hoped to see systematically taught. I remember very well that being an open-handed man, he came back from his trip to India and Japan with a collection of neckties he had bought there, which he distributed to the young instructors, of whom I was one. That was an expression of his kindness, but it was also—as I see it now—a kind of campaign button for the idea he had in mind.

The second great force behind the program of Oriental studies in

Jacques Barzun is Dean of the Faculties and Provost of Columbia University.

the College was, of course, the Carnegie Corporation, which provided, first, the means for offering the courses in the Oriental Humanities, and then the subsidy to the Columbia University Press for the series of translations of oriental classics to which Professor de Bary has referred.

Now if one ever has to justify such activities as these to persons outside the College, or outside academic life, the reasons come readily, especially after World War II. Whether we like it or not, the two things we think alien to the life of the mind—war and trade—are in fact great civilizing agents, through the simple fact of mixing peoples. Hence after World War II it is not hard to make the ordinary citizen understand why we must learn more about the remainder of the world—and particularly the East. The "small world" argument is obvious, and perhaps on that account is losing its force, and when I hear it restated I like to add a second reason which seems to me important to establish in the minds of educated Americans today.

This second reason is that in pursuing and extending our studies of the Eastern classics and civilizations, we are but continuing an old Western tradition. When Mr. Lewis Mumford reviewed Toynbee's *Study of History,* he started out by a vague denunciation of all historians but Mr. Toynbee for being provincial, nationalistic, narrow-minded, and complacent about the West. That is a grave injustice to Western civilization. For it is the only civilization which has had an unlimited curiosity about other civilizations. Mr. Toynbee could not have written his book if thousands of scholars had not stacked the shelves full of books on the twenty-one civilizations that he elected to deal with.

In Western Europe, the conscious interest in the Far East goes back to the time of Marco Polo, and since then our informed curiosity has not flagged. Besides the Christian missionaries, it was agents of the English East India Company and of all other East India companies—that is, Western traders and soldiers and adventurers and scholars and diplomats—who brought back to their home lands the knowledge and the wisdom of the East. It is thanks to them that the lore and the books of Asia have at last created important disciplines. They are founded, not on self-centered parochialism, but on a desire which now seems to be spreading to the undergraduate and the man in the street. The amateur Orientalist is a familiar figure, for whom a growing body of literature, scholarly and popular, is being produced.

A third reason for encouraging the studies represented here takes us beyond the notion that public interest in academic subjects is all to the good. It is noticeable, I think, that more and more people who profess an interest in Eastern civilizations are using their knowledge to wage war against their own culture. The latest clubwoman's fad about Zen Buddhism, the interest of a good many of our literary men in the philosophies and religions of India, and similar phenomena of our intellectual life indicate a restlessness which must be painful to those who suffer from it, and is certainly so to those who watch. It springs, as it seems to me, from a deplorable dilettantism. Men who may have been stationed in Japan or Korea and want to go back there to live are not so much caught by a culture they thoroughly understand and love, as they are repelled by a Main Street in Iowa or upper New York state which is too familiar to be endured.

If I am right, this amateur exoticism is bad for the individual and for our civilization. And it follows that the task that you are all engaged upon, of spreading the full record—the whole panorama—of Eastern life, is the only antidote to the foolishness and the snobbery which are invariable concomitants of the discovery of new cultures. I can say this with all the more objectivity because I myself am not particularly caught by any Oriental civilization, except perhaps that of Japan. My good friend De Bary tells me that this shows my lack of daring and imagination. I am simply taking a first timid step through the one country that has Westernized itself more than any other. This is probably true, and it may lamentably expose the warped mind of a professional student of European culture.

But possessing this undeserved detachment, I give my redoubled blessing to your efforts, knowing that your aim of discovering the essential humanity in various civilizations will not distort your scholarly sense of differences. Your work is not to prove ours a better or a worse culture, but to awaken the perception to things that are like us because they are human and different from us again because they are human, culture being an endless manifestation of the fundamental human diversity.

MARK VAN DOREN

Great Books—East and West

My experience with students of the great books of the West yields the following generalizations:

1. It is unwise to begin by telling students of great books that they are difficult to understand without elaborate preparation, historical, philosophical, psychological, linguistic, or otherwise. No student will have this preparation, and such of it as the teacher offers him will be harder to absorb than the text of the books themselves, assuming that the books are really great—i.e., have commanded great audiences over great periods of time.

2. This means that the teacher should begin boldly with the text, minimizing its strangeness and penetrating as soon as he can to its human center. But this is not easy. It is easier to lecture about the time and place of the book, the culture that produced it, its reputation in its own country or religion, its difference from any Western book —in other words, its unintelligibility. The hard thing is to face it as a masterpiece and to help the student find out why it is a masterpiece. The job, that is to say, is critical; and since criticism is an art rather than a science, it is probable that not every teacher in the project will have mastered its procedures. The first and chief of these procedures is to read with an open and innocent mind the words that are there; to notice what happens to one's mind as one reads the words, page after page; and to render an honest account of the result.

Now it may be objected that the great books of the East are demon-

Mark Van Doren is Professor of English at Columbia University.

strably stranger than those of the West, and more in need of prelim-
inary elucidation. But it is well to remember the objection that was
raised against humanities courses when they were first proposed a
generation ago. It was said that Greek, Roman, and medieval ideas,
having ceased to be current among ordinary modern readers, could
never be restored to their original state without the kind of scholarly
experience which an undergraduate could not be expected to have.
The great books would be read superficially if they were read at all,
and their immense significance would be missed.

Such fears, I am convinced, were unfounded. No undergraduate
ever reads Plato's *Republic* perfectly; but I have never met a scholar
who did so either—and the better the scholar, the more generously
he will acknowledge this. There is no such thing as a perfect reading
of a great book; such a book is inexhaustible, and eludes its most
learned commentators. Its wisest commentators are interested in what
new readers of it say it means. New readers often see freshly and
naturally the obvious things in a masterpiece which long acquaintance may have staled for the expert. The obvious things are probably
the essential things, and any scholar is to be pitied whose labors have
kept him among the commentators rather than in the work itself. An
expert is too often one who reads about the book, and not the book
itself. He is professional in a sense that limits his understanding. He
might have profited by the more amateur exercise of reading, re-
reading, living with, living in, living for the book he claims to have
special knowledge of, so that its contents become a portion of his
own mind and imagination, and particulars of it become the very
folklore of his life.

It might be a good idea to begin a course in Oriental humanities
by reading, or at any rate listing, the great Eastern books which are
already well known in the West. The student may be surprised to
learn how many he knows at least by name. One Oriental book happens to be the best-known of all books in the West, namely, the Bible.
It is, of course, a Near-Eastern book, or at any rate the Old Testament
is; still, it is of the East, and most students will be little acquainted

with its actual contents. They will have all sorts of "ideas" about it, favorable or unfavorable, but that will be the extent of their acquaintance. My experience with a Columbia class which annually reads the narratives of the Old Testament is that every member of this class is astonished by what he finds. They do not all find the same thing, but what they do find strikes them freshly and forcibly, and I think they will never forget it.

Perhaps the second most famous Eastern book is the *Arabian Nights*—unless it is the *Rubaiyat* of Omar Khayyam. Well, here are Arabia and Persia—again, not the Far East, but certainly the East, and the student may be interested in the fact that the farthest books (that is books from the farthest East) are the least known.

What he will have heard of in Indian literature I can only conjecture: possibly the *Bhagavad Gītā*, if not the *Mahābhārata* from which it comes, or the *Rāmāyana,* the sister epic of ancient India; possibly, too, the *Shakuntala* of *Kālidāsa,* or *Black Marigolds* by Bilhana (an adaptation of this by E. Powys Mathers is the most popular item in my *Anthology of World Poetry,* along with the Chinese section).

Chinese poetry is probably the best-known Chinese literature among us, and the same may be true for Japanese poetry, particularly the *hokku.* Yet in recent years a good many Western readers have made the acquaintance of three great novels from those countries: *Dream of the Red Chamber, All Men Are Brothers,* and the *Tale of Genji.* All three, I should think, would be read in any such course as is contemplated here.

The student should be encouraged, but not pressed, to discover parallels in Western literature. The *Bhagavad Gītā* may remind him of Plato, *All Men Are Brothers* of Homer and Robin Hood, and *Dream of the Red Chamber* and the *Tale of Genji* of sundry authors from Shakespeare to Proust. Such discoveries, however, should not in my opinion be the goal of the course. That goal, rather, should be the best possible first reading of masterpieces whose reputations and stature indicate that they deserve any student's undivided attention.

No teacher of such a course will be, need be, or should be a specialist in all of the authors or volumes studied. Ideally he should resemble the student in his initial ignorance, although, of course, he should differ from him in age, experience, reading skill, and the power to express his reading—that is, to know what really interests him as he reads and to be able to say what this is. He will doubtless make mistakes, but the only mistake he should worry about making is the mistake of not being simple enough. The "gift to be simple" is the highest pedogogical gift, and nowhere will it ever be more needed.

Education in a Multicultural World

Important as it may be, our subject this morning, "Oriental Classics in General Education," is only one aspect of a much larger subject: How to provide an adequate educational program for a multicultural world. Formerly we educated within a single cultural tradition. Now we must educate for living and thinking in a world of many cultures.

It is a big change for us all, both teachers and students. As we embark upon this new program we should be very clear about what we are doing. Concerning the Asian world especially we should ask ourselves: What are the reasons for introducing Oriental studies into American education? What is the relation between the native culture of the student and the other traditions which he studies? Though we cannot here give complete answers to these questions we can make the following observations, hoping that further discussion will clarify the basic issues involved.

First, as scholars and teachers concerned with expanding the frontiers of knowledge we realize the importance of introducing Oriental studies into the college curriculum, because they open up for students new and important realms of scholarship which must, for the welfare of our society, be intensively and professionally cultivated in the future. As more students receive instruction in these courses, more will, we hope, pursue these studies later in a professional way. Without a first introduction such as they now receive, students cannot be aware

The Reverend Thomas Berry, C.P., Ph.D., teaches Asian history and religion at Seton Hall University.

of the possibilities offered by such a career, at least not early enough to begin thinking about it as a life's work. A certain number of students should even begin in college days those linguistic studies which are so necessary and which are best begun early in a person's career.

If this first reason applies to only a limited number of students, the second reason is of more general application, for it concerns the need for universal peace in these tense years of the mid-twentieth century. Political and cultural nationalism threatens us all with disaster. These studies, rightly directed, produce in our students a better world-understanding founded on transnational and transcultural human values. The world must be educated for peace on such foundations. These studies help to establish at least some important areas of understanding. This acquaintance with other peoples begun in the earliest years of study should be fostered throughout the entire educational program until it reaches its highest level in a study of the Oriental civilizations and Oriental classics in the college curriculum. Such widespread understanding of Oriental peoples and cultures by our educated citizens is demanded in a country where the conduct of international diplomacy is carried on by a government responsible to a popular electorate.

These practical ends we seek in our educational program, yet we state a reason in itself even more fundamental when we note that essentially we study the Oriental classics for the unique vision of reality we find there. The pursuit of wisdom in and for itself is the basic reason for the education of any human personality. This reason needs a certain emphasis, for we feel at times that we are being forced into these studies more in the practical quest for survival than we are entering upon them in the pure quest for learning. Pragmatic reasons do indeed justify the introduction of these classics into the educational program. Yet we will never do our best scholarship if only such reasons inspire our work. These other reasons exist and should be appreciated for their true value. There is no opposition between the two. The pragmatic and contemplative aspects of knowledge complete rather than cancel each other.

We can say of different cultures what we say of different ages. Each offers its finest intellectual and artistic accomplishments to the other. Each completes and perfects the others. As the classical age of the West offers our age inexhaustible treasures of wisdom, art, and literature, so the classical ages of other cultures offer us similar treasures, great and inexhaustible. This mutual exchange of cultural possessions is possible because of the complex course of world history from the neolithic to the present. Not merely one, but a number of civilizations have arisen in this period throughout the Eurasian world. The five which now dominate the greater part of mankind existed in sufficient isolation from each other for each to attain a distinctive perfection and to express itself in a classical literature. Each represents a unique phase in the development of man.

Now these cultures are brought fully into the presence of each other and the revelation of each to the other is begun. We see in each literary tradition an expression of reality that we could never have known if the world entire had been formed in a single cultural tradition. It is a better world as a whole and a better world for each culture that this larger complex of cultures exists.

The intellectual and cultural wealth brought together in this assembly of cultures is overwhelming. We have not yet fully adjusted to each other. Yet we are sufficiently acquainted with these world cultures and with our new range of thought to incorporate a study of these other traditions into our educational program, traditions that offer our students opportunity for a vastly expanded knowledge of the world of man.

Our success as teachers depends upon our ability to bring this knowledge within the competence of the student whose mind is still struggling toward its full development. This involves the selection of appropriate texts and provision for teaching staffs with sufficient training in this field.

Recent efforts, financed by foundation grants, directed by teams of specialists, supported by university officials, and entered into by capable and interested students have shown what can be accomplished if we use the means that are available. So long as such interest and ability are manifested we may hope for widespread success in this country in communicating this universal fund of knowledge to our students. Our Western sense of universalism demands that we perfect the existing programs and introduce others as soon as material, teachers, and students are available.

At this stage in history no civilization is satisfied with its own accomplishments. We experience a need for the new worlds of art and literature that lie beyond the cultural frontiers of any people. Our age is dominated by this will for universalism. Horizons have broadened. This attraction for an ever-widening vision is a normal thing, for learning originates in the quest for a universal wisdom. To turn aside from the Oriental world and its literary traditions would be to neglect many of the finest possessions of mankind. It would justly stir up resentment within the Oriental peoples who would feel this rejection as a personal affront. Moreover our own accomplishments will now suffer if they are not brought into contact with these other traditions of the Asian world.

A fourth reason for introducing these studies is founded in our obligation to respond to the Orient. Our students of the present and future generations must take part in the great conversation that is going on between the various cultures of East and West, and which in fact, has been going on, to a limited degree ever since Jesuits at the courts of the Indian Moguls and the Ming Emperors of China first made available to Western readers the classical writings of these two great Oriental civilizations. This conversation has been broadened considerably in our times and is of the greatest importance for the future of man in every phase of his existence. Conversations between the nations of the West, and between the present and the past within the West, have been most fruitful in their results. Yet these inter-Western conversations will in the future be neither so fruitful nor so necessary as this new intercultural conversation between the greatest and most distinctive divisions of mankind, the Oriental and the Western.

The Oriental countries have already introduced the study of Western culture into their educational program. They are far more proficient in Western languages than we are in theirs. Their scholastic interest has been largely in scientific and technical rather than in cultural studies. Yet they have learned much of our way of life in modern times and some have read well in our contemporary literature. Many of their educators have been trained in the West. There are now many more students from the Orient studying in the West than there are Western students studying in the East. In a way, this is an advantage for us. Yet if the Asian peoples learn about us, we must also learn about them. Otherwise we cannot carry on our part in the world conversation that is now so important.

Thus far, because of Western dominance in the world during the last few centuries, we have become more accustomed to speaking to the Asian peoples than listening to them. We take for granted that the conversation should take place in Western terminology, according to Western processes of reasoning, with a great many suppositions of which the West is generally unconscious, although the Orient is acutely aware of them. This is all quite understandable when we look at the amazing Western scientific and political and economic developments of the last few centuries which have been the dynamic factors producing our present world unity. Yet it is most necessary that we be willing to listen to Asia and to learn something of those profound spiritual, emotional, and aesthetic forces which govern their deepest thoughts and most instinctive reactions. When we have done this and when Asian scholars have given more attention to the spiritual formation of the Western world in its earlier centuries, then we will both be prepared to carry on this multicultural conversation with the highest benefits to all. This conversation must become more constant and more effective in coming generations. Our duty in America is to see that our students are trained to fulfill their part in this historic mission to which they are called. What the present generation has learned we must pass on without diminution to as many Western students as are capable of receiving this knowledge.

A fifth reason for introducing these studies into our educational program is that the spiritual content of these Asian cultural traditions joins with the spiritual traditions of the West in protesting against the secularism and scientism that threaten to ruin the more profoundly human elements of our own and all other cultures. If the development of the inductive sciences is a unique accomplishment of the West, development of certain human and spiritual realms of knowledge is common to all the world. The slightest acquaintance with any of the Asian literary traditions brings with it a new awareness of the spiritual foundations of human life and the efforts men have made to discipline and perfect man and human societies according to spiritual ideals. There is difficulty in ascertaining exactly wherein we agree and wherein we differ, but there is little difficulty in seeing throughout the literature of the Orient an instinctive judgment that the final truth of things and the final goal of man are not found in the visible world. This new sense of the spiritual conveyed to our civilization from the Orient offers a healing grace to a society which in recent times has grown inured to the spiritual content of its own traditions.

One thing that needs to be well understood in this expansion of the educational program is that Western culture is more immediate to the Western student and thus takes precedence in his education.

The circumstances of birth impose upon each human personality specific racial, linguistic, cultural, and political determinations. There is no single world society, no single world language, culture, or state. There is only the pluralist world of peoples, languages, cultures, and states. We enter into this pluralist world order not as multiracial, multilingual, multicultural, or multinational beings, but as members, first, of a single distinctive society. As there is no such thing as a tree that is simultaneously oak, pine, and cedar, so there is no such thing as a person who belongs equally to all peoples, languages, cultures, and nations. We are born into a specific society and obtain our cultural formation in accord with the norms of that society. Through this society we develop mentally and emotionally and make our contribution to the universal order of human life.

To condemn the particular element in the cultures of the world is implicitly to condemn all cultures and even all human development. Every human accomplishment reflects the particular cultural form of the society in which it was produced. When we strive after an ordered world of man we are not seeking to suppress the particular cultures in favor of some universal culture. We seek rather to perfect each in a multicultural world order, to make them simultaneously more distinctive in themselves and more united in the universal society of nations.

The human order is so rich in its racial, linguistic, cultural, and political expression that no one people or culture or state can carry the full splendor of man, just as no flower can carry the full splendor of the world of flowers. The fullness of wisdom cannot be carried exclusively by any one people or age or expressed in one language. Different literary and artistic talents are distributed throughout the world so that only the Chinese of the T'ang and Sung periods in China could produce the poetry and painting characteristic of those periods. Only the Japanese could produce the Nō drama of the medieval period or the block-prints of the Edo period. None but the Indian people could produce the Upanishadic speculations or the Vedānta philosophy. Only the Buddhist world could produce the philosophy of Vasubandhu. Only the Moslem world could produce the Taj Mahal or the Alhambra.

In the same way we could go through the classical languages of the world and show that the specific genius of the different languages enabled certain thoughts to attain expression that could not otherwise have been expressed with such perfection. The world of human thought would have been far less developed if Chuang Tzu had had only Greek and Plato had had only Chinese in which to express their thoughts, if Kālidāsa had had only Japanese and Seami had had only Sanskrit.

Because of this dispersion of talents and accomplishments in every order of human life, the societies of man complete and perfect each other. Languages, cultures, and states perfect each other as one color completes and perfects the others, as one tone of the scale completes the others and gives them new meaning, as the elm and willow and walnut and maple complete each other.

This world of man and his cultures is too big for us to be, in any absolute sense, universal men. We are forced by the physical order of things to conform to some specific human type. We are intellectually committed to some particular formation of mind. A person cannot have the analytical mentality of the Western scientist and the contemplative mentality of an Indian rishi. No Western painter could have done the work of Ma Yuan or that of Hokusai. To have simultaneously the mentality of Confucius, Yājñavalkya, Aristotle, and al-Ghazālī is unthinkable.

Those who wish to be universal men in this extreme sense, without special allegiance to any particular culture or nation, become formless individuals seeking to be at home everywhere, while in reality they are at home nowhere. They seek a universal culture. They end by having no culture.

On the other hand, a fully formed person of Western culture or a fully formed person of an Oriental culture is, for that very reason, at home in his native culture and at home in all other cultures. He is one whose existence has understandable significance. In and through this native culture he enters into the universal society of man and, with a trained largeness of mind, embraces all the cultural achievements of man.

When we introduce the Oriental classics into the educational program we do this as a perfection of the cultural pattern in which our educational program is founded. Our education is Western and remains Western. Its scope is universal, its form particular. Western knowledge of the Oriental world is all that is possible for us. It is a type of knowledge distinctive with ourselves. No matter how much we learn of the Orient our knowledge still keeps its original form. Even our most capable specialists, we could say, particularly our most capable specialists, manifest the Western character of their knowledge precisely when they search deepest into the spiritual and intellectual traditions of the Orient. Our study and education, then, is unicultural in form, multicultural in content.

If we keep this in mind we will have a clear concept of just what we are doing. We will also keep the cultural traditions of the world clear of all confusion. Cultural syncretism benefits no one. Each culture should develop in its own line of perfection. Red roses are more red in a garden where there are also white and yellow roses, and the garden is more attractive. We introduce the Oriental cultures into our educational program not to make the West less Occidental, but simultaneously more Occidental and more universal. Oriental peoples also should study Western culture not to make their own culture less Oriental, but more Oriental and more universal. Perfection of understanding does not mean dislocation of life. Communication of knowledge does not mean dissolution of cultural formation.

This personal allegiance of a people to their culture is based on the normal human response of man to that cultural synthesis from and within which he has received his human formation of mind and heart. It is also based on the realization that each particular culture is necessary. All have deviations that need to be corrected. Yet each has its part to play in the universal order of human affairs. Fidelity to the universal order of mankind demands fidelity to a person's own particular culture. The world is itself impoverished if we should neglect our own cultural heritage. We ourselves and all the world are impoverished if the Oriental peoples neglect their cultural traditions. The pieces of the mosaic must be preserved if the mosaic itself is to keep a meaningful pattern. As the colors in the stained glass of the medieval cathedrals, the special qualities of these cultures should be deepened and perfected by time.

Particular cultural formation is not opposed to universalism. It is rather a preparation for a proper universalism and a protection against a false universalism. The universal does not destroy the particular, the particular does not destroy the universal. Each exists in the other. So long as each culture is vigorous, it is able to share in a profound intercommunication. When all are flattened in a common negativism, none has anything to communicate.

It is completely false to think that the American student should, as some have suggested, be taught the Oriental cultures before he becomes "narrowed" and "corrupted" through study of his own culture. This supposes that acquaintance with one's own cultural tradition incapacitates a person for an objective appreciation of others. The opposite is much more correct. The best preparation for understanding the *Mahābhārata* and the *Rāmāyana* is a thorough reading of the *Iliad* and the *Odyssey*. The finest preparation for reading the Upanishads is to read Parmenides, Plato, Plotinus, and Augustine. An understanding of Socrates is excellent preparation for understanding Confucius, although these men were different in their personalities and in their work. The tragic drama of Greece prepares us for an understanding of the Nō drama of Japan.

In this way we could go through the cultural traditions of all the world and show how well we are prepared for understanding these other cultures by a thorough training in our own culture. We could also turn the thing around and show how well a person in any of the Oriental cultures is prepared for understanding Western culture by a thorough understanding of his own culture. This applies to every phase of the intellective, moral, and aesthetic orders. Education in one culture prepares us to understand all cultures. Knowledge of other cultures offers a fine perfection and deeper tone to our understanding of our own culture.

This again is a wonderful thing about our multicultural world. We understand each culture better when we study it both in itself and in its relation to the others. Basic outlines stand forth with greater clarity. We appreciate with greater precision the different modes of thought and expression, the different visions of reality presented in the literary and art traditions of the world. These differences derive ultimately from the different subjective experiences of reality had by the different peoples of the world. These differences are seen throughout the life and thought of the various societies and furnish us with that endless series of comparisons and contrasts that enable us to "place" each element in one culture in relation to corresponding elements in other cultures.

We understand China better once we have studied the Hindu and Moslem worlds. The emphasis on negative modes of knowing in the Hindu and Buddhist traditions contrasts with the positive analytical modes of Western knowing. The delicate mood, the *mystique,* of Chinese landscape painting contrasts with the naturalism of Western landscape painting. The lack of historical sense in India contrasts with the Chinese sense of history. The feeling of social unity in Japan is seen more vividly when compared with the Western feeling of independence and individuality. The nearness of the religious and philosophical traditions of Islam to those of the West is more striking when we see the difference between India and the West in their religious and philosophical traditions.

To see each culture in itself and in its relationship to other cultures, to see each in its place in the complete world pattern of cultures and in the historical development of man from earliest times to the present, to see all this and to understand how best to guide the dynamic changes of the present into a cooperative world order in which man attains the highest development of his intellective and spiritual faculties, that is the end we seek in these studies of the Oriental world. When a sufficient number of educated people from the Oriental and Western cultures attain this understanding and see the absolute need that we have of each other, then new forces for peace will make themselves known throughout the world.

After these remarks on the reasons for studying the Oriental cultures and about the place and function of these studies in our educational program, we conclude with an observation on hospitality as the fundamental virtue which provides the conditions in which a fruitful exchange can take place between cultures. When strange peoples and cultures meet there is a period, often an extended period, during which they associate without understanding each other fully. A way must be found for this association to continue while they do become more fully acquainted. Since neither is able to explain himself adequately to the other, misunderstandings are bound to occur. Since they differ in their ways of life, they tend to irritate each other. This can be an awkward moment in the meetings of persons and traditions. Thus men and cultures face each other. The deepest values and most profound commitments of one seem to be challenged by the other. At this moment everything depends on mutual confidence and hospitality.

It is significant that we find this virtue of hospitality as a central theme in the *Odyssey* of Homer, one of the earliest books of Western civilization. Zeus himself, the Supreme God known to the Greek world, watched over this law of hospitality and gave it divine sanction. In the first choral ode of the *Agamemnon* of Aeschylus we find that Zeus is mentioned as "the witness between guest and host." The meeting of men who come from the far corners of the earth to visit each other and to discuss the common concerns of man takes place under the heavenly protection of Providence and the earthly virtue of hospitality. In ancient times the betrayal of this virtue was considered a crime second only to that of blasphemy. In the *Divine Comedy* of Dante the betrayal of hospitality is punished in the ninth and deepest circle of the Inferno. Esteem for this virtue comes down from Homer and Aeschylus through the Roman, medieval, Renaissance, and modern times to the present. It has now a new and deepened significance, for the world has become so much more tense. This tension is as all-pervading as those international contacts which are now a constant in life.

At this time it is the scholars and students of the world, those dedicated to the higher quest for truth who must preserve calm and give to the political order a mode of hospitable association and of mutual

concern for each other, not for the sake of economic gain or of superior position in the world, but for the sake of the common welfare of
all mankind and of mutual advance in the vision of truth. Each
should be prepared for the joyful acceptance of those aspects of truth
perceived more clearly by the others, convinced that all truth, wherever found, is from the one Divine Truth and leads men home to the
more perfect vision of that same Truth.

Our present efforts to introduce the Oriental classics into our educational program should be characterized by the sense of hospitality
shown by St. Augustine in his study of Plotinus, by St. Thomas, who
learned so much from the Moslem commentators on Aristotle, by
Ricci and Leibnitz and Legge, who learned from the Confucian scholars of China, and by that long list of scholars who have made it their
life's work to provide channels of communication between the Oriental and Western worlds.

As Ulysses at the court of Alcinous was hospitably received, refreshed, and then asked to tell his story, so these literary works of the
East should be received into our society so that American students
may listen as they narrate the Odyssey of the Asian civilizations down
through the centuries. Their stories are no less fascinating.

On Exploiting the Greek Analogy

My own excuse for taking part in this conference is not that I had the temerity, a decade ago, to give a course in Eastern books in translation in Columbia College, but a conviction that my own discipline, of all those in the conventional curriculum, offers the closest analogy to the kind of work which we are met here to discuss, and hence that the experience of classical literature has special applicability here. After all, the literatures we are here concerned with differ from each other almost as much as any one of them does from the Greek. If their common denominator is that all derive from longitudes east of a certain line east of Greenwich, the Greek derives from an area not very far to the west of that point, and if their common denominator is that they derived from peoples who wore their shirttails out, so did the Greeks wear their shirttails out.

One way to summarize Mr. Van Doren's eloquent and salutary paper is to say that in teaching exotic literatures to undergraduates the amateur rather than professional approach must be followed. Let me take a moment to review the tension between the two, from the beginnings of organized higher education in the Western tradition.

The earliest institutions recognizably like our own colleges and universities were two founded in Athens early in the fourth century B.C. and associated with the names of Plato and Isocrates. Plato's system was specialist and exclusive. Only people specially trained could cobble shoes, or vote, or read a book, and only privileged per-

Moses Hadas is Jay Professor of Greek at Columbia University.

sons who enjoyed close association with the master could learn: in his Seventh Epistle Plato says that anyone who claimed he had learned his doctrine from books was lying. Isocrates believed that wisdom was contained in a body of literature, which was accessible, at various levels, to everyone. Plato's notions of specialization were developed into what was in effect a series of graduate institutes by Aristotle, and it was the Peripatetics who set the tone for Alexandrian learning. But something went out of life. In the old days any gentleman was expected to be able to accompany himself on an instrument, perform competently in the gymnasium, and know how to read a book: now he must be either a virtuoso, or a champion, or a philologian.

In the subsequent history of Europe it was the Isocratean tradition, happily, rather than the Platonic that prevailed—until the last century. It was then, possibly out of a need to emulate the exact sciences, that ancient books again became specimens for laboratory study and hence a preserve of specialists. The laboratory work which was done in Germany and elsewhere is enormously impressive, but there were two bad effects: the nonspecialists were robbed of their heritage, and the specialists lost sight of the ultimate objective of their labors. A professor began a course on the *Oedipus* by pointing out what a privilege it was to study that play: it contains more grammatical anomalies than any other in the Greek corpus.

It was after World War I that the ancient books began to be restored to the larger audience for which they were intended by the efforts of interested amateurs. We think at Columbia that the prime mover was John Erskine, but even here he met with resistance, and significantly from my own department. If my senior colleagues had not opposed him the humanities courses would have been introduced some years earlier than they in fact were.

It may not be amiss to tell the story of my own conversion. In the late 1920s I taught a course in Euripides in the original with four students, and one in Greek tragedy in translation with about twenty. At the end of the term I decided not to set the Greek students the usual sort of examination, for I had heard them perform daily, but to ask instead the questions on Euripides I was setting the English readers. I had not limited my exegesis to grammar and metrics, yet even so I found that the English readers had learned more, and more enduring things, than the Hellenists.

I do not for a moment suggest that we, you and I alike, should give up or slacken our technical work in favor of popularization. We find ourselves in the position of stewards of a precious legacy, and our first duty is to cultivate and propagate the store which has been put into our hands. But to do this we must not only raise up disciples who will be our own successors but also see that the benefits of the legacy reach all who might profit from them.

To what end? I shall not speak of wisdom and understanding, for Mr. Van Doren has done that far better than I can do, but of another factor which again involves the tension between professional and amateur that I spoke of minutes ago. Again I resort to antiquity for my example.

The most impressive material achievement of the Greeks, in my judgment, was their Hellenization of the Near East in the century after Alexander the Great. The only analogy for cultural imperialism on this scale that I think of is the spread of English culture in America; but whereas English settlers found a new country occupied by a scattering of aborigines the Greeks encountered the descendants of ancient civilizations from whom their own ancestors had learned, yet they so impressed the Easterners that the Easterners came to speak of themselves as barbarians.

How did they do it? Not by force of arms, for Alexander's little army might easily have become orientalized instead of the other way around. They did it by education. No handful of Greeks settled anywhere without at once building a school, and ruins of theaters are found in every place where Greeks settled, even in far-off Babylon.

But the interesting thing is the curriculum of the schools. They taught not the techniques which made them successful and which the natives so admired, but Homer and tragedy and Plato—authors as impractical and almost as remote to them as they are to us. It was the common possession of a body of literature that enabled the Greeks abroad to retain their identity and their unity and to spread their culture in *partibus infidelium* so as to create something like an *oikoumene,* and it was that same body of literature, through several transmutations, that directed the shaping of Europeanism.

If we are not conscious of the Greek origins of specific items in our cultural store and in our general outlook it is because they have been so thoroughly assimilated. Isocrates had said that Greek is to be defined not by race but by education, and by Isocrates' definition we are all Greeks. A man from Mars who wished to understand the intellectual conventions and aspirations of Western civilization could probably do so most economically by studying the seminal books of the Greeks.

If that is so, or nearly so, then the most economical path for achieving an understanding of the other civilizations on this earth is similarly through their literary classics. But the distance from East to West is no longer as great as the distance from Athens to Babylon, hardly more, in fact, than the distance from Athens to Corinth. Physically we have achieved the ancient ideal of an *oikoumene,* wherein all men might be members one of another. To realize the ideal we must know the Eastern classics as well as the Greek. Those who believe that the ideal is a worthy one will also believe that the business of these meetings is far more important than the business of the usual academic conference.

LYMAN BRYSON

Comments

I came to this conference with some apprehension, but the remarks just now made by Moses Hadas reassure me. It seemed so likely that again we would hear the ancient doctrine, advanced for centuries by high-minded and dedicated scholars like yourselves, the doctrine that the peace of the world and a new world culture can be created by bringing together the best books, the best ideas, and the best people of all cultures and finding in their friendship the solution for the mad hostilities of war. Dr. Hadas relieved my fears—as he has often done before—and I wish I could have said what he did, except for the fact that it will count for more from him than it could from me.

It surely is not necessary for me to recall to this group the fact that there was in Europe, during part of the Middle Ages, a transnational Latin culture which transcended national boundaries and was in fact the holding system for civilization. The best people or, at least, the best educated and most enlightened people, understood one another, but that could not prevent wars. In fact, as has been remarked by some modern students of politics, any "intellectual" must be careful not to betray to his countrymen that he does not share the prejudices against strangers which are so strong in ignorant people, making them the easy victims of war-mongering demagogues. The natural tendency of the scholar is to discount the small chauvinisms out of which international hostilities are built. This does not mean that transna-

Lyman Bryson, Professor Emeritus of Education at Teacher's College, Columbia University, is director of the CBS program, "Invitation to Learning."

tional ideals are easily arrived at, or that there are not real reasons for international hostilities. It does mean that intercultural exchange is not always and in itself an obstacle to war.

If a more modern instance is needed, we can look at France and Germany. Across their mutual boundaries has gone, for centuries, every kind of cultural exchange, books, pictures, music, traveling students, and scholars. Their wars have been incessant.

Because the facts of history warn us, we have to regard our efforts toward world culture skeptically for fear our own love of the great books and the great ideas will deceive us. This does not mean that interchange of cultural treasures cannot be the basis of friendship. It only means that this is not enough.

It means also, I think, that intercultural friendship is not the best reason for teaching the great classics of all the nations to the students of every nation. There is a better reason. We make finer, richer, broader human beings by enlarging their picture of the world and their ideas of humanity's scope. That is all the reason we need for teaching the Oriental classics to Western youth. If it serves also the more pragmatic reason, so much is gained, but let us be sure we found great enterprises on great motives. If peace does come, it will come because men will no longer accept violence as the judge of right.

We need also, I think, to look more closely at our teaching of the Western classics, our own classics, to our Western students. How can we hope to make the classics of other cultures mean anything to them when we fail to give them a lasting interest in the classics of the Occident? It is time now to realize that we have, for good reasons but not to a good result, developed a system of educating American men and women aesthetically, morally, and politically, for a world in which they will not spend their adult lives. After they get out of college, unless they become teachers and probably not even then, they are not likely to talk much at the family dinner table about Aeschylus or Marlowe. It would be wonderful if they did, but we are evidently not good enough teachers to implant that kind of lifelong interest in the classics in their minds. They are going to get their ideas and their art mostly from television, radio, movies, magazines, paperbacks, and familiar talk. We can deplore this. We can complain about the violence and shoddiness of popular art. But we evidently produce the consumers of popular art in great numbers in our colleges. The potentially popular taste is probably better than the producers believe; my own experience in getting a million or so free persons to listen to the discussion of significant books once a week would indicate a need somewhere for more substantial offering. And there are signs that reading habits are generally improving. But the current stimulation of modern American life is popular art.

This should not suggest that we give them less work with the great books while they are young and are open to impressions and in an atmosphere of intellectual excitement. We give them far too little of the great things in our own tradition and almost nothing of the great things in other, especially the Eastern, traditions. It does mean that we are missing the chance to show them that there are, in all the classics, enduring and universal principles which can be applied even to the ephemeral art of the day. We can make them discriminating consumers of popular art and—believe me—that art will improve if any substantial number of its consumers want something better.

In the meantime, however, we ought to realize what the sociologists are finding out about changing cultures elsewhere in the East and in Africa and especially as recently reported in the Middle East. I venture to cite a sociologist, even among humanists, because Daniel Lerner's recent book, *The Passing of Traditional Society,* bears directly on our problem. This is the report of a series of interviews with the ordinary inhabitants of the towns and villages of the Middle East, from Teheran to Cairo. They were taken and repeated after a span of years by trained native students, and they are reported by Lerner in this book after an exhaustive analysis. The book is formidable with tables and technicalities, in spite of Lerner's gifts as a writer, but for us it shows one fact of the greatest importance. It shows that the ancient ways are breaking up under the impact of modern communications, the radio, movies, cheap prints that we look down on, and that this is not a degradation of ancient culture, but an enlargement of the human spirit.

What is happening in the Middle East, and no doubt elsewhere in free or reasonably free populations, is the breaking up of the old ways of life in which men knew one single pattern, lived by one single pattern, and did not even admit the possibility of any other. This is the real ancient society, Fustel de Coulanges to the contrary notwithstanding, the society in which men do not know and do not care how other men live.

Lerner takes the growth of empathy, of interest in new or strange human possibilities, as the measure of the advance of modernity and finds that it can be correlated with the growth in the use of modern means of communication. Some of you may have seen Lerner's story in *Harper's* Magazine about the grocer of Balgat, in Turkey. When he saw his first American movie, the grocer went back to his village fired with enthusiasm. With a silly love story or a vision of violence? Not at all. With the first realization that there were grocery stores in the world in which the goods were canned, where customers who could read and hence could find their own needs went in and made their own selections from the shelves. His whole life—which was, after all, his grocery store—was changed. Nothing else for him or his grocery-keeping father before him, or his grandfather before him, had ever suggested a new way of living and working.

The new world is a world of interchanging ideas. You may not believe that these ideas are significant enough, or changed at a high enough level. If so, it is our business as teachers to make the interchanges more significant. We need the classics for undergraduates and for ourselves too, more of them, not less; better understood, not merely scanned. We need also to face the fact that all the people of the next generation, our own students included, will live in this modern world, and that it is our work, and our privilege if we can do it, to make the great ideas and the great beauties of the past seem relevant to these modern ways of living.

BARRY ULANOV

Comments

Critics and scholars have often noted the close connection between the modern arts and the classics of the Orient, but they have not examined that connection closely. The association needs to be examined. For the fact is that poets, painters, composers and dancers have gone far ahead of us. They have made embarrassingly large their acquaintance with the East, demanding much of those of us who attempt to explicate their performances. In the case of dancers, the embarrassment is minimal. The translation of gesture and grimace from East to West has been accomplished at such a low level that a passing acquaintance with Rodgers and Hammerstein gives one small talk on the subject and the ability to extend the neck muscles in more than one direction makes one an expert. With composers, one must make more of an effort. The considerable substance of Gustav Mahler's *Das Lied von der Erde,* for example, rests upon the translations into German made by Hans Bethge from the Chinese of Li Po. The words require explication as well as the music, the kind that follows careful reflection upon their meaning for Mahler and for other musicians who were influenced by him. Is this merely a wine-glass pessimism or is it more significant than that? Do the poems sustain the symphonic structure built about them? For many, *Das Lied* is Mahler's greatest work because it remains a song-cycle, with the intimacy the Chinese verses require, despite the massive proportions of the orchestral setting. For Arnold Schönberg and Alban Berg, Mah-

Barry Ulanov is Assistant Professor of English at Barnard College.

ler's procedure in joining these brief lyrics to large-scale symphonic statements was instructive: upon it, they based the pattern of several of their principal works.

Modern painting has Oriental sources. We all know that. The story has been told several times; the documentation is complete, at least back to the French Impressionists. But the documents merely report Manet's fascination with Japanese art or Degas's. They do not make coherent the association of the cultures of Japan and France as a student expects us to do in lecture or seminar: They say too little about the content of the painting of the Orient and its influence on the content of the painting of the West.

This is where the poet has the advantage and where the instructor can be at ease. Two examples may make clear what I mean.

In T. S. Eliot's "The Dry Salvages," the third of his *Four Quartets,* the poet offers what may be the briefest possible redactions of Krishna's admonitions to Arjuna in the *Bhagavad Gītā.* He speculates:

I sometimes wonder if that is what Krishna meant—
Among other things—or one way of putting the same thing:
That the future is a faded song, a Royal Rose or a lavender spray
Of wistful regret for those who are not yet here to regret,
Pressed between yellow leaves of a book that has never been opened.
And the way up is the way down, the way forward is the way back.

He meditates—or perhaps one should say contemplates:

Here between the hither and the farther shore
While time is withdrawn, consider the future
And the past with an equal mind.
At the moment which is not of action or inaction
You can receive this: "on whatever sphere of being
The mind of a man may be intent
At the time of death"—that is the one action.

As a guide for Western readers of the *Gītā,* these lines may be of some small help. For an understanding of Eliot's mystical doctrine, drawn from St. John of the Cross, Lady Julian of Norwich, and others equally oblique, they are very helpful lines indeed. With the supplementary aid of their source, the *Gītā* itself, they help illuminate many dark passages in Eliot.

In the summer of 1935, William Butler Yeats wrote to a friend a description of a large piece of lapis lazuli someone had sent him. On it a Chinese sculptor had carved "a mountain with temple, trees, path, and an ascetic pupil about to climb the mountain." Yeats commented: "Ascetic, pupil, hard stone, eternal theme of the sensual East. The heroic cry in the midst of despair. But no, I am wrong, the East has its solutions always and therefore knows nothing of tragedy. It is we, not the East, that must raise the heroic cry." A few days later, he wrote again: "To me the supreme aim is an act of faith and reason to make one rejoice in the midst of tragedy."

The meditation on the Orient lasted for a long time, for a year. In the summer of 1936, Yeats wrote "Lapis Lazuli" and declared himself quite pleased with it. He should have been. It is a wise poem, a moving consideration of the nature of faith and reason and the frame tragedy provides for both. If tragic heroes and heroines are worthy of their parts, they will not "break up their lines to weep." Hamlet and Lear, Cordelia and Ophelia show gaiety in "all that dread"—or at least they ought to, as the Chinese in his great jewel does. He delights, he says,

> . . . to imagine them seated there;
> There, on the mountain and the sky,
> On all the tragic scene they stare.
> One asks for mournful melodies;
> Accomplished fingers begin to play.
> Their eyes mid many wrinkles, their eyes,
> Their ancient, glittering eyes, are gay.

The imperturbable Chinese of Yeats's poem, gay in the face of tragedy, may be as dubious an image of the true people as the inscrutable Chinese of folklore. And yet Yeats performs a valuable service. He reminds us of the meditative texture of Chinese culture and in comparing his Orientals with their Western counterparts makes his own quiet protest against the shallow and the shabby in our culture.

Father Berry invoked for us the hospitality shown by Augustine to Plotinus and by Thomas Aquinas to Averroes. I should like to add some of our contemporaries to the list. In their glosses and commentaries on Oriental materials, many of our artists have already offered the hospitality of the West to the East. It is time for us to extend it and even to expand it in our classes.

Synopsis of Discussion: First Session

The open discussion in the first session covered a wide range of questions posed by the two major topics of the conference. In a broad sense, the question how best to present Oriental books to a Western audience applies, Lyman Bryson first indicated, not only to Oriental but to any classics: Aeschylus is great, but the *Agamemnon* is read today in order to pass examinations, not to consult it about life. It is read, in short, for devious reasons, as is shown by the fact that most people do not demand it over the "trash" that radio and television usually offer them. The reason this is so, he said, is that most people lack a taste for greatness, and this is the fault of teachers. When teachers inculcate a love of greatness in their pupils, he concluded, those pupils will demand better things of radio and television—and will get them.

Are the students on whom the change is to be worked, however, likely to be interested in Oriental classics? If the experience of Thomas Berry was typical, there is reason to be optimistic. If a book is presented properly, Father Berry found, the students are sometimes amazed at how much they understand. Classics, so many of them written for popular understanding, are distinguished by universal qualities, often enshrined in them with particular differences, but not essentially strange. In fact, students are often attracted by what is familiar as much as by what is strange.

Yu-kuang Chu felt that the preference of people for "trash" over great books may be partly owing to differences in the style of language. It is important, he said, that great books should be presented in modern language. Perhaps new translations should be made periodically.

Other remarks were directed to the question why such books deserve to be read. Barry Ulanov emphasized the value of reading Oriental classics as an aid to the understanding of modern Western works of art. Donald Keene dissented. He considered such an approach peripheral to the modern works mentioned, since they rested on European foundations, and also to the Oriental classics, which did not depend for their value on the modern uses of them. Their importance, he said, is in themselves; they have their own contemporaneous qualities.

Mr. Ulanov, nevertheless, considered it important to a full comprehension of modern writers that their references to Oriental works and themes be understood. His own understanding of Yeats, for example, had benefited greatly from learning some of the techniques of Nō drama. He was not, on the other hand, proposing that his approach was more than a secondary reason for taking up the Oriental classics.

An aspect of the question that Hellmut Wilhelm considered noteworthy was the pioneering role of the artist. Mr. Keene had pointed out that the Western artist who found inspiration in Oriental works sometimes did so through poor translations. The amazing thing was, Mr. Wilhelm said, that despite that handicap, the Western artist could express some of the spirit of the Oriental work. It was this ability of the great artist to be first in understanding that made his role important.

Several speakers commended the classics as inspirations to their readers to be better men. Wing-tsit Chan maintained that an educated man should read great books because his imagination would be stimulated and his outlook broadened. If, he added, a man studied other cultures through classics, his knowledge of the range of human values would grow, and he might become nobler.

Bernard Phillips, however, protested against any idea of timeless principles. If we assume any timeless principle, the classics are immaterial; any one great thinker will tell us as much as two. Everything, he maintained, must be of its time and in some sense unique. Yet he said finally that the only reason for reading Oriental classics was not to be informed by them but transformed.

Murray Fowler supported strongly the idea of reading for information. It was likely that students would find great inspiration in reading, for example, the *Bhagavad Gītā,* and he would not deny the worth of that. It was important, however, to point out that there are differences of opinion, even in India, about what parts of the *Gītā* mean. The way to explain those differences is to approach the book historically. It must be made clear, he concluded, that people are different. Barry Ulanov, whose earlier remarks had prompted Mr. Fowler's statement, said that he was sympathetic, by reason of his training, to the historical position. He had wanted, however, to call attention to the eloquent witness that contemporary men have provided for great Oriental works. The commentaries of poets, artists, and composers were as important as those of scholars, he thought.

Earlier Mr. Bryson had suggested that to work toward a world culture, the teaching of humanities might benefit from alliance with other disciplines. The approach of sociology, he mentioned, might help explain the human beings that the classics introduced. Allan B. Cole proposed that if sociological methods could help the humanities, psychological insights might, too. Cooperation between the humanities and social sciences might avoid, he felt, the danger of being too fragmentary, as was possible in relying on great books alone.

JOHN T. MESKILL

Books and World Culture

In the light of the very thoughtful discussions you have had during the course of the day and are likely to have tomorrow, you must not expect me, in these lighter moments of the conference, to say anything novel or even useful. All that I hope to do is perhaps to add a personal accent to some of the thoughts around the theme of this conference which you will be expounding and annotating with a distinction all your own.

It is pleasurable to take part, in whatever humble capacity, in a conference which is essentially concerned with books. We are living in an age of books. This is not just a truism. I believe that today, more than in any other epoch in history, there are books on almost every conceivable subject under the sun. Actually, I should say that we are living in an age of words. But if you exclude printed words, what remains? The millions of words impinging on the ionosphere that emanate from politicians, propagandists, and quiz masters. These, for the moment, we can ignore. Between ourselves, I do not think that we shall be ignoring anything very valuable. So let's return to books.

Those of us who during the last war were separated from our own or any other important source of books, who were perhaps in a remote

The late Professor Bokhári, who was Under-Secretary for Public Information of the United Nations and former Ambassador Plenipotentiary and Extraordinary of Pakistan to the United Nations, delivered this address to the conference at dinner, September 12, 1958. His death, which came as these proceedings were going to press, is a particular loss to those who felt the warmth of his presence on that occasion and came to admire his fine qualities of mind and character. [Ed].

part of the world, must have shared with many in my part of the world, in addition to the horror of murder and pillage and destruction, the horror of being separated from books. Books were not plentiful, editions were limited and were exhausted as soon as they were produced. I know of some people who made difficult journeys during those first hazardous days of 1939-40, in order to get closer to books.

But if books in plenty are a blessing, they also create a difficulty. The difficulty is not that there are books, but, alas, that there are too many books, and to make a choice is a baffling task. Sir William Haley, the editor of the London *Times,* who, as you know, was for many years a book reviewer on the *Manchester Guardian*—one of those book reviewers who did read the books he reviewed—said in a lecture that if he read at the rate of a hundred pages an hour, which, mind you, is a difficult pace to keep, and that if at this rate he read for four hours a day for forty years, he could not hope to read more than about 6,000 books. This means that persons who could have read 10,000 books are extremely rare. Six thousand books out of the millions that are produced—what would we not give for the choice to be made easy!

This conference is concerned, among other things, with making the choice somewhat easy and telling us what good and significant books there are to read. I'm grateful to any organization, any discussion, any intellectual cooperation, which makes me aware of the gold so that I can keep away from the dross. It would be a great service for any teacher to perform in this age if he but confined himself to suggesting the books that his students should read. I therefore welcome a conference like this. I know that its avowed aim is limited, but, while you pursue your specialists' interests, the larger aim is also fulfilled.

There is another aspect also which these books that you have chosen and value and are determined to pass on to the next generation have in common. They have a moral standpoint. In the last resort, they're concerned with what is valuable. They are concerned with problems of good and evil, and for those of us who believe, as I do, that the moral and the aesthetic and the great are but aspects of the same elevation, a book with a moral standpoint elevates a man in all these ways. These books are concerned intensely with the problem of the evaluation of human conduct. They may differ from each other in many other ways, they may differ from the classics which have their origin in other lands and other ages, but in all such cases it's not the answer that's important. The important thing is that they all raise the same important question.

It is good to remind ourselves that that question is an eternal question to which every man within the sanctity and solitude of his own soul, with whatever help he can get from fellow human beings, must find an answer. In our age and time there are many forces, and many currents of thought which are deterministic and fatalistic in their effect and which make one's awareness of the value in conduct or of transcendental values somewhat dim.

I suggest to you an experiment which I've tried with some students, both my own and others. If you ask an average young man or woman to name what he or she considers to be, say, the six most important virtues, you will seldom get a clear or a prompt answer. In fact, you will probably cause great confusion. First of all, the word "virtue" will fall strangely upon the ear. It is a word which is gradually falling into disuse. And secondly, it would take an average student brought up in our environment a long time before he could think of or name such qualities as kindness, love, tolerance. He will think of various other things, but on the whole he will be on the rack trying to define what those qualities of human conduct and human attitudes are which he must inculcate.

The need for bringing to the notice of everybody including ourselves books which have a moral standpoint is, I venture to suggest, very great, apart from the fact that these books have already inspired large numbers of people over centuries. For a long time amongst the illiterate and the untutored people of the East, a book meant a good book. In my home town in my childhood, and I dare say even now, you would find a man—illiterate—come across a stray piece of paper in the street. He wouldn't know what's written on it, but he would pick it up carefully and carry it until he came to a niche in a wall into which he might safely tuck it, because if it is paper with something written on it, it must be sacred and it must not be trampled upon. This is the attitude that he has toward books, and it is the attitude that I think we might try to inculcate amongst ourselves and amongst our students. For that purpose, the classics of the Orient will stand you in good stead, as, indeed, would similar books from other regions. I do not wish to give the impression that such literature is confined to the Orient.

There is a great need for mutual understanding in the world today. We are living, as you heard from a very thoughtful teacher, Father Berry, this morning, in a multicultural world. Now that does not mean that we are living at a time when many cultures co-exist, because that would not be a statement worth making. There was no time when there were not many cultures in the world. What, therefore, do we mean when we say we are living in a multicultural world?

What we mean is that each one of us today is exposed to many cultures as he never was before. In fact, some of the advances made in the first half of the century have made this exposure so easy that it is inescapable. The development of printing, the development of color photography (which has made paintings available to people who had never hoped to see them); and, above all, the development of scientific anthropology, which has brought other cultures nearer us so that we can study them in a spirit of humility or at least open-mindedness and which has taught us that cultures, simply because they are foreign and exotic, need not be shunned as corrupting the mind—all have helped the process. It is in this sense that we are living in a multicultural world. We cannot escape the impact on our minds of various cultures across and around the globe. In fact, one might borrow a phrase from Mr. André Malraux, who talked of "the imaginary museum" in which an artist today lives. An artist today is much more aware of art all over the world than, say, Leonardo da Vinci. What is true of the artist is true of the scholar, and what is true of the scholar is true of the common man, in varying degrees. It is imperative, this exposure being there, to know what to do with it. If some attempt is not made at understanding other cultures, we shall be living in a neglected manner.

I do not believe that the study of Oriental literatures by the Occident, or of Occidental literatures by the Orient, will immediately bring about an era of peace on earth. An era of peace on earth is a matter of the heart, not of the head. But it is quite true that a large number of mistakes could be avoided if one knew the motives, the moral and intellectual background of other nations.

Take the political problems posed by Islamic movements today. It would be impossible, I think, fully to understand the urges of Muslim countries or even the urges of the Arab world without studying the Qur'ān which laid down not merely a religion but the requirements of a new society. To understand the Muslims, one is driven to a study of the book from which the conception of Islamic society takes its origin.

There must be some people who keep up such studies in the hope that they will somehow find the means of passing their understanding on to those who are in a position to act. Those who act have no time to think and others who think are not in a position to act, and the problem always has been how the benefit of the studies of those who think, which preeminently includes this group, can be passed on to those who act. The passage between them, the channel, has never been very easy. How to give every Alexander an Aristotle? And would he listen to Aristotle after he is at the peak of his glory? That is the great question. Your efforts, in your own sphere, could, I believe, lead to a better education of those who are in a position to act and with whom lies the comparative tranquillity of the world, if not the total abolition of war.

Even, therefore, if we take a pragmatic, a politically international view, it should be an asset for a nation to know other people. I don't believe anyone roams the globe more than the Americans. They do it partly because they have lots of money. But, aside from that, I think they have a wanderlust. Also, their new duties and their position in the world will force them to look into the four corners of the earth and to be pioneers not in one place but in a thousand. Therefore, it is far more important for the young generation of this nation, more than of any other, to try and lay the groundwork for that kind of understanding which will make its wanderlust rewarding.

There is yet another purpose which this kind of study might have. I have seen the learned paper of Father Berry which he read this morning. Many wise men hold the view that he holds (and I probably belong to the undistinguished minority in this matter) that there is no universal culture, that a universal culture is not a dream, but an illusion. Well, with me it's a dream and not an illusion. Father Berry strongly holds the view—and so do many other distinguished thinkers —that the best equipment for the study of other cultures is to be firmly implanted in one's own.

I think a difference of opinion might be permitted on this issue. You can either think of the scholar (by the scholar I mean the inquirer, any inquirer—a student, a teacher), you can either think of him after the image of Donne's lover, resembling a pair of compasses with one leg firmly implanted in the center and the other leg out and moving around and coming back home whenever required. Or you can conceive of him as a dome with many colored windows. I conceive of him as the second. There are green windows and blue and yellow, and the light that comes through each takes the hue of the glass. But in the mind itself the various colors do not lie snugly side by side. They mingle and form a new and rich and subtle color which represents my dream of a universal culture.

Is this obtainable? Yes, but it is yet a hazardous and a difficult task. It imposes on the scholar a great mission and a great loneliness. He will find his community not always around him, but across the seas and across continents. I think this aristocracy (I use the word with trepidation in a ferociously democratic country) is the aristocracy which eventually might solve some of the worst problems of the world. It is not an aristocracy to which a person has to be born; anyone can be admitted to it, and therefore I hope that some of the objections that might have arisen in your mind at the first sound of the word will in the end be quieted. It is an aristocracy to which one can belong by the bond of understanding. There's a growing number of people in the world today—cosmopolitan, if you like to call them —who beckon to each other across the darkness—whenever it is dark —and get much moral support from each other.

This does not mean any dissipation of loyalties. One of the characteristics of our age is that loyalties are being reexamined in a curious topsy-turvy way. The loyalties of friendship are becoming somewhat undervalued and yet, as Mr. E. M. Forster reminds us, Dante put Brutus into hell for betraying his friend. Other loyalties are being substituted for the older ones, and perhaps most of us are undecided and confused. But I ask for no dissipation of loyalties. I only ask for higher and higher loyalties as one goes on.

Let this not have us a-trembling. As Mr. Justice Frankfurter has said, "The true mark of a civilized man is the confidence in the certainty and the strength derived from an inquiring mind." That is the citadel within which you will sit and not within the citadel of any temporary or valueless loyalty which we might hear preached.

I also remember a quotation from Mr. Clark Kerr, the distinguished Chancellor of the University of California. He said, "The difficulty, the danger, is not that loyalties are divided today. The danger is that loyalties might be undivided tomorrow. I would urge upon every individual to avoid total involvement in any organization." For his "organization," I would substitute "culture." I would urge upon every individual to avoid total involvement in a culture, and to look around him freely, because what is human is worth studying, perhaps worth embracing, and it makes no difference where the source lies. It is what we bring to it, the readiness to learn, and to feel warmth, which is the essential factor.

Let me remind you, also, that what you're undertaking is not an isolated project. There are, I learned the other day, about six hundred organizations of private citizens in America which are concerned with intellectual cooperation with and study of Asian countries. Six hundred is a very large number. I do not believe that any other country in the world can come anywhere close to this in studying foreign cultures, and in intellectual cooperation with people not born in one's native land. That's an achievement of which you can justly be proud. The program you have set before you, therefore, forms a very important sector in the total attack upon human ignorance and cultural isolation.

One word more and I would have finished. There's one other reason why I welcome this conference and the attention that you pay to Oriental classics. With your help, shamed by your efforts, and inspired by your challenge, some of us in the East—myself most of all— might, let us hope, read a few more of their own classics.

PART TWO

Some Great Books of the Oriental Traditions

ARTHUR JEFFERY

The Qur'ān

The Qur'ān is the Bible of Islam, the sacred scripture of those 280 to 300 million people who call themselves Muslims and whom we more familiarly know as Muhammadans. These are the people whose sacred city is Mecca, the forbidden city to which the Muslim pilgrimage is annually made, whose Prophet is Muhammad, the Apostle of Allāh, whom they revere as unique among the prophets and peerless among mankind. The Qur'ān is the body of "revelations" set forth by Muhammad as instruction from Allāh for the guidance of the Muslims and a statement of His mind and will and purpose for mankind. As such it is given by them a reverence surpassing even that given by Jews and Christians to their Scriptures, and has a claim to be the most studied, even at the present day, of all the sacred books known to and believed in by men. Now in our modern world these almost 300 million Muslims constitute a considerable segment of world population, some groups of them being, for a variety of reasons, prominent in matters of international concern, so that the book which is so highly regarded by them, which has influenced and continues to influence their lives profoundly, necessarily has a major claim for consideration among the classics of Oriental literature.

THE SIGNIFICANCE OF THE QUR'ĀN

Curiously enough, however, that seems to be the Qur'ān's sole claim to a place among such classics. On the thought and literature of Mus-

Arthur Jeffery is Professor of Semitic Languages and Chairman of the Department of Near and Middle East Languages, Columbia University.

lim peoples its influence has been enormous, but elsewhere it has left
hardly a trace. In our Western languages and literatures there is nothing from the Qur'ān save its name. Our European vocabularies have
been enriched by many Arabic words—algebra, logarithm, cypher;
cupola, sofa, muslin; sherbet, coffee, apricot; lute, tambourine, guitar
—but none of these words, nor of the scores of others of Arabic origin,
is from the Qur'ān. "Confucius said" and "Also sprach Zarathustra"
have become so familiar to us as to be humorous, but neither our
learned nor our popular speech has any echo of what Muhammad
proclaimed in the Qur'ān. Even our familiar saying about Muhammad and the mountain comes to us from the Byzantines and not from
the Qur'ān. Nor has the Qur'ān as a religious message had any effect
on Western thought.

From the medieval period onwards there was a considerable contribution made to the West from Arab sources, but this was from
Arabian scientific and philosophic thought quite remote from the
religion of the Qur'ān. Year after year our students of comparative
religion complain that they find far less of interest in the Qur'ān than
in the other sacred books of the East. It presents no new religious
insights, makes no discernible advance toward the solution of the
perennial problems of religion, scales no new heights, plumbs no new
depths of religious experience, so their feeling in reading it is that
they are getting only a secondhand treatment of religious matters
dealt with much more adequately in the scriptures of the older religions.

The same absence of Qur'anic influence is equally apparent in the
literature of the non-Muslim Orient. Into the languages of India and
the Far East have come elements of Arabic vocabulary, coming for
the most part as a result of commercial contacts with the Arab world,
but there are no noticeable traces in either language or thought of
contact with the Qur'ān. When we turn to Muslim areas, however,
the contrast is startling. Persian, Turkish, Urdu, Malay were for
centuries written in a script derived from the Arabic script employed
in the Qur'ān, and their vocabularies have been enormously enriched

by the incorporation of Qur'anic words. To a lesser extent this is true of other Central Asian, Indian, Indonesian, as well as of some African languages where there is an important Muslim section of the people using these languages as a vernacular or maybe as a language of literary expression. This is not to be wondered at, for one thinks of the number of Greek words introduced through the Christian Church into the languages of Western Europe, and of the Sanskrit terminology which entered Tibetan, Mongolian, Burmese, Siamese, Chinese, and Japanese with the spread northwards and eastwards of Buddhism.

What is more surprising is the extent to which the text of the Qur'ān has become woven into the literature of these various Muslim peoples. We are familiar enough with the statement of how much the German language owes to Luther's translation of the Bible, and of how little intelligible English literature of certain periods is without an acquaintance with the King James version. The impress of the Qur'ān on the literature of Persian, Turkish, Urdu, and Malay, not to speak of Arabic, has been even greater. Even in quite secular literature among Muslim peoples one commonly finds that the turn of a phrase, the choice of a word, though the subject may have no immediate connection with religion, is decided by the writer's familiarity with the Qur'ān. One may even suspect that the fondness for rhymed prose so characteristic of public speaking in the Muslim East derives from the fact that the Qur'ān is in a form of rhymed prose.

The Qur'anic legislation, which often enough deals with details of personal and community behavior, has necessarily had a profound effect on the social life of Muslim peoples, deciding indeed the very pattern of their social structure. The Qur'anic determinism with its tremendous emphasis on the transcendence of Allāh and the immutability of His eternal decree, in accordance with which all things ever have been, are, and ever will be, has had its equally profound influence on the manifestations of their spiritual life.

What is less often remembered is that Qur'anic teaching has also largely controlled the aesthetic life of Muslim peoples. It is no accident that until comparatively recent times the drama has been almost unknown as a serious literary genre, that the dance has never risen above the lowliest popular level, that music and representational art have flourished only in very limited areas and under severe restrictions, while formal art, both in the minor arts and in architecture, has developed in a unique way in areas of Muslim dominance. While we may well look askance at certain modern attempts to read weird mystic meanings into the structural forms of Muslim architecture and the details of arabesque design, there is a sense in which it is true to say that Qur'anic teaching is at the back of these things.

THE REASONS FOR THE QUR'ĀN'S MUSLIM SIGNIFICANCE

When we ask why the Qur'ān has had this profound influence on Muslim culture the answer is easy to give. It comes directly from the Muslim doctrine of Scripture.

The Qur'ān is a scripture. The word *Qur'ān* is itself derived from the Syriac *qeryānā* used for the scripture lessons used in church services. Muhammad knew about the scriptures of contemporary religious groups. He mentions not infrequently the "People of the Book," i.e., the peoples who had scriptures which they studied and from which they derived their Rule of Life, and he expressly refers to the *Torah* (Law) of Moses, the *Zabūr* (Psalter) of David and the *Injīl* (Gospel) of Jesus, in each case conceiving of the scripture as a corpus of revelations "given" to a prophet.

From this derives the Muslim doctrine of Scripture. God has not left mankind without a knowledge of His mind, His will, His purpose. Man may learn something about God from nature, something about Him from history, something about Him from reflection on experience, but for the religious life that is not enough. So God has chosen from time to time men to whom He has given revelation about religious matters.

These men are the prophets, the envoys, the messengers, of whom Adam was the first and Muhammad the last. Revelation is progressive. A very simple revelation was all that was necessary during the earliest years of man on earth. As life developed and became more complex this simple revelation given to Adam no longer sufficed and so another prophet was sent with a fuller revelation, which preserved all that was still useful of the previous revelation but abrogated what was not. Some revelations given to these prophets were put into written form, others were not. After a long succession of such prophets Muhammad was sent to be the seal of the prophets. His revelation in its written form is the Qur'ān. It confirms and preserves all that is still valid and useful of the earlier revelations but abrogates the rest. It is thus the final expression of the mind, will, and purpose of Allāh and His final Rule of Life for mankind.

But how did God give this revelation to the prophets? By inspiration (*wahy*). The angel of inspiration is Gabriel who transmits to the prophets the messages they are to deliver to mankind as the Word of God. This Word of God, however, had already been recorded. Before the foundation of the world the Pen had written on the Preserved Tablet all that was to be from the beginning of time till time shall end, including, of course, the material to be revealed to each prophet in turn. Gabriel thus merely transmits from the Tablet what the prophet is to transmit to men for their instruction and guidance. As Muhammad transmitted what Gabriel brought to him, it, according to orthodox theory, was recorded by the Prophet's amanuenses, and after Muhammad's death this material was gathered together and issued in Codex form under direction of the Caliph 'Uthmān. Orthodox theory also claims that Gabriel and the Prophet each year collated what had been revealed that year with the original on the Tablet and on the last year of the Prophet's life they so collated it twice, so that the Qur'ān as we have it is an exact transcript of all that Gabriel was charged to transmit as the final revelation from Allāh to mankind.

This, of course, makes the Qur'ān unique among the scriptures of the world. Other scriptures also claim to be the Word of God, but according to this Muslim theory the Qur'ān is the *ipsissima verba* of God himself and consists of nothing but His words. If we look at the

Qur'ān, we find that, with the exception of the little opening prayer and the two little charms at the end, it is always God (Allāh) who is speaking to man, never man speaking, as is the case for the most part in other holy books. From this it follows that, since the Qur'ān is in Arabic, Arabic must be the Divine Language, and for that reason the Qur'ān cannot really be translated into any other language. This explains why the Qur'ān is always recited in Arabic, why Arabic is used in all the cult practices of Islam, especially in the prayers, and why all over the world of Islam there is such eagerness to learn and to use Arabic.

From this follows also the inerrancy of the Qur'ān. God cannot be wrong, so any statement He makes in His word must *ipso facto* be correct. Therefore the Qur'ān contains ultimate wisdom and knowledge. Human knowledge and wisdom are of necessity fallible and imperfect, but the Word of God must always be right and true and adequate. We are not ignorant of the fact that in both Judaism and Christianity there have been at times groups defending the inerrancy and sole adequacy of the Bible, and in modern Hinduism there are those who make the same claim for the Vedas, but nowhere has this sense of the ultimate authority of the written Word of God been so profound or all pervasive as in Islam.

From this there developed in time two other beliefs about the Qur'ān, namely, the belief in its uncreatedness and the belief in its miraculousness. That it was preexistent follows from the fact that its material was all there on the Preserved Tablet before the creation of this world. Muslim theologians, however, had learned from their contacts with learned men of the older religions something of what we call the Logos doctrine, i.e., of the eternal Word of God. In Christian theology this is concerned with the person of Christ, but the Muslim theologians, not understanding this, attached it to the preexistent Qur'ān, and spoke of the eternal Word of God in that sense. There may well have been Jewish influences at work here also, for the rabbis spoke of the Torah as preexistent. Since God's Word was obviously with Him before the Pen wrote it on the Tablet they could speak of His Word being in that sense "uncreate." Then, as the Qur'ān is also the Word of God, the teaching came to be that the Qur'ān is uncreate.

This in itself would be proof of its miraculousness, but there is something more. In the Qur'ān there are passages in which men, or even men assisted by the jinn, are challenged to produce anything like it. From the context it would seem clear that the challenge refers to content. Those being addressed are the pagan Arabs who are slow to accept the message, and to admit the claim of the messenger to be in the succession of the prophets, so they are challenged to produce anything which, like this message, brings them the content of the old prophetic religion known to the People of the Book. Muslim orthodoxy, however, has taken the challenge to refer not to the content but to the form. If this book is the Word of God, it is necessarily inimitable, and so the doctrine of *I'jāz* has come to mean the miraculous beauty of diction, the matchless elegance of style, the linguistic perfection of the Qur'ān.

Since Arabic is the divine language, and the Qur'ān a matchless, miraculous example thereof, it naturally has been taken as the norm for Arabic grammar and rhetoric. There has been within Islam a highly interesting division of opinion on this matter. What we refer to as Islamic orthodoxy has been shaped by the labors of the Muslim theologians and jurists. Grammar and rhetoric on the other hand were the province of men of letters, and in the older days men of letters were often far from orthodox. They had their tradition that the source of correct Arabic was the speech of the old desert poets, and so they preferred to quote verses of the poets as normative for and illustrative of rules of grammar and rhetoric. In this, of course, from our point of view, they were right. With the triumph of orthodoxy, however, the claims of the men of letters had to be denied, and so we find writers, such as al-Bāqillānī, writing elaborate treatises to show how the diction of the Qur'ān is far superior to that of the pagan poets. Since the criteria for judgment have already been drawn from the Qur'ān they have, of course, no difficulty in doing this.

While this may seem to be a matter of little more than academic importance, certain other deductions from the miraculous character of the Qur'ān have been of the utmost practical significance. Part of a prophet's mission was to provide men with a Rule of Life, and so the Qur'ān contains a good deal of instruction on moral and ethical questions, as well as regulations for both individual and community life. For Muslim orthodoxy this is not fallible human instruction, but is the word of God for man. Thus the Qur'anic prescriptions are for them the ultimate and unquestionable authority on all matters of social and ethical concern.

On an Export Line vessel threading the Mediterranean toward Alexandria one summer a bright young Egyptian girl was animatedly advocating one morning the feminist position on the equal rights of the sexes, and rather contemptuous of the old-style Muslim leaders who opposed feminism, when an Afghan doctor, on his way home after a year of special study at Harvard, quietly dismissed the whole feminist position by a quotation from the Qur'ān which states plainly and unequivocally that men have been given by Allāh a superiority over women. When that kindly, urbane scholar Mustafā 'Abd ar-Rāziq was gently chided by a German friend of many years for taking to himself an additional wife, he answered, "Allāh allows each Muslim four wives. I am not going beyond what the Almighty Himself has declared is quite right." When Shaikh 'Abd al-Ghanī was somewhat severely taken to task by the American head of the school in which he taught for divorcing the wife of his youth, the mother of his five children, for no other reason than a financial gain to himself, he was frankly astonished and wanted to know why he should be considered as having done wrong when he had done only what Allāh had permitted as right. When Ibn Sa'ūd in his famous conference with Franklin D. Roosevelt wanted Mr. Roosevelt to stop the British interference with the slave trade between Africa and the Hijāz, he could not understand why he should regard as an evil a thing which Allāh in His much greater wisdom had regarded as not evil. What God has decreed on such matters surely cannot be gainsaid.

To Western observers perhaps the most characteristic thing about life in Muslim lands is its deeply rooted feeling that life is lived under the immutable and inscrutable decrees of Allāh. *Mā shā' Allāh* (what Allāh has willed), and *In shā' Allāh* (if Allāh wills), both derive from the predestinarian teaching of the Qur'ān. If the emphasis of Judaism has been on the wisdom of God, and the emphasis of Christianity on the love of God, the great emphasis of Islam, even from the beginning, has been on the will of God.

This, of course, has its good side, and all the great religions have stressed the importance of discovering and doing the will of God. But in Islam it does not have to be discovered. Its teaching is that all we do is done because that, and that alone, was the will of God for us, and who are we to question what Allāh has decreed for us?

Some years ago a young American in Egypt, distressed at the appallingly high incidence of eye disease among the peasants, interested a student group in spreading information about preventive measures. They selected a village as a demonstration center, and found the mayor and village head-men cooperative, so they started a clinic. All went well till the religious teacher heard about it. He peremptorily called a halt to their treatments. "If it is the will of Allāh that this man go blind he will go blind. If it is not the will of Allāh that he go blind he will not go blind. Why do you think that with your treatments you can interfere with the will of Allāh for him?" The young American had the last word, for he countered: "And would I have come all the way from America with treatments for this man's eye if Allāh had not willed I should? Are you questioning the will of Allāh?"

One further extension of this idea of the miraculousness of the Qur'ān has been that of regarding it as the sole source of wisdom. This amiable weakness seems to be common among peoples who possess a scripture, for we know of Jewish groups who would draw all wisdom from the Torah, of "Bible" Christian groups who shun all save Bible knowledge, and Marathi Hindu saints who hold that the Vedas embrace all knowledge. In two passages (XII, 111 and XVI,

91) the Qur'ān claims to contain a clear exposition of everything, where doubtless what was meant was everything necessary to salvation. This, however, was often taken quite literally, so that on the one hand we find Qur'anic statements quoted as the final and authoritative truth on a variety of matters, and on the other come upon highly ingenious attempts to discover many modern scientific ideas hidden in various phrases of the Qur'ān.

THE PROBLEM OF WESTERN USE OF THE QUR'ĀN

All this raises the question of how a Western teacher can approach the study of the Qur'ān and use it as a representative classic of Oriental literature. We can regard it as the Word of God only in the very limited sense that it was Muhammad's interpretation of some of the things he thought the Word of God to be. From the beginning to the end it is Muhammad's book, bearing the impress of his personality, revealing his interests, his passions, his very limited knowledge about many things, and his complete misunderstanding of many others. Read in a more or less chronological order it reveals very clearly the development of his thinking, and in particular the development of his own understanding of his mission. What is even clearer is its reflection of the milieu in which the Prophet lived and labored in seventh-century Arabia. Its technical religious vocabulary is very largely drawn from the languages of those religious communities with which the Prophet was in contact. The stories used so effectively as illustrations in his preaching are for the most part stories of Biblical "worthies," but the details of these stories, it is curious to note, are derived rather from midrashic and apocryphal embellishments on the Biblical narrative than from the more sober Biblical accounts.

It is thus obvious that we cannot approach the Qur'ān as a Muslim does. To us it is Muhammad's book in the same sense as we consider the *Book of Mormon* to be Joseph Smith's book. Thus we can only expound it as the substance of what Muhammad set forth to be the fundamental teaching for the religion he founded in seventh-century Arabia, and which is still the basic teaching for Muslims. Nor can we ever convey to Western students the effect the book has on Muslims when they listen to its message. In the Orient scripture is not read, it is cantillated. Thus in a way the closer comparison would be with our hymnody.

When Marmaduke Pickthall was in Cairo in the 1920s he made much of the fact that he had seen audiences both moved to tears and stirred to religious enthusiasm by the recitation of the Qur'ān, which, he held, demonstrated its Divine origin. Many a Methodist could similarly tell of audiences moved to tears, and audiences stirred to ecstatic fervor, by the singing of Wesley's hymns at Class Meeting. In both cases it is emotional conditioning which is the efficient factor and not the message conveyed by the words.

Furthermore the peculiar beauty claimed for the language of the Qur'ān is a beauty inherent in the Arabic language which cannot be conveyed by any translation. The same is true of the old Arabic poetry. This poetry had its conventions as to rhyme, rhythm, and structure, and the poets showed themselves at times extraordinarily skillful and ingenious in utilizing the resources of the language to produce variety, charm, delicacy of expression, within the framework of those conventions. Zuhair, we are told, was a poet who would take a month to compose an ode, then spend a year polishing it, then read it to a few connoisseurs for their criticism and only then recite it publicly. Now ash-Shanqītī tells us that the most poetical verse Zuhair ever wrote was:

> There strove in her the likeness of the wild cow, and the
> pearl of the sea, while her similitude is the gazelle.

In English that seems nothing much, but Arabs still gasp in wonder at the skill with which that verse has been composed, the subtle choice of words, the daintiness, the delicate harmony and smoothly balanced rhythm the poet has attained. So in the Qur'ān where, it would appear, Muhammad has shown considerable skill in handling the Arabic language within the conventions he observes as those appropriate for setting forth a religious message, the force of this is lost on those who cannot appreciate the original Arabic diction.

The meaning of the Prophet's message we can give in English or in any other modern language, and there are passages which, even in translation, can convey something of the rugged strength, the emotional intensity, the deep conviction of the Prophet. We can see him striving to understand and express the significance of his message. We can hear him arguing his convictions as he struggles with his opponents. We can catch something of his hopes and fears, and share in a measure his prophetic experience, just as we do that of Amos, or Jeremiah, or Mani, or John Wesley. But on the other hand his message is so bound up with the mentality of seventh-century Arabia that it is often very difficult to make it really relevant to the conditions of our modern world. Muslims themselves are aware of this, so that in recent years there has been a great deal of labor in certain Muslim circles in Turkey, in Egypt, in North Africa, in India and Indonesia, to find ways of interpreting the Qur'ān which will make its message more acceptable to the modern mind. The basic principle here, of course, is sound. The Word of God is timeless and as it speaks to every generation may be re-expressed in terms of the life and thought of each generation. So, *if* the Qur'ān is the Word of God, why should not its message be reinterpreted in the language of our time?

That still does not relieve us, however, from responsibility for trying to understand and expound what it meant to those to whom it was originally addressed. Our fundamental problem with the Gāthās of Zoroaster, for example, is not how they can be interpreted to suit the life situation of a Parsi community living in the highly industrialized conditions of modern Bombay, but what Zoroaster meant by the words he uttered and how they were understood by those who first heard them. So Markwart, Lommel, Nyberg, or Duchesne-Guillemin in their labors at interpreting the *Gāthā ushtāvatī* strive to place themselves in thought in that ancient Iran where the prophet lived and taught. In taking the Qur'ān as one of our classics of Oriental literature it must similarly be our primary task to set it in its environment of seventh-century Arabia, and seek to understand and then explain what it meant to those who first heard it.

This poses for us a problem. With regard to the Qur'ān we are in no such favorable a position as we are for interpreting the original message of Zoroaster or Mani, for the helps are not at hand. The translations of the Qur'ān with commentary by the Ahmadiyya groups, or that by Yūsuf Alī, are interesting as showing how modern Muslims are trying to adapt the Qur'anic teaching to modern ideas, but scientifically they are worthless. Some of the more modern translations, particularly that of Marmaduke Pickthall, are highly tendentious and should be avoided at all costs, while others lack the provision of notes necessary to make the text intelligible. From the scholarly point of view the best translation in English is that of Richard Bell (2 vols., Edinburgh, 1937, 1939). Bell's Introduction has been published since his death (Edinburgh, 1953), but the publisher still refuses to face the cost of printing his body of notes to his translation. Régis Blachère's French translation is even more up-to-date (Paris, 1949, 1950), and his Introduction has also appeared (Paris, 1947), but the long-promised final volume of annotations has not yet appeared. For teaching purposes Rodwell's translation in the Everyman series is still the best. It is hardly up-to-date, for it appeared in 1861, but it arranges the material in roughly chronological order, translates into dignified Biblical-flavored English, and has a number of footnotes giving a good deal of useful information. The standard Introduction is still that of Nöldeke-Schwally-Bergsträsser-Pretzl, *Geschichte des Qorans* (Leipzig, 1919–1938), and there is a useful subject-index in H. U. Weitbrecht Stanton's *The Teaching of the Qur'ān* (London, 1919).

R. BAYLY WINDER

Comments

In commenting on Professor Arthur Jeffery's presentation on the Qur'ān, I must express my great diffidence in venturing into the realm which Professor Jeffery has preempted as uniquely his own. It is a case of a neophyte and a master. However, there are two general points which I would like to raise.

The first relates to the initial sentence of Professor Jeffery's paper, namely, "The Qur'ān is the Bible of Islam." This is apparently a truism, but closer examination may reveal that it sets up an erroneous analogy. This point, I hasten to add, is not original, but rather has recently been made by Professor Wilfred Cantwell Smith, the director of the Institute of Islamic Studies at McGill University.[1] The point is that there is an almost automatic tendency to equate Christ and Muhammad on the one hand and the Bible[2] and the Qur'ān on the other and yet the parallel does not really work. To quote Professor Smith directly:

We suggest that much more insight is gained if one realizes that the role of St. Paul in Christianity and that of Muḥammad in Islām are much more closely comparable. Both are apostles. St. Paul preached a message, as did Muhammad; only his message, and the message of Chris-

R. Bayly Winder is Associate Professor of Oriental Languages and Literatures at Princeton University.

[1] In *Islam in Modern History* (Princeton, Princeton University Press, 1957), p. 17, n. 13; p. 18, n. 14. See also a forthcoming article by Professor Smith in which Christianity and Islam are more systematically compared than in these references.

[2] I assume that Professor Jeffery is using the word Bible in sense 1 of the definition of it in *Webster's New Collegiate Dictionary:* "The book made up of writings accepted by Christians as inspired by God and of divine authority."

tianity, is the person of Christ. If one is drawing parallels in terms of the structure of the two religions, what corresponds in the Christian scheme to the Qur'ān is not the Bible but the person of Christ—it is Christ who is for Christians the revelation of (from) God. And what corresponds in the Islamic scheme to the Bible (the record of revelation) is the Tradition (*Ḥadīth*).[3]

Naturally, Professor Jeffery is aware of this difference and in fact brings it out in the section of his paper entitled "The Reasons for the Qur'ān's Muslim Significance," and in particular by his reference to it as the *"ipsissima verba* of God himself." Nevertheless, this framework established by his initial sentence seems to constitute an almost overpowering hypothesis which the latter discussion does not completely break down.

My second observation is of a more practical nature having to do with teaching the Qur'ān in an undergraduate program in general education. It seems to me that there is in the Qur'ān quite enough to interest and enlighten the student even though he has no background on seventh-century Arabia. Naturally, the more we can give our student of that background the better, but in our general education program there will be little that we can do. I do think that the text provides enough material of intrinsic value and interest (it must of course be carefully selected) to enrich measurably the young student exposed to it. The poetical visions of many of the short *sūrahs,* the utter awesomeness of the divine will, or the dramatic retelling of the story of Joseph, unite to form the particular synthesis which is Islam. Possibly the fact that I happen to have at least a limited knowledge of that "lawful magic" which is the Arabic original precludes me from facing the text as an undergraduate does, but as Professor Van Doren's paper opening the conference advised us: give the student the text; don't tell him how difficult it is.

Finally in regard to translations, I must make a mild objection to Professor Jeffery's comment on the Pickthall version. It is true that Pickthall's translation is overly enthusiastic (he was a convert to

[3] Smith, *Islam in Modern History*, p. 17, n. 13.

Islam), even "highly tendentious" if you like, but the fact remains that for me it has two major advantages in undergraduate teaching. First, it is readily available and cheap; second, and more important, it catches the flavor of the Arabic more feelingly than do any of the others. To inflict the Bell translation on an undergraduate in general education would seem to me as regrettable as to give any English one other than Bell's to a graduate student.

MAAN MADINA

Comments

In his paper Professor Arthur Jeffery has referred to the belief of orthodox Muslims that the Qur'ān is perfect, both in content and in form. To Muslims, the Qur'ān is not only a great book, it is the greatest book that ever existed. It must also be remembered that, according to Muslim orthodoxy, the Qur'ān is the first and basic source of right knowledge. All other sources, regardless of the actual extent of their contribution to knowledge, are designed only to amplify and supplement the teachings of the Qur'ān. To Muslims the infallible Word of Allāh is cherished as the measure of all things.

Most Western scholars, it is true, are unable to share this high estimation of the Qur'ān. They criticize its religious teachings, its originality, its method, and its style. Yet they do not exclude the Qur'ān from the ranks of the classics of the East. For they acknowledge that if it has no other merit, the Qur'ān still deserves consideration for the command it has held of a substantial portion of the world's population over a period of many centuries.

Professor Jeffery has also shown how the Qur'ān has influenced Muslim life and thought, and what its significance is to the Muslims. In this connection it should be emphasized that the Qur'ān has been instrumental in developing a new type of thought and character, transforming a heterogeneous tribal order into an effective and victorious force which created a world empire. It has established a vast politico-religious community, the impact of which we feel even today.

Maan Madina is Assistant Professor of Modern Arabic at Columbia University.

Therefore its significance must be seen in relation to the distinctive way of life and civilization which takes the Qur'ān as its basic inspiration.

The Qur'ān poses a special problem for the Western student. Its literary form is different from anything the Westerner has known, and as a text to be read it has the added disadvantage of being somewhat repetitious. He must therefore be reminded that the Qur'ān, though referred to as a book, is not a book in the strict sense of the word. It is rather a collection of proclamations, admonitions, promises, and teachings which Muhammad uttered on various occasions as the situation required. It was only after the death of the Prophet that these utterances were compiled into one volume without regard to their chronological arrangement or subject matter.

The teacher should also point out to the student the great identity that exists between the Qur'ān as a literary work and the mind of Muhammad, the man who produced it. There is no doubt but that a great deal of the power of the book reflects the strong personality of Muhammad. That is why the Qur'ān must be understood in terms of his life and mission.

Westerners often point to the weaknesses of Muhammad's ethical system when compared to their own. It is, of course, useful and natural for anyone to compare other religious and ethical systems with his own when confronted with them, and all the more so in the case of the young student, for it is the best means of enabling him to see his own religious and ethical beliefs in perspective. We cannot attempt here an estimate of Muhammad's character as a man and his sincerity as a prophet. But in fairness to him and the Qur'ān, the religious and ethical standards which Muhammad proclaimed should be judged in comparison not only to Western ethics, but also to the religious and ethical practices of pagan Arabia which they were meant to replace. We must not forget that although the Medinan Sūras abound with polemics against Jews and Christians, Muhammad was devoted throughout the Qur'ān to the task of raising the religious and ethical standards of pagan times to the higher level established by the revealed teachings of earlier prophets.

Concerning the charge that the Qur'ān is lacking in originality, it must be admitted that there is some truth to it. Many of the ideas and information in the Qur'ān are taken from outside sources. As Professor Jeffery has pointed out, Muhammad was attracted by the idea of scripture, i.e., of having a book in which God himself reveals to men something of his will and his mind. Muhammad was aware that the Jews and Christians had their own scriptures, and he repeatedly refers to them as the "people of the Book." He also repeatedly emphasized that his own message is a confirmation of those earlier revelations. And although several other new elements influenced Muhammad's conception of his own role as a prophet, the desire to bring to his people the religious message of the earlier scriptures must have always remained with him. As Professor Jeffery suggests, this is one reason why Christians and Jews find so much of the Qur'ān familiar.

Still, it must be pointed out that in the case of material borrowed from earlier scriptures, originality is not to be looked for so much in terms of the novelty of the ideas as it is in the way they are presented and utilized. We must not forget that in Muhammad's conception of revelation there is very little room for originality, and if originality is to be sought, it must relate more to the spirit than to the content. Whatever ideas or information the Prophet of Islam received from outside sources became impregnated with his own spirit and bore the marks of his own distinctive style.

This dominating spirit, the ultra-emotional expression of Muhammad's religious zeal toward Allāh, is what the student must be made to feel and realize. For it is this spirit, in its multiple manifestations at all levels of Muslim thought and endeavor, which is the distinctive element of the Islamic tradition.

Ibn Khaldūn

Ibn Khaldūn's "History" (especially the Introduction and
Book One, which treat the general problem of history and the "science
of culture" respectively and which are known together as the *Muqad-
dimah* or "Introduction") is presented to the reader with the following
claims made for it by its author: 1) It speaks directly to him concerning problems lying at the foundation of his thought and views about
the nature of history and society; it attempts a critical and scientific
investigation of the opinions commonly held, and the axioms consciously or unconsciously accepted or rejected, by previous writers on
these subjects. Since the generally admitted desirability for a correct
historical account and for correcting existing historical accounts requires, among other things, an understanding of the nature and causes
of human association or culture, it becomes necessary and useful that
these opinions and axioms be brought to light and those of them that
prove valid be made the premises of a comprehensive science useful
for writing a correct historical account and for correcting existing historical accounts. 2) Such a science of culture had not been attempted or
constructed before; Ibn Khaldūn's work is saying something that had
not been said before, except for incomplete beginnings and primitive
efforts in the same direction. 3) This science is deeply rooted in philosophy or wisdom, and deserves to be considered one of the philosophic
sciences. It fills a gap in the established philosophic sciences through

Muhsin Mahdi is Assistant Professor of Arabic, Department of Oriental Languages
and Civilizations, University of Chicago.

the application of their general principles and methods to a new field. These claims were in substance accepted in the subsequent history of Islamic civilization. Since Ibn Khaldūn's time, his work has continued to have a unique and permanent place in Islamic thought on history and society, in Arabic literature as well as in the newly emerging literature in Turkish and Urdu. The role of the "History" in the history of Islamic civilization, not only substantiated Ibn Khaldūn's claim, but supplied further evidence of its importance: 1) Most of the important works on the nature of history and society had to face the challenge of Ibn Khaldūn's work irrespective of whether they admitted or rejected them; 2) In a number of cases, Ibn Khaldūn's work had great impact on the writing and interpretation of history by Muslim authors, especially, though not exclusively, in Turkey; 3) To all appearances, Ibn Khaldūn's work seems to be there to stay, and its value seems to increase with the greater attention given to the problems of history and society in the Islamic world; 4) Finally, and for reasons that will be discussed in detail, the value of Ibn Khaldūn's work seems to transcend the boundaries of Islamic civilization. More specifically, it has been translated and studied in the West, not merely as representative of Islamic thought or the Islamic world-view, but as saying something directly relevant to modern scientific thought, a thought which aims at transcending all previous world-views. This seems to indicate that Ibn Khaldūn's work may have something to contribute to the understanding of the nature of history and society as such.

This paper will attempt to indicate some of the didactic problems faced in teaching this work on the undergraduate level, both in general courses on Islamic civilization and as a great book of a non-Western civilization. It will attempt to anticipate the probable reactions of students to a first reading of Ibn Khaldūn's text, and to indicate the direction in which the discussion is to be led in order to elicit Ibn Khaldūn's intention, make possible a more thorough understanding of the fundamental principles underlying his thought, and arouse in the student the incentive for reexamining his own opinions on the issues brought to light by a more genuine confrontation with Ibn Khaldūn's position.

It will be found in general that the peculiar obstacle in the way of understanding Ibn Khaldūn's thought is not its alien or singular character, but an assumed similarity, if not identity, between it and modern thought. This has invariably been the reaction of his modern readers, and there is no reason to suppose that it could be avoided except through a more critical effort on the part of the instructor to understand the reasons for such a reaction, and to devise effective methods for challenging it and leading the student to realize the significant difference between the foundations of Ibn Khaldūn's science of culture and those of modern social science.

It is perhaps trite to say that Ibn Khaldūn addressed himself to the educated Muslims of the fourteenth century. But his art of addressing the educated Muslims of his time, when intelligently studied, can raise problems which transcend the particular cultural and historical context of his time. The contemporary tendency toward cultural relativism needs to be counterbalanced by asking where and in what manner Ibn Khaldūn, while writing for the educated Muslims of his time, has something to say to the educated non-Muslim of our time.

The central problem of Islamic thought, which is everpresent throughout Ibn Khaldūn's work, is the conflicting claims of the religious-legal sciences and the philosophic-rational sciences that each offers the only proper set of principles and methods for the study and understanding of history and society. Ibn Khaldūn made the most massive and comprehensive attempt in Islamic thought to steal away the study of history and society from the religious-legal sciences and to incorporate it within the sphere of the philosophic-rational sciences in general and of the natural sciences in particular. This required, not only a theoretical, scientific effort to apply the principles and methods of the philosophic-rational sciences to a new field, but also an extremely subtle art of communication through which he sought to convince the educated Muslim, trained in the religious-legal science,

that the principles and methods of these sciences are insufficient and
inadequate for the proper understanding of the nature of society and
of the real meaning and use of history, to show him the need to turn
to philosophy, and to suggest to him the superiority of the explana-
tions offered by the latter.

Yet the general run of educated Muslims, and the learned uphold-
ers of the religious-legal sciences, were suspicious of the philosophic-
rational sciences and openly antagonistic to the protagonists of Greek
philosophy, especially when these sought, as in this case, to challenge
them in a field most intimately related to the way of life of the Islamic
community. They also had effective ways of persecuting, silencing,
and eliminating them. In such a context, it would have been, of
course, disastrous for Ibn Khaldūn to make a frontal attack, both for
his own person and for the success of his enterprise. Therefore, he
chose the more effective method of openly aligning himself with the
religious-legal sciences, while gradually undermining their authority
in the specific field he chose as the object of his investigation. In this,
he followed a well-established and well-known art of communication
which Muslim philosophers had inherited from their Greek and
Hellenistic masters, and which they elaborated to meet the particular exigencies they faced in their own religious community.

In a liberal society in which rationalism and science have tri-
umphed, and in which religion seems to have been for a considerable
time suspected and persecuted, and at a time when religion, rather
than reason and science, seems to be struggling to lay claims to do-
mains for long monopolized by science, the student is not likely to
become excited over such problems as hiding one's intention to gain
an initial hearing or to escape the censure and wrath of the religious
community—problems which could not escape the trained mind of
an educated Muslim of Ibn Khaldūn's time. In addition, the modern
educated man suffers from an almost complete forgetfulness of even
the existence of what were once commonplace ways of writing, especially among great authors of the past. Consequently, he is not at all
equipped properly to read their works. He seems to think that only a

confused author would not say exactly what is in his mind; and he is more likely to admire an author's rashness than his prudence.

These are the most formidable obstacles in the way of the appreciation and understanding of many of the important Islamic classics, including Ibn Khaldūn's work. Because of them, these classics remain mute and helpless to communicate their message to the educated modern man. The most notable contribution that an instructor can make is to remind his students of these issues by pointing them out whenever encountered in the reading of these classics, and thus aid their authors by establishing a wider channel of communication between them and their modern readers.

Perhaps the simplest approach would be for the instructor to appeal to the student's desire for historical understanding, which demands the appreciation of the particular context within which an author like Ibn Khaldūn wrote, the specific problems he intended to solve, and the alternative methods which were open to him in pursuing his aim. But once these issues are reopened, he could enhance the interest of the student in them by directing his attention to what he could learn from an author like Ibn Khaldūn concerning the character of public dogmas in all societies, including his own, of the restraints and limits they impose on public expression, and of the ways and means followed in suppressing or persecuting those who challenge them in societies most dedicated to the free expression of thought. The student will thus be brought to face the theoretical and practical considerations which make prudence rather than rashness the more desirable virtue in a writer.

In its positive teachings relative to history and society, experience has shown that, unlike many other Islamic classics, Ibn Khaldūn's work is able for the most part to command immediate acceptance, if not admiration, by the modern educated man. Its modern reader is drawn to its subject matter and to its scientific approach. It reminds him of a science, and of a critical approach, which he had thought to be specifically modern and to which he is usually already committed. Thus he begins to trust its author's scientific intentions, and to accept his analysis and interpretation of Islamic history and the Islamic society. Ibn Khaldūn has thus been able to escape the fate of many Muslim authors who aroused only the interest of the antiquarian, or were subjected to a historicist interpretation, i.e., were placed in a particular historical context and explained accordingly as a representative of a particular world-view. He is admitted in the company of modern scientists as a fellow-investigator in a common endeavor for objective knowledge.

This, however, is a mixed blessing. It certainly lightens the work of the instructor who is freed from the burden of attempting to arouse, at the outset, sufficient interest in, and respect for, the author, both of which are necessary conditions for a sustained dialogue between such an author and his reader. Therefore, this initial acceptance and trust should at first be encouraged. But in fairness to Ibn Khaldūn's text, the instructor must sooner or later turn this surprising *rapport* into a problem, and raise the question as to its reasons and the degree of its validity. He will soon discover that it is based on a conception of science and its method which, though at certain points coinciding with that of Ibn Khaldūn, differs from it on fundamental issues. The most important of these is the deep gulf that separates the modern conception of natural science and its relation to the science of society from that of Ibn Khaldūn.

Both Ibn Khaldūn and modern social science have attempted to develop a natural science, or a physics, of society. There are, of course, important differences in the reasons for following such a course and in the uses contemplated from the results, and in general in the place of the resulting science of society within the totality of human knowledge. Nevertheless, it could be said that in both cases it was thought that a science of society drawing its principles and methods from the wider study of nature, of which man is but a part, would be more exact and more explanatory, and would do least violence to the data which are being investigated, than a science of society based on principles whose only justification is tradition, faith, or common opinion.

But as soon as we stop to inquire into the precise character of Ibn Khaldūn's natural science, the similarity ends. For we find that for Ibn Khaldūn, natural science meant traditional Aristotelian natural science as found in that part of Aristotle's corpus which begins with the *Physics* and ends with the *De Anima,* together with the commentaries of Muslim philosophers in general and of Avicenna in particular. Our modern social science, on the other hand, was patterned after modern classical and post-classical physics with its radical departure from, and rejection of, traditional natural science or natural philosophy. How could then a science of society based on traditional natural philosophy be as scientific, and its conclusions as worthy of our consent, as a science of society based on modern physics? Is it that it makes no difference what kind of natural science one starts with? Does this mean that our modern physics has no higher claim to validity, at least in so far as its implications for social science are concerned, than traditional natural philosophy?

The central importance of Ibn Khaldūn's work lies in that it forces us to raise such questions, and in that it may be of use in seeking answers for them; for it is the only comprehensive attempt to develop a science of society on the basis of traditional natural philosophy. As one pursues such questions through his text, the real differences between his science of society and our modern social science begin to emerge. It will be found for instance that, in spite of the fact that he lays special emphasis on material and efficient causes, his conception of the "nature" of man and society is wider than that of modern social science: it includes their purpose and end, the good, and happiness.

It is, of course, not to be expected that when this fact is pointed out to the modern reader, he will continue to admire or trust Ibn Khaldūn's conclusions and judgments. What would be didactically useful and significant is that the shock resulting from the loss of initial and naive admiration and trust be taken as an opportunity to raise the important question of the status of modern physics, to question the naive acceptance of its presuppositions, to question the uncritical faith in its principles and methods as the only ones which can lay claim to being unquestionably scientific, and to question the character and the degree of explanation offered by a social science patterned after this physics.

Ibn Khaldūn certainly did not know of our modern physics in its specific details. But he knew of physical theories that had something in common with it, e.g., ancient materialism, and Islamic atomism and occasionalism. Yet, for the purpose of explaining the nature of society, he decided in favor of Aristotelian natural philosophy because he believed in its superiority as natural philosophy and in the superiority of a science of society that could be based upon it. He did not seem to be of the opinion that, so far as the science of society is concerned, it makes no difference what science of nature one chooses; and he seemed to place more confidence in Aristotelian natural philosophy, and in the usefulness of its principles and methods for the science of society. Thus he seems to challenge rather seriously the superiority of our modern physics as well as of our modern social science.

At a time when both modern physics and modern social science have begun to entertain doubts about their presuppositions, and to be concerned with problems of a more philosophic nature, such a challenge should be made to command more attention, and to offer an additional reason for a more serious examination of the claims of traditional natural philosophy and of the science of society based upon it.

One of the aspects of traditional natural philosophy that needs special attention in this respect is its place within traditional philosophy or science as a whole. For the fact that it was an integral part of general philosophy made the understanding of the relationship between nature, soul, and intellect more accessible. Consequently, Ibn Khaldūn's study of the nature of man and society, though based upon the principles and methods of natural philosophy, could still take into account such human and social phenomena as the sciences, inspiration, and prophecy, and in general things that are specifically human and superhuman, and for whose understanding natural philosophy alone is not sufficient.

It was this belief in the accessibility to reason of the principles of all things natural and beyond nature, and in the possibility of knowing what is best for man as man, that made it possible for Ibn Khaldūn to arrive at the necessary detachment from, and to pass judgment upon, the opinions and actions of his own community. Modern students uniformly admire his objectivity, his intellectual honesty, and his severity in judging the shortcomings of his community. On the other hand, they see that he is definitely committed to the proposition that the principles upon which the religious Law of his community was based made it superior to other communities. Their initial reaction to this seemingly contradictory position is usually that his toughness is the result of his positive scientific attitude, while his belief in the superiority of his own community is socially conditioned. This is the characteristically modern conception of the universal character of positive science, of which Ibn Khaldūn is supposed to have been a precursor, and the relative and socially conditioned character of cultural values, from which he is thought to have been able to free himself.

It will no doubt prove extremely difficult to convince the modern reader of the dogmatic character of this position. But it should at least be pointed out that the attempt to understand Ibn Khaldūn on this basis is liable to prejudice the issue and close the mind of the reader to what Ibn Khaldūn could teach him concerning the relation between science and cultural values. Here again, and at the risk of another shock and additional loss of confidence in the scientific character of Ibn Khaldūn's thought, the instructor will have to point out, perhaps with the aid of suggesting the need for an objective understanding of his thought, that Ibn Khaldūn's attachment to science or philosophy, as he understood it, made tough and polite judgments equally possible; and that for him praise and blame, and the recognition of superiority and inferiority, are both equally grounded in the understanding, or at least in a dim vision, of what is best for man and society.

In this respect, the understanding of Ibn Khaldūn's text requires an approach which substitutes for the modern distinction between facts and values the distinction between events, commonly known and generally accepted opinions and beliefs, and the pursuit of knowledge, the results of which, when fulfilling the requirements of logical reasoning, constitute science. Opinions and beliefs may agree or disagree with, may be identical with or contradictory to, or may come close to or may be remote from, scientifically demonstrated conclusions. All existing communities are based on opinions and beliefs; and differences among the opinions and beliefs of different communities, and among their ways of life which are based on such opinions and beliefs, are not only possible but to a certain extent natural. But such plurality does not exclude the possibility of scientific knowledge on the basis of which one could transcend the opinions and beliefs of his own community. Therefore, all men are not fated to accept blindly the opinions and beliefs of their community as being identical with truth or the good. Yet men of science are not those who simply dismiss opinions and beliefs as mere opinions and beliefs, but those who, on the basis of their scientific knowledge, and experience and prudence, can correctly judge the degree of truth contained in, and the practical use of, different opinions and beliefs, including those of their own community.

The reader must first be made to see how Ibn Khaldūn was able to do this with respect to the communities with which he was acquainted, and particularly how this approach enabled him to understand and judge his own community, its opinions and beliefs, and its way of life. This becomes rather delicate when he studies matters such as revelation, prophecy, and religious law. But when the reader becomes acquainted with his art of writing, he will begin to see that the general approach outlined above holds even in the study of such matters.

Since Ibn Khaldūn's work was on the whole concerned with the Islamic society, it will be easier for the educated Westerner to accept his critique of that society, as his own opinions, beliefs, and way of life, and those of his own community, are not immediately at stake. Indeed, it would be useful to reveal the various facets of Ibn Khaldūn's critique of the Islamic community as thoroughly as possible, yet insist throughout upon the theoretical foundation on the basis of which such a critique was possible. The instructor will find that, because the student's own preferences and those of his own community are not directly involved, he is more likely to be openminded and more willing to be tough. If sufficient control is exercised to prevent this from becoming a free indulgence in common prejudices against other communities, it will prove an excellent training ground for developing his power of critical judgment, the exercise of which can and must eventually be transferred to the critical study of his own community, its opinions and beliefs, and its way of life.

For ultimately, Ibn Khaldūn's study of the nature of man and society will prove of little value for general education if it fails to arouse in the modern reader a genuine concern for understanding himself and the character of his own community. A necessary prerequisite for such an understanding is the readiness to question the generally known opinions and the commonly accepted beliefs of his own community. The general tendency has been to see in Ibn Khaldūn a confirmation of established opinions and beliefs. The continued use of his work for this purpose will mean the perpetuation of a misunderstanding of Ibn Khaldūn's thought and intention. Further, since it will encourage opinionated complacency, it will prove harmful to general education. The task of the instructor is to initiate a dialectical process in which the reading of Ibn Khaldūn serves to help the student to question his own opinions and beliefs, and then use this critical attitude for a more thorough and a more critical understanding of Ibn Khaldūn's text.

It is to be hoped that the preceding remarks have shown that the problems confronting the teaching and the study of Ibn Khaldūn's text are not primarily philological or historical in character, at least not in the narrow sense of philological and historical criticism. The text has been preserved in numerous copies, many of which were excellently transcribed under the supervision of an author who also prided himself on writing in a clear and free manner, upon which modern philology need not presume that it can improve. Ibn Khaldūn himself also supplies in the same text all the historical background relevant for understanding it. He was, after all, a great authority on the history of his time.

There are, it is true, difficulties related to the appreciation of his art of writing, the understanding of the precise character of his scientific investigation of society, and the recapturing of his conception of the nature of scientific knowledge in general and its place within the social order in particular. But these difficulties are for the most part not faced, but only sidetracked, by modern philological and historical criticism. These latter are the scientific offspring of a modern philosophic attitude which has invariably supplied the premises (sometimes accepted dogmatically by these specialized disciplines) in the light of which Ibn Khaldūn's text has been interpreted. Since the proper understanding of the text seems to require, and to lead to, the questioning of the dogmatic character of this attitude, it is evident that the reader, if he is to profit intellectually from his reading, must regain a certain innocence, and be willing to think, to doubt, and to question both his own ideas as well as those presented to him by the author.

If the reader is an undergraduate student, he will need an adequate translation of the text prepared for him with the assumption that he is a serious reader, and an instructor trained to arouse his curiosity about important issues in general, and direct his attention to the specific issues raised by Ibn Khaldūn's text in particular.

There are a host of summaries, paraphrases, and selections in the various Western languages, but very few of them are executed with proper care. They subscribe (at least the most popular among them) to the notion of the modern character of Ibn Khaldūn's thought. Thus they omit or mistranslate the sections that do not harmonize with this notion; they rearrange the text, modernize its expressions, and in general try to present it in a perspective intended to prove or suggest the modern, scientific character of the thought of its author.

The student should be encouraged to turn to the two complete translations of the "Introduction," that of Baron de Slane in French and that of Franz Rosenthal in English. He will find them of much greater use in learning about the scope of the work and of its internal structure. Of the two, the English translation is the more recent and the superior one. However, under the influence of previous summaries, selections, and monographs, it accepts the notion that the text is "modern in thought yet alien in language and style," and a great effort is made throughout to make the text comprehensible to the general reader through an extensive use of the modernizing type of rendering. Therefore, the careful reader, willing to spend the time and effort required by a more exact (even if less literary and more dry) rendering of the Arabic style and of the technical terms, with the hope of a sounder understanding of the text, will still find himself severely handicapped. Thus the burden is shifted to the instructor, who will have to control the translation.

This, of course, is the most elementary task that will be faced by the instructor, and one which is by no means the most difficult to overcome. The teaching of Ibn Khaldūn's text as a great book and for the purposes of general education makes demands on the instructor which very few specialists in Arabic and Islamic studies are at present prepared to meet. This is not an accident. It is intimately linked with the past and present status of these studies. Arabic and Islamic studies as scientific academic disciplines are relatively recent ventures. They developed in the nineteenth century as special branches of philology and history; were influenced by the current trends in these two disciplines; and continued to remain loyal to them in the critical editions of texts and in textual criticism, and in the critical study of Islamic history. It would be sheer folly at this juncture in the development of these studies to detract from the value of the type of specialized training they offer, to say nothing of disrupting a tradition built with great dedication and effort. Yet it must in all honesty be recognized that such a training does not by itself supply the required background for the critical reading, understanding, and interpreting, of the great Islamic classics. If one had enough courage, he might even dare to say that they are not, strictly speaking, an indispensable requirement for such a work. (Averroes and Aquinas were able, without them, to understand the text of Aristotle better than most, if not all, modern philologists and historians.) The normal trend within these studies has been to have recourse to the theories that happen to be popular at the time (historicism, sociologism, psychologism, etc.), or other commonly accepted beliefs and opinions, and to adopt them in interpreting these classics, thus enjoying the advantage of following the latest scientific style.

Such scientific interpretations are usually harmless exercises, and they can, on rare occasions, be useful in providing certain insights into the Islamic classics. But they tend also to become substitutes for the direct critical reading of these classics with the intention of finding what one can learn from them. And they even get incorporated into the texts of these classics through the modernized type of rendering. Perhaps no great Muslim author has suffered from this tendency as much as Ibn Khaldūn. Thus when the innocent student proceeds to read and understand his text with an open mind, he is likely to have before him a not-so-innocent version of it, and to have as his guide an instructor who seems to know all about Ibn Khaldūn's background, his psychology, the social forces that determined his thought, the reasons for his belief in God and superstition and religion, etc.— in short everything except how to critically read the text before him, analyze it, closely follow the steps of Ibn Khaldūn's argument, enjoy his "doubletalk," appreciate his hints and allusions, and arouse and encourage in the student a passion for reading the text, appreciating it, and criticizing it as a great work of the mind. He seems often to have been trained to explain the text away, and to lack the readiness for allowing the text to explain away his own notions, to form his mind, and to train it in dealing with the great issues of life and of the world.

The grafting of this latter attitude upon the existing structure of Arabic and Islamic studies requires a concerted effort on the part of educators and Arabists and Islamists alike. Nor should the latter be thought of as immune or insufficiently responsive to new demands, especially if coupled with the expectation of more solid rewards. Many Arabists and Islamists have, for instance, proved obligingly willing in recent times to meet the demand for popular versions of Islamic history and civilization—sometimes even at the expense of their own scientific conscience, and in spite of the reproachful and censorious attitude of their colleagues. The teaching of the Islamic classics as great books, however, is of a completely different order.

There is already in existence an established academic, and even para-academic, tradition with respect to the introduction of the classics of the Western world into programs of general education. By now, educators have a rather clear idea of what the problems and prospects of this enterprise are, and the training required of a successful instructor in this field. This experience must be made available to specialists in Arabic and Islamic studies so that they would gain a precise notion of the nature of the new needs. It should, in particular, be impressed upon them that the critical reading, analysis, understanding, and interpretation of an important text requires a special skill and training that cannot be acquired in one's spare time, that need not be subjective, nor the work of an undisciplined amateur.

If Arabists and Islamists find that the history and character of their discipline make it difficult for them at present to offer such a training, then the best practical arrangement will be for them to encourage the student to acquire such training through interdepartmental committees, in fields where such a training is offered, such as in philosophy, and in classical and modern literatures, i.e., in fields where the classics are made the backbone of the program of study. This is certainly a second-best arrangement, since it involves the task of subsequently transferring the skills thus acquired to texts of somewhat different character. But in addition to substantially meeting the present need for qualified instructors to teach the Islamic classics, the result will no doubt prove a significant gain to Arabic and Islamic studies themselves. For no matter how necessary or useful philological and historical criticism may be, they should never be separated from the study of Islamic classics as classics.

GEORGE BOSWORTH BURCH

The Upanishads

THE UPANISHADS AS LITERATURE

The Upanishads [1] are outstanding in world literature for poetical, philosophical, and historical interest. If they are, as it seems, older than either Plato or Lao Tzu, they are the most ancient strictly philosophical work now extant. And in Indian philosophy, just as in Western and Chinese philosophy, the oldest extant philosophical work has seldom if ever been surpassed either for profundity of thought or for beauty of style.

Of the many books called Upanishads there are a dozen, more or less, which are recognized as the principal or classical ones. All together these make only a small volume. The *Brihadaranyaka, Katha,* and *Chāndogya* are perhaps of greatest interest. The *Brihadaranyaka* is the longest, and is the most explicit source of the nondualist philosophy. The *Katha* contains the dialogue between the god of death and Nachiketas, who demanded of the god, who had promised him a boon, that he explain to him the meaning of death. The *Chāndogya* contains the famous formula *Thou art That,* interpreted by the nondualist school as asserting the identity of the Self with the Absolute.

The Upanishads have inspired endless commentary. If Western philosophy can be called, as Whitehead said, a series of footnotes to the Dialogues of Plato, Indian philosophy may equally

George Bosworth Burch is Fletcher Professor of Philosophy at Tufts University.
[1] The best English edition is R. E. Hume, *Thirteen Principal Upanishads* (Oxford University Press, 1931).

well be called a series of footnotes to the Upanishads. In both cases the commentary is sometimes negative, but in both cases the influence persists to the present day, and the old texts maintain their position as the basic documents of the wisdom literature of the two great cultures. But the Upanishads need no commentary. They stand on their own merits as wisdom and as poetry. The way to approach them is to read them, not read about them. To read the Upanishads with Shankara's commentary is like reading the Book of Genesis with St. Augustine's commentary—great philosophy, but hardly the way to introduce a beginner to the text. The many commentaries on the Upanishads are important for students of Vedanta philosophy, but they should be read only by persons already acquainted with the texts themselves. Like Plato or the Bible, the Upanishads appeal to readers at any stage of intellectual advancement, and can be reread many times without failing to offer fresh insights.

THE UPANISHADS AS TRADITION

An appreciation of these ancient books requires some consideration of their place in the cultural history of India. Philologists can trace the literary history. The Vedic hymns are the oldest extant works, the *Brāhmanas* are later, the Upanishads still later, and the Sanskrit language evolved from the older to the later works. But to trace the Upanishads back to the Vedic hymns is about as sensible as to trace Locke's essay back to *Beowulf*. The language of Locke is indeed derived from the language of *Beowulf*, but his ideas have their sources in earlier non-English literature. The language of the Upanishads developed from that of the hymns, but the genealogy of the thought is another question.

Any theory of the origins of Hindu culture must be based on two facts. One fact is the relation of Sanskrit to the other Indo-European languages. This fact implies no theory as to when, where, or by whom this language group originated, but the fact itself is undeniable. The other fact is the existence of the Indus Valley cities.

The time, race, and language of their inhabitants are matters for speculation, but the ruins themselves are a fact. These two facts can be related by the hypothesis that the Indus cities were destroyed by invaders who brought the Sanskrit language into India, and many historians hold that this is a plausible view. This theory is only a hypothesis, and even if correct it is an extreme simplification of what must have been a very complicated situation. But it has the advantage of providing categories of thought in terms of which we can discuss the origins of Hinduism. It presents the problem of sorting out the elements of historical Hinduism into two groups, those contributed by the Aryan invaders and those contributed by the non-Aryan earlier inhabitants. The Aryan invaders contributed the Sanskrit language and the class distinctions which eventually developed into the caste system. The non-Aryans, to make a guess on the basis of the archaeological evidence, probably contributed most of the arts, sciences, and techniques. There is some evidence, though not very strong, that the Saivite and Tantric religions had their source in the Indus cities. But how about the Upanishadic philosophy?

The evidence for this is only negative. We have no information about the philosophical theories taught by the wise men of Mohenjo-daro. But we know something about the thought of the Aryans, because we have their hymns. We should of course be cautious in going beyond the evidence. A future historian who tried to reconstruct the culture of twentieth-century America from a Methodist hymnal would certainly get an inadequate picture of our many-sided civilization. Still it is better than nothing. And if anything is clear about the thought of the Aryans, it is that their thought was not Upanishadic. Nothing could be less Hindu than the Vedic hymns. The militant, this-worldly, animistic Aryan invaders knew nothing of reincarnation, nothing of karma, nothing of the illusoriness of the world, nothing of the Absolute Self, and the last thing they wanted was liberation from individual existence. Wherever the Upanishadic philosophy came from, it did not come from the

Aryans. It might conceivably have some completely unknown foreign source, but presumably its source was in the thought of the pre-Aryan Indians.

If this perspective is correct, then the people of India, especially the Dravidian-speaking people, can look to the Upanishads as the oldest extant documents of the immemorial tradition of their ancestors, although written in the alien language of the invaders. It is something like the situation of India today, where original books of Vedanta philosophy are written in English. Those fanatically anti-Aryan Dravidians of South India, who at the present time delight in hanging Rāma in effigy on the festival when northern Indians hang Rāvana, might well venerate as an ancient Defender of the Faith that king of Mohenjo-daro whose bust, now in the New Delhi museum, has an expression of unutterable disdain, indicating extreme contempt for somebody, perhaps for the Aryan barbarians pouring through the Khyber Pass, against whom, like his successors throughout the ages, he defended India most unsuccessfully.

As in other parts of the world, such as Greece, the Indo-European speaking barbarians, conquering because of superior military techniques, especially chariots, imposed their language on the conquered people, not simply by force but largely through the intrinsic merit of the language itself. But the superior culture of the defeated peoples eventually conquered the inferior culture of the invaders as the ancient wisdom, perhaps driven underground by the military conquest, again asserted itself. The Indo-Europeans were strong on poetry but weak in philosophy. As Plato points out in the *Republic*, Homer's poetry is magnificent but his ideas are scandalous. Nestor, the wisest of the Achaeans, was not the intellectual ancestor of Pythagoras and Plato. Nor were the Vedic hymnographers the intellectual ancestors of the Upanishadic philosophers. The Vedic hymns in Hinduism, like the Psalms in Christianity, are venerated as revealed scripture and incorporated into the liturgy, but their ideas are either interpreted allegorically or simply ignored.

There is good reason to suppose that the Vedānta tradition, of which the Upanishads are a text, has flourished in India from pre-Aryan times, probably alongside other philosophical traditions, such as the Jain and Tantric. The Upanishads themselves are the glorious manifesto of the Vedānta tradition as it reasserted itself, in sublime literary form, after the period of cultural darkness which must have followed the Aryan conquest, and established its position as a new orthodoxy. The language of the Aryans and the wisdom of the Dravidians combined to form a new literary foundation for Hinduism.

UPANISHADS AS REVELATION

This speculative attempt to consider the Upanishads in historical perspective is not, to be sure, the way in which Hindus look at them. For Hindus the Upanishads are revealed scripture, what they call *shruti*. The whole corpus of revealed scripture, including hymns, liturgy, and Upanishads, is called the *Veda*. This is analogous to the Western Bible, but the Hindu notion of revelation is different from the Western. While the books of the Bible are supposed to have been written by inspired prophets, the *Veda* is supposed to be eternal, with no author and no beginning. It is not exactly "revelation," because it is not revealed to anyone or by anyone. It simply is.

Nevertheless, the problems presented by shruti to Vedānta philosophers are strictly parallel to those presented by inspired scripture to Christian philosophers. The *Veda* is an autonomous source of knowledge, coordinate with reason and experience. It is to be accepted by faith as authority, and anyone who does not accept it is no good Hindu. But, like the Bible, it needs interpretation, application, and understanding. First, since it is largely ambiguous or figurative, even those who agree on its infallibility may disagree as to its meaning. Second, those who have faith, that is, accept it as true, still need what St. Paul calls a living faith, that is, to base their lives on it. Third, those who believe its doctrines may still desire, like St. Augustine, to understand them by reason. Such rational understanding of revealed truth is the Vedānta philosophy.

The doctrines taught in the Upanishads are the basic doctrines of metaphysics, the existence of God and the soul. Underlying the phenomena of the world is a substance, Brāhman, of which the world is a creature, manifestation, or illusory appearance, and underlying the events of consciousness is a substance, Ātman, which is the subject of knowledge. Brāhman and Ātman, however, are to be translated "God" and "soul" only in the most metaphysical meanings of those words, and they must not be confused with a personal God or a conscious mind. They mean the Absolute Reality and the Absolute Self.

These truths can be known only by revelation. It is not necessary, of course, to read the Upanishads. A Hindu learns these doctrines from his guru, and they are also taught in non-Hindu religions. They can be known, in fact, without any religious instruction. You do not have to go to Sunday School in order to hear about God. These truths are not esoteric. They are handed down in the cultural tradition of all civilizations, and are available to everybody. But their source is always superhuman. They must be learned from a teacher, who likewise learned them from a teacher, and so on, the first in the line necessarily relying on revelation. Other cultures may have their own revelations, but the tradition can always be traced back to a superhuman source. This is necessarily so, because these truths cannot be learned from any human source. Neither experience nor reason teaches the existence of God or soul. We cannot know God by sense-perception, because we do not meet Him in experience, and we cannot know the soul by introspection, because this, as James rightly observed, reveals nothing beyond the stream of conscious events. There is no rational demonstration of the existence of God which will convince a person not already convinced on other grounds, and reason, even if it may convince me that "I think therefore I am," never shows that I am a substantial soul. If we relied only on experience and reason, without any revelation either immediate or transmitted, we would never even think of God or soul.

Revelation, therefore, and ultimately the primary revelation or shruti, makes a radical difference—in the West between Christianity and humanism, in India between Hinduism and Buddhism. Hindus, like Christians, in the formula of the old Muslim distinction between infidel and heathen, "have a book." The book is all important, because without it we are restricted to the resources of experience and reason. In the West philosophers thus restricted are called positivists. They reject all authority except that of experience and reason. Consequently they deny not only the existence, but even the meaningfulness of God, soul, and all metaphysical entities whatsoever, and they do so quite rightly, granting their initial position. In India this is the position of the Buddhists, who likewise reject all alleged revelation. The religious consequence of this is to describe life as suffering, as we know it to be by experience, rather than as sin or illusion, as we cannot know it to be except by some information not given in experience. The philosophical consequence is to deny that there is any soul or self, to deny that there is any God or Absolute, to deny in general that there is any substance whatever, and to assert that reality is process. The Buddhists, like the positivists, are quite right. Without shruti we have no ground for believing in the existence of anything beyond the phenomenal processes given in experience.

But Hindus, like Christians, do have a source of metaphysical knowledge, the revealed scripture of the Upanishads. Knowing from these that God and soul exist, they can consider the relations between God, soul, and world, and seek to realize their destiny in terms of this revealed knowledge—something which Buddhists, be their dialecticians ever so subtle and their saints ever so magnanimous, cannot do. This, at least, is the Hindu view.

THE UPANISHADS AS PHILOSOPHY

In the West some philosophers, like Comte, reject the Bible; others, like Descartes, accept it but do not let it influence their philosophy; while others, like St. Augustine, base their philosophy on it. Likewise in India some philosophers, like the Buddhist school, reject the *Veda;* others like the Sānkhya school, accept it but do not let it influence their philosophy; while others, the Vedānta school, base their philosophy on it. Vedānta is the philosophical superstructure erected on the *Veda,* that is, the Upanishads. The standard classics of Vedānta philosophy are commentaries on the Upanishads, on the *Vedānta Sūtras,* and on the *Gītā.* The Upanishads are shruti itself. The Sūtras, composed by Bādarāyana, founder of Vedānta, are a concise summary and reconciliation of shruti. The *Gītā* is not shruti, but is just as good as shruti. The purpose of the commentaries is to understand the revelation by reason.

But philosophers do not see eye to eye, in India any more than elsewhere. The Vedānta school, united by historical tradition, faith in the *Veda,* and certain categories of thought, has developed many philosophies radically different in epistemological, metaphysical, and ethical doctrines. These philosophies are called dualism, nondualism, qualified nondualism, and dualistic nondualism. All were established in the Middle Ages, when their classical expositions were composed, all have developed various sub-schools, and all still have enthusiastic advocates at the present day.

Dualism, founded by Madhva, teaches empiricism, realism, pluralism, and theism. The highest good is eternal bliss in heaven, attained by devotion to God and service to fellow men.

Nondualism, founded by Gaudapada, teaches that Brahman is the only reality, the Self is Brahman, and the world is illusion. Identity of Self with Brahman does not need to be attained, since it exists eternally, and the highest good is simply the awareness of this truth.

Qualified nondualism, founded by Rāmānuja, teaches a sort of pantheism, that all things are real because permeated by the Brahman which is their essence. The highest good is union with the personal god, Vishnu, attained by love for him responding to his love for us.

Dualistic nondualism, founded by Bhāskara, teaches an all inclusive philosophy stressing the equal validity of monism and pluralism. The highest good is that self-expansion by which we renounce our limitations, retrace the steps by which we became finite, and return to the original unity of Brahman.

Dualism explains things by the logical law of discrimination, nondualism explains things by the epistemological law of ignorance, qualified nondualism explains things by the moral law of karma, and dualistic nondualism explains things by the metaphysical law of causality. Outstanding contemporary advocates of these systems are Professor Nagaraja Sarma of Madras for dualism, Professor G. R. Malkani of Amalner for nondualism, Professor P. N. Srinivasachari of Madras for qualified nondualism, and Mrs. Roma Bose Chaudhury of Calcutta for dualistic nondualism. In general students will do better to begin a study of the Vedānta schools through the clear English writings of these contemporary philosophers than through the difficult Sanskrit commentaries of the medieval āchar-yas.

The whole body of Vedānta works, ancient, medieval, modern, and contemporary, constitutes a vast system of philosophical literature in which it would seem that all philosophical problems are explored and all possible solutions critically examined. The historical and dogmatic foundation of the whole tradition is the Upanishads. These short books, which Max Müller compared to the light of the morning and the air of the mountains, teach those simple and profound insights which generations of philosophers have elaborated with infinite detail and analyzed with infinite subtlety.

THE UPANISHADS AS NONDUALISM

Among these Vedānta philosophies, nondualism is preeminent in two respects. On the one hand, it does seem to represent most closely the implicit teaching of the Upanishads. Thibaut, the translator of Shankara's commentary on the Vedānta Sūtras, came to the paradoxical conclusion that Shankara's nondualism misrepresents the Sūtras, which are closer to Rāmānuja's system, but correctly represents the Upanishads which the Sūtras purport to summarize. On the other hand, nondualism has appealed perennially to the most profound philosophers of India and alone among Vedānta systems has also appealed to non-Indian philosophers. No other Indian philosophy, says Thibaut, can be compared with it "in boldness, depth, and subtlety of speculation."

The most rigorous statement of nondualism is found not in the extensive commentaries of its great popularizer Shankara, but in the concise *Karika* of its founder Gaudapada. The first chapter of this 215-verse work is an interpretation of, and often considered part of, the *Mandukya Upanishad,* which has only twelve verses itself. Karmarkar, a translator of Gaudapada, argues that it is not really part of the Upanishad, because Gaudapada was a man, while the revealed Upanishads have no human authors. Bhattacharya, another translator, believes on the contrary that the Upanishad is a commentary on Gaudapada. Be this as it may, Gaudapada's work is inextricably associated with the Upanishads. A reader of the Upanishads should be sure to include the *Karika,* and he may find it the most interesting book of the whole collection.

Gaudapada presents explicitly, systematically, and rationally the ideas which are implicit in the poetry of the Upanishads. In so doing he lifts them from their literary context and makes them universal. The Upanishads are just as thoroughly Indian as Plato's Dialogues are thoroughly Greek, but Brahman is no more exclusively Indian than the Good is exclusively Greek. Nondualism, if true anywhere, is true everywhere. These books are to be read for their beauty as poetry and for their illustration of Indian culture and ways of thought, but they are also to be read for their insight into eternal and universal truth.

The search for the objective reality in our largely subjective experience cannot stop short of the absolute *That* which is the ground of all relative appearances. The philosopher's quest to "Know Thyself" cannot stop short of the absolute *Thou* which is thy real self. The relation between them can only be expressed ultimately by asserting *Thou art That*. This is taught by the Upanishads, demonstrated by Vedānta, but realized only by those who go beyond both faith and reason to immediate awareness.

Indian and Greek Epics [1]

One who undertakes a comparative study between two
cultures is usually guided by a half-conscious bias which can assume either of the two following forms. He may so handle the
material at his disposal as to concentrate almost exclusively on the
similarities, real or apparent, of the terms of the comparison. Or
his mind may react more spontaneously to the differences and unconsciously exaggerate them.

The first attitude—which we could conveniently call "cultural
syncretism"—is often the characteristic of a generous yet shallow
mind. Generous, because it is anxious to bring about harmony and
unity and naturally refrains from extolling one culture at the expense of another. Shallow, because, in order to achieve its ideal of
harmony, it rests satisfied with a superficial view of things and
avoids the labor of deeper analysis for fear of seeing its conclusions
challenged.

The second attitude—to which we give the name of "cultural
chauvinism"—is that of a mind whose natural sharpness is placed
at the service of partisan spirit. It seeks to establish the superiority
and uniqueness of one culture and, in pursuing its end, exercises
its ingenuity either to undermine any attempt at comparison or to

Father Robert Antoine S.J. is Professor of Sanskrit Literature, Xavier College,
Calcutta.

[1] Reprinted and revised, with the permission of the Editors, from *Quest* (Calcutta),
April–June 1958, pp. 37–49.

prove that all similarities are the result of dependence or plagiarism.

Is it at all possible to combine the syncretist's generosity and the partisan's acuity while avoiding the former's simplicity and the latter's parochialism? A perfectly unbiased mind, if it could at all exist, would probably remain inactive, for the human mind never acts as a passive mirror, but rather as an actively selective organ. Facts, and especially human facts, never speak for themselves. They are made to say what the human observer prompts them to express.

Should we, therefore, give up all comparative studies on the plea that perfect impartiality is impossible? I do not think so. It is enough to know, and to guard oneself against, the dangers which such studies entail. If we keep in mind that, within the general pattern according to which human societies arise and evolve, there remains ample room for individuality and originality, we can safely undertake the fascinating task of comparing cultures.

THE GENERAL PATTERN OF HEROIC SOCIETY

All the great heroic traditions owe their existence to tribal culture. The basis on which tribal society rests is the principle of kinship and its social unit is the family group. Whereas the higher culture of the territorial state is founded on the idea of individual citizenship and gives rise to urban civilization, the tribal organization ignores national feeling and finds its social expression in feudalism. Feudalism is essentially an exchange of services between defenseless peasants and the military lord. In return for the protection which the lord gives them, the peasants offer him their land and promise to man his armies. When, to the economic necessity of finding a protector, is added the element of personal devotion to the leader, the cult of the hero is born.

On the other hand, epic poetry is usually retrospective. It develops at a time when tribal society enters into contact with a higher civilization and tends to project into the past certain elements of urban culture which give to the old capitals an anachronic aspect of modernity. It is this marginal character of epic poetry which explains how tribal heroes can gradually be transformed into national heroes.

It is interesting to note how epiç poetry, in three different historical contexts, blossomed at an intermediary period, a kind of "Middle Ages" between two urban civilizations. In India, after the disappearance of the Indus civilization and before the rise of the Mauriyas; in Greece, after the decline of Aegean culture and before the emergence of Athenian dominance; in Europe, after the fall of the Roman Empire and of the short-lived Carolingian renaissance and before the urban civilization of the fourteenth century.

1. *The aristocrats at war.* Heroic society is an aristocratic society. In the Greek epic, the heroes are called the *"aristoi,"* i.e., the best among men. Stereotyped adjectives are used, referring probably to some well-known quality of some ancestor, and the name of the father or a patronymic *"taddhitānta"* continually reminds us that nobility is hereditary. The feuds which result in bloody battles have never the character of national wars in which the common people play the prominent part. In fact, the common people do not appear at all except as a necessary background against which the valor and prowess of the heroes stand out in greater splendor. Most of the fights are single fights, extraordinary duels witnessed by a crowd of spellbound soldiers and retainers.

The origin of the great battles is, in all cases, the personal offense of a hero's honor. And it is generally a woman who supplies the occasion. In the *Iliad,* it is self-evident. The Greek tribes, personified in their leaders, agree to avenge the honor of Menelaus whose wanton wife has eloped with the Trojan Paris. There is not the slightest hint of a national campaign, and the leadership of Agamemnon has no other reason than the necessity of a concerted attack. Again, it is the wounded pride of Achilles which proves fatal to the Greek armies and brings the Trojans within an ace of victory. The young lady whom Achilles had received as a prize for his bravery is arbitrarily taken away from him by Agamemnon. Finally, if Achilles decided to enter the fray, it is not out of a sense

of solidarity with the routed Greeks, but of the purely personal desire to avenge his friend's death. National feeling, if it exists at all
in the *Iliad,* is to be found among the Trojans. For them, everything is at stake, as it will be for the Greeks at the time of Mara-
thon and Salamis. Yet, in spite of the simple solution of returning
to her lawful husband the woman who is the cause of their extreme
misfortune, they choose to fight because the Greeks have challenged
them. It is a question of *panache* and it overrides the security of the
city.

The tragedy of the *Rāmāyana* begins with the foolish claim of
a vain woman, Kaikeyi. King Dasaratha who knows her claim to
be unreasonable considers himself bound by the sacred duty of keeping his word. The welfare of his subjects and their undisguised dis-
approval count for nothing before his misconceived obligation toward Bharata's mother. And thus Rāma, Sītā, and Lakshmana
leave for the forest. Bharata is the only one whose attitude must have
made sense to the more enlightened. But his efforts are all in vain.
The capture of Sītā by Rāvana constitutes a lesser national problem
than Helen's elopement, for the people of Ayodhyā have nothing
to do in rescuing her. It is a personal injury to Rāma who, instead
of calling on his own people to fight with him for their beloved
princess, gets involved in the family dispute of a monkey tribe and
gains the allegiance of the winning side. After Rāvana's defeat and
the recovery of Sītā, it may be argued that Rāma gives up the arbitrary rule of feudal lord and rates very high the feelings and opinions of his subjects. The fire ordeal and the second banishment of
Sītā are undeniable proofs of his new policy. Yet, one wonders if
that new policy heralds the dawn of a new era. It is so much in
keeping with Rāma's submissiveness at the time of his banishment.
Rightly has Rāma been given as the ideal of the "shānta" hero and
one aspect of his love for peace seems to be that trouble should be
avoided at any cost: neither his right to the throne, nor his absolute
conviction that Sītā is innocent can arouse in him the passion necessary to resist the trouble-makers.

The destinies of the Pāndavas and the Kauravas are decided in a game of dice. This is typical of a feudal setting where the rulers dispose of their kingdoms as they would of their private fortunes. The overbearing pride of the winners and the spiteful humiliation of the losers reaches its climax in the Draupadī incident. It is around the ill-used Draupadī that the personal antagonism of the feudal lords crystallizes. The terrible imprecation of Bhīma against Duhshāsana, "I shall split his breast and drink his blood" (*Mahābhārata,* Sabhaparva, 90.57), is the real declaration of war and the long exile will be unable to delete its memory. Its gruesome realization can easily bear comparison with the savage profanation of Hector's body at the hands of Achilles.

After the exile, when the Pāndavas delegate Krishna to Duryodhana in order to reach a compromise, it is Draupadī, with her untied hair as a perpetual reminder of her humiliation, who passionately opposes all kinds of peaceful settlement. The way in which Krishna conducts the interview with the leader of the Kauravas is strongly influenced by the bellicose attitude of Pāncālī.

2. *The aristocrats in peace time.* Success in war being at the same time the condition of survival and the highest glory to which the heroes aspire, it is quite natural to see the young aristocrats apply themselves enthusiastically to their military training. Under the wise guidance of Drona, the young Pāndavas and Kauravas vie with one another in the display of their skill, while the elders and a crowd of simple admirers look on with immense delight. Their loud acclamation fills the air (*Mahābhārata,* Adi-parva, 144.39).

In the *Rāmāyana,* young Rāma receives his training from Vishvāmitra. The expedition against the demons is not just a game but is meant to give Rāma an idea of the evil forces with which he will have to grapple in his maturity. Homer has not depicted the early training of his heroes. Old Phoenix, however, gives us a glimpse of Achilles' education. Pleading with the sulking hero, Phoenix tells him: "My noble Lord Achilles, if you really think of sailing home and are so obsessed by anger that you refuse to save the gallant ships from going up in flames, what is to become of me without you, my dear child? How could I possibly stay there alone? Did not the old charioteer Peleus make me your guardian when he sent you off from Phthia to join Agamemnon? You were a mere lad, with no experience of the hazards of war, nor of debate, where people make their mark. It was to teach you all these things, to make a speaker of you, and a man of action, that he sent me with you; and I could not bring myself to let you go, dear child, and to stay behind, not if God himself undertook to strip me of my years and turn me into the sturdy youngster I was when I first left Hellas, the land of lovely women." (*Iliad,* Rieu trans. [Penguin], Book X, p. 172.)

Skill and strength are the necessary qualities of warriors. But these qualities have also a social importance which cannot be ignored. They are rated so high that a king is ready to give his daughter in marriage to the strongest, irrespective of the caste to which he belongs. Dhrishtadyumna, brother of Draupadī solemnly declares: "Be he a brahmin or a king or a merchant or a shūdra, he who will string this excellent bow will get my sister in marriage." (*Mahābhārata,* Adi-parva, 203.19–20.)

Sītā is won by Rāma because he alone can bend the bow. Draupadī is won by Arjuna for the same reason. Arjuna, to avoid detection, had come in the guise of a brahmin. The amusing scene describing the misgivings of the brahmins as one of them rises to perform a feat which the well-trained princes were unable to accomplish makes us guess the pride and joy they felt when Arjuna defeated the kings at their own game. At the end of the *Odyssey,* Ulysses, having reached Ithaca after his long peregrinations, finds his place occupied by the suitors. Penelope, prompted by Athena, decides to put them to the test: "Listen, my lords, you have fastened on this house in the long absence of its master, as the scene of your perpetual feasts, and you could offer no better pretext for your conduct than your wish to win my hand in marriage. That being the prize, come forward now, my gallant lords; for I challenge you to try your skill on the great bow of King Ulysses. And whichever man among you proves the handiest at stringing the bow and shoots an arrow through everyone of these twelve axes, with that man I will go, bidding goodbye to this house which welcomed me as a bride." The suitors fail. No doubt, they are grieved at the loss of Penelope, but, as Eurymachus puts it, "What does grieve me more is the thought that our failure with his bow proves us such weaklings compared with the godlike Ulysses. The disgrace will stick to our names for ever." Like Arjuna, Ulysses appears unrecognized and humbly asks to be allowed to test the strength of his hands. The suitors are annoyed: "We don't want the common folk to be saying things like this, 'A poor lot, these; not up to the fine gentleman whose wife they want to marry! *They* can't string his bow. But in comes some casual tramp, strings the bow with the greatest ease and shoots through all the marks!' That is the kind of thing they will say; and our reputation might suffer." (*Odyssey,* Rieu trans. [Penguin], Book XXII, pp. 317–18, 324.) We live here in the same world and breathe the same atmosphere as in Drupada's palace and Janaka's capital.

3. *The aristocrats facing the mystery of life.* Life in the Epic Age was essentially active. Games, gambling, conquests, and military campaigns kept the heroes occupied, while the recital by bards of the glorious deeds of their ancestors gave an ever new luster to the flame of chivalry. Before the compilation of the main epic narratives as we have them today, there must have existed a great number of independent lays celebrating different families or dynasties. The *Mahābhārata* contains a great wealth of such stories quoted as examples to the heroes. The *Iliad* and the *Odyssey,* though less rich than the *Mahābhārata,* use the same device and the Greek tragedy testifies to the existence of numerous epic cycles not incorporated in the works of Homer. The teaching which appealed to the knights of old was a concrete teaching which left out abstruse speculations.

It may be reasonably surmised that Arjuna and the Krishna of the *Bhagavad Gītā* belong to a later age when speculation had taken precedence over action.

In fact, a life of action has its own problems. Man realizes that his plans are often thwarted and that he is not the sovereign master of his destiny. There are mysterious forces at work which must be reckoned with. Above all, the great mystery of death is ever present in the precarious life of warriors. The heroic mentality acknowledges the presence of the mystery, is deeply impressed by it, but does not attempt to give it an abstract solution.

In the face of the mystery of life with its passions, its failures, its cruelty, the hero, while feeling responsible for his actions, knows that the divine power ordains and guides everything. To our rationalistic minds, his position may seem to be illogical: either one is a fatalist and denies human freedom and responsibility, or one believes in freedom and denies the supreme power of fate. But our argument would not disturb the hero's belief. It is reality which interests him and reality is complex. The human and divine worlds are not juxtaposed, they intermingle so intimately that to consider one apart from the other destroys the very texture of reality. It is the divine world which gives to human existence its third dimension and makes of it a living and full-blooded tragedy. Who would be so devoid of sensitivity as to affirm that the epic heroes are mere marionettes activated by the mechanical device of a hidden magician?

Naturalism which has cut off human life from its mysterious roots and claims to explain everything by an analysis of superficial psychology would have made our heroes smile. They knew better and the modern tendency to reaffirm the mystery is much closer to the heroic mentality than the so-called realism of the last century. It is not without significance that depth psychology borrows from the epic some of its most important symbolism. The inner mystery it tries to penetrate may not be without connection with the transcendent mystery which the heroes of old acknowledged with awe and trembling.

Death, the lurking and inevitable menace, is a constant reminder of life's precarious stability. Sadly recalling the forebodings of defeat in a long and beautiful threnody, old King Dhritarāshtra, in a crescendo of despair punctuated by the recurring refrain "tadā nāshamse vijayāya Sanjaya,"² concludes by expressing his desire to leave this fruitless existence: "O Sanjaya, since life is such my desire is to die without delay, for I do not see the slightest advantage in keeping alive." (*Mahābhārata*, Adi-parva, i. 245.)

In true epic fashion, Sanjaya replies by quoting the examples of hundreds of kings and warriors, far superior to the Kaurava princes, who have lived, fought, and died. Their death takes nothing away from their fame and valor, and life is worth living as long as fate does not snatch it away. Sanjaya does not speculate about future life or rebirth, he states the mystery of life and death and accepts it as a matter of fact: "There is no reason to lament over what is to be. Who can, through endeavor, change the course of fate? Time is the root of everything, of life and death, of happiness and adversity." (*Mahābhārata*, Adi-parva, i. 271–72.)

In the *Iliad,* the scene between Hector and Andromache has the same message to convey. Andromache is frightened by the bellicose enthusiasm of her husband: "Hector, you are possessed. This bravery of yours will be your end. You do not think of your little boy and of your unhappy wife, whom you will make a widow soon. Some day the Achaeans are bound to kill you in a massed attack. And when I lose you I might as well be dead. There will be no comfort left, when you have met your doom—nothing but grief." Hector is not indifferent to his wife's appeal. He loves his son and his wife dearly. Yet, he is a warrior and fate calls him to battle. "My dear, I beg you not to be too much distressed. No one is going to send me down to Hades before my proper time. But Fate is a thing that no man born of woman, coward or hero, can escape.

Go home now, and attend to your own work, the loom and the spindle, and see that the maidservants go on with theirs. War is men's business; and this war is the business of every man in Ilium, myself above all." (*Iliad,* Book VI, pp. 128–29.)

INDIAN AND GREEK PERSPECTIVES

Although much more might be said about the similarity between the Indian and the Greek epic, we must now turn our attention to what makes them different. For they are different. There is an atmosphere, a spiritual climate proper to the Indian epic, as there is an outlook and a perspective which characterize the Homeric world. Why is it, for instance, that not a single Greek hero decides, after a life full of activity, to end his days in the peaceful retirement of the forest? Or how is it that the *Rāmāyana* and the *Mahābhārata* have been and still are religious books from which millions draw spiritual comfort and guidance, whereas the *Iliad* and the *Odyssey,* which have shaped the Greek temperament, have never been sacred books?

The mystery of death is ever present in the life of epic heroes. But the Indian temperament, so well depicted in the boy Nachiketas of the *Katha-Upanishad,* seeks to penetrate the mystery which the Greek temperament is rather inclined to accept. Hence, a fundamental difference between the two outlooks. The more deeply the Indian soul meditates and reflects on the transitoriness of life, the less importance it gives to purely human achievement. The more forcibly death appears as inevitable to the Greek hero, the more urgent also the necessity to live fully the short time which destiny allots to man. The similarity which we have pointed out in the first part of this essay is the similarity of a spontaneous and prospective tendency which precedes all metaphysical reflection. The Greek epic remains all through spontaneous and prospective. The Indian epic shows a gradual evolution toward a more reflexive and meditative attitude. In Greece, epic poetry and the metaphysical quest have remained two separate achievements. In India, both have met and blended, and that blending has conferred on the epic itself a character of its own. It has been the work of long centuries, especially for the *Mahābhārata*. Each generation had its contribution to make, and the whole work was not written under guidance of a logical mind anxious to safeguard the logical consistency of the various portions, but under the inspiration of the vital unity of a living people whose growth and development are reflected in its numerous verses as the changing landscape in the waters of a powerful river. What we are looking for in our study of the epic is not an abstract system which could be neatly summarized in a few clear and definite propositions, but human and concrete attitudes which reveal not the vision of a few philosophers but the temperament of living peoples. Our aim is not to pass a verdict or to decide that one temperament is better than the other, but to vibrate in unison with both temperaments since both are able to reveal to us hidden depths of the human soul.

1. *The Indian and the Greek temperament as revealed in the composition of the epic.* When we read the Greek epic, we are forced to concentrate on the story and on the heroes. Without preamble, the *Iliad* begins with the narrative of Achilles' wrath. In spite of lengthy speeches and inconsistencies in the narrative, the story of the Achaeans' gradual discomfiture proceeds apace, and we are never allowed to forget the central theme. The sulking Achilles remains ever present, and we are anxiously waiting for the relenting of his stubborn resentment. The death of Patroclus arouses Achilles from his inaction and the doom of Ilium is sealed. The *Odyssey* is perhaps the first novel ever written. Ulysses drifting on the high seas, among unspeakable dangers, pursued by the vindictiveness of the god Poseidon, relates his adventures and finally reaches his dear Ithaca, while his son Telemachus, unable to solve the difficulties which he faces at home, undertakes a long and vain quest for his father. Both finally meet at Ithaca and defeat the suitors.

The *Mahābhārata* has been called "a vast repository of Hindu traditional lore, philosophy and legend." Its bulk is eight times as great as that of the *Iliad* and *Odyssey* put together. It would be ridiculous to look for a well-focused narrative without digressions. It is not meant to be a simple story, and its greatness lies in the fact that, around the main story which occupies about one fifth of the whole work, the folklore, the wisdom, and the religious aspirations of long centuries have clustered into an immense florilegium of Indian life. The Ādi-parvan, after announcing the great tale, keeps us waiting for sixty chapters (i.e., over 2,000 verses) before beginning the story of the Pāndavas and Kauravas. Then, like a majestic river, the story follows its slow development, with many interruptions. The Sabhā-parvan with its 2,500 verses brings us to the exile of the Pāndavas. The Vana-parvan is a real storehouse of legends and beautiful tales and spreads over more than 17,000 verses. It is a real forest of myths, legends, and instructions of all kinds. The Virāta-parvan is like a short interlude of more than 2,000 verses. After the failure of a peaceful solution and the preparation of the armies (Udyoga-parvan with nearly 8,000 verses), Sanjaya's account of the great battle begins. The Bhīsma-parvan (close to 6,000 verses) ends with the pathetic sight of Bhīsma dying on a bed of arrows. The Drona-parvan (about 9,500 verses) relates the fall of Jayadratha and the end of Drona. Bhīma's revenge over Duhshā-sana and Karna's death at the hands of Arjuna are related in the Karna-parvan (about 5,000 verses). After a long interruption devoted to the relation of Balarāma's pilgrimage to the Sarasvatī, the battle comes to an end with the unfair victory of Bhīma over Duryodhana. That is the Shālya-parvan (about 4,000 verses). The remaining Kauravas attack the Pāndavas at night and massacre their armies. The five brothers and Krishna escape death (Sauptika-parvan with 800 verses). In the Strī-parvan (800 verses), the Kaurava ladies, headed by Gāndhārī, visit the battlefield. The story is ended. But the great poem goes on with the Shānti-parvan (14,000 verses) and the Anushāsana-parvan (8,000 verses) embodying the teachings of Bhīsma. They are the richest portions of the *Mahā-*

bhārata as a treasure-house of Indian tradition: artha-shāstra, dharma-shāstra, civil law, strategy, popular wisdom, cosmogony, theology, yoga, psychology—all the branches of knowledge are represented in that immense discourse which must have taken centuries to be written. The story is resumed with Yudishthira's Ashvameda. Dhritarāshtra, accompanied by Gāndhārī, Kuntī, and Vidura, retires to the forest and is granted a vision of the deceased warriors. After the death of Balarāma and Krishna, the Pāndavas renounce the world.

Although the *Rāmāyana* is much more similar to the Greek epic than the *Mahābhārata,* there are elements in its composition which differentiate it sharply from Homer's poems. Like Homer, Vālmīki is a historical poet who has composed a great epic of startling literary qualities. There is even a great similarity between the general theme of the poems: the great war brought about by the abduction of a princess, the siege of the abductor's capital, the victory of the lawful husband, and the return of the princess to her conjugal home. There is little doubt that the origin of the *Rāmāyana,* like that of the *Iliad* and the *Odyssey,* is to be found in the heroic traditions of warring tribes. Yet, like the *Mahābhārata,* although to a lesser extent, the *Rāmāyana* incorporates an imposing collection of interpolated legends and myths which have no direct connection with the central theme. More explicitly than in the *Mahābhārata,* the hero of the *Rāmāyana* has become a divine incarnation, and the human interest of the story, without being destroyed, is sublimated into a divine episode.

2. *Humanism, Greek and Indian.* From a purely literary point of view, we might be tempted to conclude that the Greek epic avoids many of the defects of the Indian epic by a greater fidelity to the objective it has in view. Yet, we may wonder if the lengthy digressions of the Indian epic and the tendency to divinize its heroes have nothing else to reveal than bad literary workmanship. Is there not a fundamental difference between the Greek and the Indian conception of humanism? "Conception" is perhaps the wrong word,

for we are not comparing two systems of philosophy, but two literary testimonies. It would be better, perhaps, to speak of two tendencies, two innate visions which try to find an expression without ever succeeding in reducing it to a clear-cut system. Have you ever heard the same story told by two persons of different temperaments? An extrovert will tell the story with passion, but a passion for the story itself, and he will leave out his personal reflections and subjective impressions, because he obscurely knows that the story can speak for itself. An introvert will allow his mind to wander and try to find in the incidents of the story props for his personal considerations regarding life and destiny. His passion is more interior, and the story itself will gradually lose something of its importance, without, however, disappearing completely. The thread of the narrative will be loose yet continuous. Am I far off the mark when I qualify the Greek epic temperament as extrovert, and the Indian as introvert?

The extrovert humanism of Greece. Spengler's remark that the soul of European antiquity is "pure present" is certainly very true of the Greek epic. We have already remarked on the hero's attitude toward death and what follows. It is a mystery which he recoils from investigating and which he accepts without question. Similarly, the mystery of human suffering and human wickedness is solved summarily. "Are not the gods responsible for that, weaving catastrophe into the pattern of events to make a song for future generations?" That is how King Alcinous consoles Ulysses for the loss of many of his dear friends. What the king is interested in is the story which Ulysses has to tell: "Explain to us what secret sorrow makes you weep as you listen to the tragic story of the Argives and the fall of Troy." (*Odyssey,* Book VIII, p. 138.)

What matters for the Greek hero is to make the most of the time allotted to him. Too much speculation is of no avail; it will not postpone the fatal day foreseen by the gods. To fight, to enjoy the pleasures of love and of congenial company, to make a name for himself, "to listen to a minstrel, while the tables are laden with bread and meat, and a steward carries round the wine and fills the cups," that is life, and the rest does not count. The transitoriness of human existence never prompts the Greek hero to give up the world to retire to the forest. Death is the great retirement and it will come in its appointed time.

There are no demons in the Greek epic. The Cyclops himself is just a savage of immense physical strength who does not represent in any way the dark power which resists the ruling of the gods. Both evil and good in human behavior have a divine origin. They remain human and we witness in them that strange blending of fatalism and responsibility which are the two facets of all human activities. Listen to Helen after her return to her husband's palace. She is fully conscious of her sin when she declares: "The Achaeans boldly declared war and took the field against Troy for my sake, shameless creature that I was." Yet, she also knows that it was not her independent doing: "Aphrodite blinded me when she lured me to Troy from my own dear country and made me forsake my daughter, my bridal chamber, and a husband who had all one could wish in the way of brains and good looks." (*Odyssey,* Book IV, pp. 68, 71.)

But the gods themselves are so very close to man. Except for the blind submission which they command regarding their arbitrary decisions and partialities, they behave exactly like the heroes of the poem, more recklessly even, for they have nobody to fear. Those humanized gods of the Homeric pantheon will remain "a fit inspiration for an athletic contest, a statue, or an ode, but [they are] of little use to the philosopher, and entirely unsympathetic to the simple everyday sorrows of mankind." [2] Although they rule everything, they never rob the heroes of their humanity. Their quarrels are reflected in the conflicts that oppose man to man, they positively help their protégés and are personally engaged in the battles of men. But the human warriors do not rise above their human status. We may compare, in this connection, the decisive fight between Achilles

[2] A. R. Burn, *Minoans, Philistines and Greeks* (New York, Knopf, 1930), p. 256.

and Hector, and the final struggle between Rāma and Rāvana. We are in two different worlds, the Greek world in which man would be what he is without divine interference, the Indian world in which man, a mere instrument raised to a divine efficiency, breaks his human limits. The Greek heroes are so human that they make one forget the divine operation which sustains them. The Indian gods are so prominent that they blur the human outlines of the heroes.

The introvert humanism of India. This last remark of mine should not lead one to conclude that I have failed to respond to the deep human appeal of innumerable passages of the Indian epic. I shall try to explain my meaning by a concrete example. I, who am not a Vedāntin, have great friends who are Vedāntins. In our usual human relations I fully appreciate their humane qualities. But I know that, deep down in their soul, they have a vision which is incompatible with that human distinction between "I" and "Thou" which is the very foundation of friendship. And that makes me feel uneasy. My attitude towards the Indian epic is something of that kind. I love Rāma and Sītā. Yudhishthira arouses my admiration. The Strī-parvan brings tears to my eyes. Arjuna's grief at the news of his son's death moves me deeply. As long as I forget the pattern to which they belong I feel one with them. But there is a pattern. Before trying to describe it, let us first understand how the Indian epic completes and deepens the Greek vision of life.

The simple fact that the *Mahābhārata* and the *Rāmāyana* are acccepted, even today, as the divine answer to the religious aspirations of millions is a clear indication of the depth of their message. They have given an answer to the eternal questions of the "why," the "whence," and the "whither" of human existence. The epic story has become an occasion to reflect on the instability of things mundane and to seek for stability. The great heroes who survive the heroic struggle for power realize that power is an empty shell which must be discarded. Evil is a reality which is at work in the world, and the demons are bent on checking the divine control of

the universe. They represent a terrible force, both external and
internal to man, against which it is the duty of all, according to
each one's situation, to fight. Human destiny is not to find its fulfillment in this world. Wisdom more than bravery has the key to
the mystery of life. The heroes are continually invited to make the
decisive struggle an internal struggle towards final emancipation,
while the external struggle is nothing but a passing phase of the
world of appearances. With the Indian epic, we enter into a vast
pattern in which human life, human emotions, human values are
assumed and transformed.

In the *Rāmāyana,* that pattern is outlined in the first book which
is certainly a later addition revealing to a nicety the Indian temperament. The gods are much troubled by the demon Rāvana who cannot be destroyed except by man. But, in order to kill him, one
would need divine power. Hence, Vishnu agrees to be born as a
man. The divine struggle weaves itself into a human fabric.
Dasharatha begets four sons. Rāma is the full incarnation of
Vishnu, his three brothers are partial incarnations. We may forget about that divine prelude when we read the story of the exile,
of the siege of Lankā, and of Rāvana's defeat. But what we discuss
here is not whether or not the addition of the first book fulfills its
purpose, but the fact that the first book has been added. In the
perspective of that first book, the whole human story of Rāma and
Sītā, the abduction of Sītā by Rāvana, and the battle between Rāma
and Rāvana, become a kind of camouflage of the real story. A
camouflage, as we have pointed out, which is not always successful,
since the heroes often lose their human dimensions.

For the *Mahābhārata,* the pattern is much more complex. Toward the end, we come to know that all the heroes are divine incarnations. But let us consider one instance, the *Bhagavad Gītā.*
There is Arjuna, deeply moved at the prospect that he has to fight
against his relatives, and his gurus. Krishna encourages him to
do his duty as a worthy Kshatriya, and that remains within the
boundaries of the Greek epic. But when Krishna teaches Arjuna

about the eternity of the Self and the illusion of the bodily individuality, the whole struggle, viewed from that perspective, vanishes into something unreal. The whole thing is a big puppet show in which the actors are moved by supernatural agencies.

The Indian pattern, as distinguished from the Greek outlook, is characterized by the fact that there is no strict division between the divine, the demonic, and the human. The Law of Rebirth allows the spirit to move across the three worlds in its pilgrimage toward liberation. How many demons do we not see released from their bondage once the heroes, under divine guidance, act as the unconscious instruments of a superior power? That fluidity of the Indian universe dissolves, as it were, all that is specifically divine, demonic or human, into an immense current of mysterious and predetermined events which follow their course under the appearance of spontaneity.

Appearance or reality? That is the question which the confrontation of the Greek and the Indian epic brings to our minds, but which it does not solve. Both the Indian and the Greek heroes have a keen perception of "that void, that nothingness at the bottom of things," but are inclined to react differently to it. While the Greek hero feels that human existence is a gift which must be enjoyed, the Indian hero tends to see in it a bondage from which one should escape. The greatest passages of both epics are those where the gift-aspect and the bondage-aspect are blended into that energizing humility which is man's closest realization of what he is.

GEORGE T. ARTOLA

Comments on the Rāmāyana and Mahābhārata

American college students who are encouraged to seek parallels for Oriental literary works in the classical and vernacular literatures of the West should be made cognizant of the fact that the Indian epics, while inviting comparison with the poems of Homer and the popular and learned epics of European literature, can be read, indeed should be read, for their own special significance in world literature. Although epic in their motive and spirit, the *Mahābhārata* and the *Rāmāyana* are unlike any of the epic poems of popular origin which arose in Medieval Europe. The Indian works characterize a period of highly developed intellectual and social culture, and this cannot be said, for instance, of *Beowulf,* or the *Chanson de Roland* or the *Cantar de Mio Çid.* The *Mahābhārata* and the *Rāmāyana* are *itihāsa,* that is, works of legendary tradition, on a large scale and with a massive purpose. The *Mahābhārata,* especially, is the creation and expression not of a single individual mind, but of the mind of a whole nation. In it are found the power to embrace great events and vast spaces in a total view, and the tendency to fill them with an abundance of minute, effective, vivid and significant detail—a kind of unanimism *avant la lettre.*

George T. Artola, a specialist in Sanskrit and comparative literature, has prepared an anthology of classical Indian literature which will be published shortly by Jaico Press, Bombay.

For over two thousand years the Indian epics have been molding the lives of countless generations in India because of the profound influence they have exerted on the minds and hearts of the Indian people. The story of the great Bhārata war and the story of Rāma have been listened to with devotion and pleasure by Indian children whose imaginative minds have been particularly receptive to the recitation, whether in Sanskrit or in the vernacular languages, of the tales and legends which are their cultural and folk heritage. At school they would read selections from the epic poems from either the Sanskrit works if they were studying Sanskrit, or from the various versions and adaptations in their native languages. Later, if so inclined, they were given opportunities of attending free public lectures on virtually every aspect of the poems. Today, throughout the length and breadth of India, and especially in South India, pandits and religious thinkers comment publicly on the *Mahābhārata* and the *Rāmāyana*. Their lectures are announced daily in the newspapers; they are gratis and available to all. The artistic productions which owe their inspiration to the characters and events of the great epic poems are readily visible everywhere, in the form of temple sculpture, at museum exhibits, or in the theaters and music academies and at the cinema.

In addition to the aesthetic value of the poems—for they have a generous portion of lyric and descriptive poetry of a matchless beauty—they are also the key to many aspects of Indian civilization which have contributed very considerably to the development of human thought and culture. Moreover, the *Mahābhārata* and the *Rāmāyana* constitute an important source of the cultural history of India because of the flood of light they shed on so many aspects of Indian life of a remote era. Life in ancient India is delineated in both poems with a great force of intellectual conception and living presentation. A truly remarkable feature shared by both works is the peculiar blending of the natural breath of an early, heroic, swift, and vigorous force of life with a strong development and activity of the ethical, intellectual, and philosophic mind. It is this feature which distinguishes them from any other productions of world literature.

In the Indian tradition the *Mahābhārata* has been held in a special esteem, and for this we have the statement of the *Mārkandeya-purāna* to the effect that the *Mahābhārata* is the best Treatise on Moral Law (*Dharmashāstra*), the best Treatise on Material Gain (*Arthashāstra*), the best Treatise on Love (*Kamashāstra*) and the best Treatise on Deliverance (*Mokshashāstra*), which is equivalent to saying that it teaches better than any other literary work the harmonious development of the powers of man to ensure happiness in this life and liberation from rebirth and eternal bliss in the here-after.

Broadly speaking, the *Mahābhārata* and the *Rāmāyana* occupy in time an intermediate position between the Vedic epoch and the period of classical literature. In the evolution of the Sanskrit language, the prose and verse of the *Mahābhārata* echo the simplicity and directness of language of the *Brāhmanas* and the Upanishads. The language and the style of the *Rāmāyana,* on the other hand, point forward to the period of ornate and elaborate poetry (*kāvya*), to writers like Kālidāsa and Bhavabhūti, Kshemendra and Bāna. For the themes and plots of their works, classical poets and drama-tists are indebted to a very great degree to both poems. In fact, the sum and substance of classical Indian literature may be said to be dependent upon, to have its source in, three gigantic works of an earlier period: the *Mahābhārata,* the *Rāmāyana,* and the lost *Brihatkathā* of Gunādhya. This statement is not to be wondered at, if one considers that the corpus of these writings would occupy several bookshelves and would constitute an extensive library of Indian wit and wisdom, fiction and philosophy, mythology and theology. In teaching the words of later Indian authors, constant reference to both poems and to abridged adaptations of the *Brihatkathā* is inevitable. Moreover, the genesis of technical works such as the *Arthashastra* of Kautilya, of the philosophical systems (*darshana*) and of the artistic treatises on polity (*nītishāstra*), such as the *Panchatantra* and the *Tantropākhyāna,* must necessarily be sought in the *Mahābhārata* and the *Rāmāyana.*

The *Rāmāyana* differs from the *Mahābhārata* by a greater simplicity of plan, and a finer glow of poetic warmth and color. While the *Mahābhārata* owes its sacred character to the didactic sections (found principally in the twelfth book, called *Shāntiparvan*) which were subsequently added to it, the *Rāmāyana* owes its sanctity to the inherent purity and goodness of its hero and its heroine, Rāma and Sītā. The *Rāmāyana,* in particular, points out the strength and the weakness of the Aryan character. The superiority of the Aryans lay in the sternness of their character, their spirit of sacrifice, their supreme regard for truth, their love of adventure, and their perseverance. Rāma is the embodiment of the high ideals of Aryan life. In him is presented the unique combination of a faithful and dutiful son, an affectionate brother, a loving husband, a stern and relentless hero, and an ideal king. It is not a willful paradox to assert that originally the poet Vālmīki started his work as a treatise on polity (*nītishāstra*) in order to instruct princes in the high principles of political and ethical conduct, drawing on the Rāma story as an illustration of perfection of such principles; but in the course of his composing, the narration of Rāma's story became his all-absorbing interest, so that the character of the work as a "mirror for princes" remained subordinate to its other features. The author of the *Mahābhārata* who first began to piece together the ballads (*ākhyāna*) and legends (*itihāsa*) of the great Bhārata war—Indian tradition has maintained that his name was Vyasa—was primarily concerned with relating what to him was an historical event. In the course of time and with the expansion of the text, the *Mahābhārata* took upon itself the character of a treatise on polity (*nītishāstra*) and even on moral law (*dharmashāstra*) by dint of an abundant addition of political, ethical and religious matter.

Both of the Indian epic poems have come to hold a prominent place in the larger context of Eastern literature, for at an early period they migrated eastward to Java, Indo-China, Thailand, and Tibet. There are Old and Middle Javanese translations of four

divisions (*parvan*) of the *Mahābhārata,* and they have been edited
and studied in recent times by Dutch scholars and utilized in the
preparation of the critical Sanskrit text. The influence of the *Rāmāyana* in local literature, art, and music is found not only in
Java and Bali, but in Cambodia, Laos, and Thailand. The entire
Rāmāyana in the form in which we have it today, including the
final chapter (*uttarakanda*), was known in Champā (modern Indo-
China) in the seventh century of the Christian era. Also, fragments
of a Tibetan version have been uncovered, but they do not seem to
correspond to the work of Vālmīki since they contain a somewhat
different and peculiar Rāma story. We may conclude from this that
popular Rāma narratives were current at an early period and that
they reached India's eastern neighbors possibly through Nepal.
Indications are that such Rāma stories are found written in Ma-
layan, Laotic, and Thai. The Old Javanese translation was made on
the basis of a seventh-century poem (*kāvya*) entitled "Slaying of
Rāvana" (*Rāvanavadha*) and generally referred to as *Bhatti-kāvya*
after its author.

Acquaintance with the Indian epics was not made in Europe
until the latter half of the eighteenth century. However, it must be
remembered that a portion of the *Mahābhārata* reached the Western world in the Middle Ages, although the selection was not—
nor could it have been—known at the time as emanating from the
Sanskrit *Mahābhārata.* Three animal stories from the twelfth section of the *Mahābhārata* were incorporated into the Pahlavi work
which was called after the names of the jackals in the first *tantra*
("thread") of the *Panchatantra,* Karataka and Damanaka. The
Arabic version of Ibnu 'l-Muqaffa' entitled *Kalīlah wa-Dimnah*
was translated into Syriac, Byzantine Greek, Modern Persian, Medieval Spanish, and Hebrew over a period of time from approxi-
mately the middle of the eleventh century to the middle of the
thirteenth century. The humanists of the Renaissance knew of the
fables through the Latin translation of the Hebrew, the work of
a Jewish physician, John of Capua, which bears the title *Directorium
Vitae Humanae.* How and why the fables of the Emergency Friend-

ship between the Cat and the Mouse, of the Prince and the *Pūjāni*-bird, and of the Pious Jackal who served the Lion as Minister entered the Bidpai tradition has not yet been satisfactorily explained.

In the nineteenth century complete translations of the *Mahābhārata* were made into French and English. The *Rāmāyana* was translated in its entirety into Italian, French, and English. Some idea of the enthusiasm with which the *Rāmāyana* was received may be gained from the words of the French historian Michelet, referring to the year 1863, at which time he first read the Fauche translation: "That year will always remain a dear and cherished memory; it was the first time I had the opportunity to read the great sacred poem of India, the divine *Rāmāyana*. If anyone has lost the freshness of emotion, let him drink a long draught of life and youth from that deep chalice."

We cannot be optimistic enough to expect that American college students will understand and appreciate so enthusiastically the Indian epic poems through the verse or prose translations they will read. In the main, students will be required to read extracts and not complete texts. One may anticipate that objections even to extensive selections will be voiced by many students, but it must be borne in mind that such objections are merely expressions of a difference of mentality and aesthetic taste. The vastness of the plans of both poems and the leisurely minuteness of detail are baffling to a Western mind accustomed to narrower limits, tiring to a more easily fatigued eye and imagination, and exasperating to those keyed to a faster pace of life. Exception has especially been taken to the didactic matter in both poems. However, if students are encouraged to approach the *Mahābhārata* and the *Rāmāyana* holding in abeyance their alien canons and aesthetic standards, eventually they will come to feel a profound admiration for Vyasa and Vālmīki. Their efforts will be rewarded when they are enriched with a body of mature thought and uplifted by a refined nobility and gravity of ethical tone.

JOHN D. MITCHELL

A Sanskrit Classic: Shakuntalā

Although there can be no disputing that East and West are alike in having a common basis in humanity, the Oriental classics sometimes present very real challenges to our powers of comprehension. In the case of the classical Sanskrit drama *Shakuntalā,* a staging of the play for an audience, which would be true to the spirit of the play and evocative of the Indian culture out of which the play arose, is likely to be the most satisfactory solution to the problem of appreciating *Shakuntalā.* However, since most Western readers and students will be dependent for their understanding and appreciation of it upon reading the text, the use of several disciplines can provide helpful insights, and perhaps the essential key to unlocking the door to this play.

"During the last two decades in archeology, linguistics, anthropology, and psychology, awareness of new evidence along with revised insights regarding older evidence has begun to provide us all, translators, teachers, and common readers, for a world-size view of the process of the creative imagination. . . . Alert to the common basis, both our comparisons and our contrasts in our discussions of world literature may acquire more pertinence. We shall also be released from two perilous superstitions which still haunt the literature classroom: The illusion that ideas never crossed language barriers until the day before yesterday; and the fallacy that

John D. Mitchell, a drama consultant in New York City, was U.S. delegate to the first World Conference on the Theater, held in Bombay in 1957, under the sponsorship of the International Theater Institute of UNESCO.

irreducible temperamental differences divide East from West."[1]

A deeper satisfaction to be derived from *Shakuntalā* lies in discovering how different it is from what we are accustomed to. To get at the difference requires its being placed in a context. Here is the advantage of experiencing the play as a member of an audience.

The knowledgeable producer, through production design, style of acting, decor and costuming, and use of music will delight the eyes and ears of the audience with the rich diversities of the Indian play and evoke what is both universal and particular in the play. I stress the importance of seeing the classics of the East in performance, because one of the most important characteristics of the theater of the East is that its total theater is greater than the sum of its parts. A play should be read as if it were a blueprint for performance in a theater before an audience. When one reads the printed text of an Eastern play, this is most evident. In a sense when we read a play we are taking on the roles of producer, designer, director, and actor. For a challenging play remote from our own culture, we should recognize that we need to prepare ourselves very much as would the producer who has a responsibility to his audience, to make the play for them meaningful and deeply satisfying.

We may make still another parallel. Just as the director has to do the major research in respect to the play in order to guide competently his actors to a true and valid understanding of the play, so too must the teacher, like the director, marshall his experience, talent, and competence through research to guide his students to an interpretation and to an experiencing of the play.

As is true of many dramas, there are at least three levels to *Shakuntalā*. Bearing in mind that the playwright Kālidāsa wrote for a particular contemporary audience, as does any playwright at any time throughout the world, his most conscious concern was with what we may characterize as the first level; namely, the level of *immediate appeal*. It is at this level that we may examine the

[1] Jeremy Ingalls, "Urban History and Urbanity in Literature," *Indiana University Conference on Oriental-Western Literary Relations*. (Chapel Hill, University of North Carolina Press, 1955), pp. 193–203.

play as a theater-piece; it is the telling of a story; it provides a vehicle for the artistry of the actors and his fellow theater artists; it is the opportunity for the poet-playwright to demonstrate and to exercise his special talents.

When the classics are in translation and are being presented to readers of a different culture, at this level of immediate appeal there is likely to be both very great loss and also some special difficulties. In respect to the Sanskrit plays, the scholars make known to us the very great and substantial differences between the structure and the poetic devices of the Sanskrit originals; even the most inspired of translations in English cannot hope to reproduce the innate characteristics of the Sanskrit poetry of the originals.

"Most translations of Sanskrit poetry in English are unbelievably bad and even those which are passable are little read. . . . Sanskrit poetry remains like Sleeping Beauty. It is hidden in a castle behind a hedge of thorns. And this is a great pity." [2]

Aided by the Sanskritists, our first objective should be to find, if such does exist, the best translation of the Indian play. The verse translation by Arthur Ryder seems to be such a translation of *Shakuntalā*. However, it is well to bear in mind that translations undergo change with time. Changing popular tastes influence our degree of receptivity to older translations of classics, and often we feel the need for contemporary poets to attempt new and fresh translations. Sometimes this has been justified on the basis of the findings of improved scholarship; sometimes it is simply that the verbiage of a previous generation is no longer acceptable or appealing to the present generation of readers.

In the annals of the contemporary stage, there have been instances of the collaboration of resource persons, all of whom are aiming at the re-creation of a classic on the stage for a contemporary audience, which have brought forth a fresh and authoritative translation of a classic. Under ideal conditions, the producer of a classic

[2] Daniel H. H. Ingalls, "Sanskrit Poetry and Sanskrit Poetics," *Indiana University Conference on Oriental-Western Literary Relations* (Chapel Hill, University of North Carolina Press, 1955), p. 4.

may turn to several resource-type persons: the scholar, the poet, and the actor. Working together with the encouragement and the incentive of a theatrical producer, the scholar and the poet produce a blueprint in English of the classic for testing in the crucible of the theater. During a long period of rehearsal, the sensitivities of the actors are able to indicate to the scholar and the poet changes in words, word order, and even images truer to the speech of the contemporary stage, and more acceptable to the ears of the contemporary audience. Just as the scholar and the poet should be appreciative of the validity of the insights of the actor, so too, must the actor heed the scholar's knowledge of the original. If there could be more of this pooling and sharing of skills and insights, it might mark the beginning of a new era in making translations of the world classics highly attractive and more fully appreciated by contemporary readers and even contemporary audiences.

As the producer of the Indian classic *Shakuntalā* would have to familiarize himself with the conventions of the staging of an Indian play, so is it important for the reader of these Indian plays to have some knowledge of the classical theater of the East. Research on the theater of India has been lacking and is still today inadequate. However, some audio-visual materials are available and help to make up for this deficiency. Two films come to mind. The recent prize-winning film, *Pather Panchali,* gives one an experience of India which is true to the life of the masses of India. Likewise, there is in the film an episode in which a touring company of actors perform for the villagers. These roving bands of players who travel about through India performing in the villages are perpetuating a type of staging which derives from the staging of the Sanskrit plays.

The performing of Indian plays was and is highly theatrical and stylized. It is traditional Indian theater practice to have the audience seated in a circle, viewing the play from all sides. The popularity of arena staging in the United States will make the Indian practice of the performing of the plays in-the-round seem less remote to us.

The film *The River* has great merit for providing a background for visualizing and appreciating the Indian propensity for stylization and color. In defense of including such a commercial film in a program of films providing a broad and diverse view of India, I would draw upon a personal experience of mine there. Once I flew in a small plane of the Indian Air Lines from Bombay to the Deccan; the route of the plane takes one from the west coast of India, rising sharply to fly above the Western Ghats, getting one onto the broad plateau which is known as the Deccan. From such a small plane, one gets one type of perspective on India. Never before had I realized how very beautiful India is. The diversity and the luxuriance of this terrain as seen from the air are impressive and moving. When one is at closer range and is driving through this countryside, one gets quite a different impression. It is not possible to question the validity of each of these perspectives of India; for both are true. Likewise, the film *Pather Panchali* reveals the simple way of life of most Indians, the poverty, and even the melancholy drabness of India. It cannot be disputed that this is true to India. The commercial film, *The River,* in its context chooses to focus upon the festivals, the colorful arts, and the fantastic and richly varied rituals of India. These, too, without dispute, are true to India. If one has the selective view and the broad view in one's frame of reference, one has a richer context out of which to attempt to understand and appreciate Indian plays like *Shakuntalā.* One may also recommend for a broad and basic understanding of India—80 percent of whose people live in small villages—the fine documentary film made by Louis De Rochemont on village life in India.

Since time would be limited for readers of these plays, there is no need to cite all the many audio-visual materials which might be valuable in building up a background for study of them. However, I would urge the reader, just as I would a producer, of these plays that he turn to UNESCO's book of reproductions of the Ajanta frescos. In reading plays, one attempts to visualize in one's mind's eye a performance of the play. The beautiful Ajanta frescos will be evocative of the costuming, posturing, and movements of the actors performing *Shakuntalā*. So as not to neglect the aural aspects of the production, it would be beneficial for the reader also to turn to recordings of Indian music, since music has always played an important part in the presentation of these plays, as it does in the theater of India today.

Thus with a relatively small investment of time and effort and with such aids to the visualization of these plays in performance, one may be able to reach the play on the first level, the level of immediate appeal. If one goes no further than this, one may still derive from his reading of the plays a valuable art experience.

The second level has to do with the deeper significance of the play for the people of the culture out of which it was written. The nature of the modern contemporary theater of the West, which we characterize as having become basically a prose theater of ideas and social comment, inclines us of the West to look to the playwright as a thinker. The "playwright as a thinker" has served as the title of a book evaluating the contemporary theater of the West. It seems to me that if we bring this attitude, one may even say this prejudice, to the *Shakuntalā* of Kālidāsa, we are likely to be disappointed in the play and to reject the poet-playwright, Kālidāsa. In fact, if we stop to think about it, such a demand upon the playwright would result in our rejecting almost the whole corpus of dramatic literature of the world. This is not to deny that there have been playwrights who have been original and substantial thinkers. However, in the long history of the theater throughout the world, this has not been the function nor the responsibility of the playwright. One may venture that this phenomenon of the playwright as a thinker is only likely to occur at a time when the audience for theater is limited, and when the theater is supported and favored by an elite, as is at present the case in the United States. The historic function of the theater has been basically to refine our feelings concerning what we already believe. If we examine the play

Shakuntalā in the light of this function, we reach its second and deeper level. It is also at this level that we gain some added insights concerning historical India, and also, in view of the impressive continuity of Indian civilization and culture, we gain insights regarding contemporary beliefs and convictions of Hindus.

When King Dushyanta falls in love with Shakuntalā "at first sight," his initial concern is her social status. He is apprehensive lest caste prove a barrier to his love. In this way, too, the romantic tone of the meeting of the young king and Shakuntalā is tempered by the king's realistic and practical considerations. Only when he is satisfied that no barrier exists between them by reason of the taboo against certain inter-caste marriages does he set out to court Shakuntalā. We can see that Kālidāsa's young hero is by no means a revolutionary or a rebel; he acts upon the conservative acceptance of the strictures of his social milieu. His relief upon learning of her caste and her parentage is expressed in the following: "And so my desire has really scope for its indulgence" [3] (p. 23).

In this way we see how caste is acknowledged as of singular importance, and by indirection deference to the taboo of intermarriage between certain castes is respected even by a king. This is one instance in which it is evident that the audience, through its becoming identified with the heroes and heroines of *Shakuntalā,* would have its feelings refined—reinforced—concerning beliefs and convictions already held. The obligations to family binding upon the individual, respect and submission to the mandates of the religious, deference and obligation to one's parents—these are likewise characteristic of the Indian culture and are reflected in *Shakuntalā.*

Elements of tension are developed by the end of Act II. When King Dushyanta is put in the position of a conflict of duties, he declares: "This places me in a dilemma. Here, on the one hand is the

---

[3] Page references to the play in the remainder of this paper are to *Śakoontalā,* trans. by M. A. Monier Williams (New York, Dodd, Mead, 1885).

commission of these holy men to be executed; and, on the other, the command of my revered parent to be obeyed. Both duties are too sacred to be neglected. What is to be done?" (p. 50).

This conflict of duties for King Dushyanta would have seemed very real for the audience for which the play was written, and even today in India it would be appreciated by modern Indian youth.

The whole of the play is grounded in the very basic Hindu tenet that the individual is on the wheel of life, experiencing a series of rebirths. This is known in Hindu doctrine as karma. Kālidāsa gives this overt expression with poetic effect: "Can it be/that the dim memory of events long past,/or friendships formed in other states of being,/flits like a passing shadow o'er the spirit?" (p. 108).

Again at the close of the play the final wish expressed by the king is a confirmation of the Hindu's belief in karma: "And may the purple self-existent god, whose vital Energy pervades all space,/ from future transmigrations save my soul!" (p. 205).

In pursuing the function of the drama as a refinement of our feelings about what we already believe, we may note instances in this play of a reinforcing of social-ethical principles of Indian society. Although it is used in the context of the play by the king to rationalize his action in rejecting the girl Shakuntalā, the following quotation reiterates an ethical concept of Hindu society at the time of the play: "The virtuous man is master of his passions,/and from another's wife averts his gaze" (p. 128).

There is ample evidence of a marked inequality in the status of men and women in ancient Indian culture. An inferior status for woman exists today as a problem with which modern independent India is struggling. Such stage classics of the West, as the plays of Ibsen and even Molière, have been found by the average Indian audience to be controversial, inflammatory, and even revolutionary. The defense of woman's right to equality in plays of the former, and the questioning of family relationships in the plays of the latter, are viewed by conservative and reactionary Hindu groups as destructive to the Hindu way of life.

The hermit Kanwa, the foster-father of Shakuntalā, gives advice to his foster-child before sending her to the city to rejoin her husband the king: "Honour thy betters; ever be respectful/to those above thee; and, should others share/thy husband's love, ne'er yield thyself a prey/to jealousy; but ever be a friend,/a loving friend, to those who rival thee/in his affections. Should thy wedded lord/treat thee with harshness, thou must never be/harsh in return, but patient and submissive" (p. 100).

When Shakuntalā has been brought to the court, presented to the king, and rejected by the king, the hermit Sharadwata, who has escorted her to the king's court, leaves Shakuntalā with these parting remarks: "Śakoontalā is certainly thy bride;/receive her or reject her, she is thine. Do with her, king, according to thy pleasure—/the husband o'er the wife is absolute" (p. 127).

Since we know that Sanskrit was almost exclusively the language of men, we may assume that the play *Shakuntalā* by Kālidāsa was performed for a male audience. In view of the structure of the Indian family and the hierarchical nature of Indian society, it need not surprise us that this play of Kālidāsa confirms male superiority. Kālidāsa is obviously no revolutionary thinker nor a critic of his own times and culture.

"It was the regular language of conversation between educated men of different provinces . . . the conditioned reflexes of childhood and the emotional needs of adolescents played little part in its development. One's mother in those days, one's wife, one's children, never spoke Sanskrit . . . as a general rule Sanskrit was never what one may call a language of the family." [4]

We may now turn to the third level of a play—the psychological. This level is by far the most difficult to investigate and requires adventurous analysis.[5] However, the rewards are most substantial, for

[4] Daniel H. H. Ingalls, "Sanskrit Poetry and Poetics," pp. 7–8.

[5] "When a worker in one field presents to those in another field some of his conclusions in the hope that they may be of interest and use when applied to other data, it behooves him to do so in a duly tentative and modest spirit. This attitude is particularly called for when a sphere of activity possesses such peculiar character-

only through such an analysis of the play does one come to discover its very deep and pervasive universality. At this basic level it is most easy to understand how the play survived as a deeply meaningful fantasy, both for its contemporary audience and also for the audiences of succeeding generations. I would call it the level of wish-fulfillment fantasy.

Fantasy is here used in the same sense as it may be used in referring to a dream or a daydream. On this basis, we would proceed with our analysis: if this were a dream of the author, Kālidāsa, we could speculate as to what personal meaning it had for him; if this were a dream with whose heroes and heroines members of the contemporary Indian audience did identify, we could discover what deep satisfactions it provided them. For indeed it must have provided a potent unconscious wish-fulfillment, both for its contemporary audiences as well as for successive generations of audiences in India, to account for its remarkable survival, when so much else has perished. It is no dangerous assumption that it was both an effective theater-piece and a play with deep meaning for its audiences—a timeless and universal meaning.

We may assume that members of the male Indian audience would readily identify and become involved emotionally with the hero, King Dushyanta. At the opening of the play, the young king is seen in the forest on a hunt. Through the poetic dialogue, he is presented to the audience as a formidable warrior, noted for his prowess with bow and arrow. The hero as hunter and the hero distinguished for his skill with bow and arrow would readily be accepted by literary critics, without benefit of psychoanalysis, as symbols of youthful virility.

The king is in the act of taking aim to transfix with his arrow a

istics as does that of psycho-analysis, where he knows that he can count only on incredulity and opposition from those not familiar with the subjects. The instinctive resentment, however politely disguised, which is felt toward an intruder who ventures to make suggestions concerning work in a strange group can only be intensified when those suggestions are unwelcome and unflattering as so many psycho-analytic ones are." Ernest Jones, "Psycho-analysis and Anthropology," *Essays in Applied Psycho-analysis* (London, Hogarth Press, 1951), II, 114.

deer. With poetic diction the king gives an appealing description of the deer (again there would be little or no objection to accepting the deer, so described, as a foreshadowing image of the heroine, Shakuntalā). At this moment, a voice behind the scenes, calls out to the king that he must not kill the deer. This is but one of many successive instances in which there are voices from behind the scenes. In some cases the voices from off stage are motivated and explained realistically. However, in several other instances, these voices are almost disembodied, nonrealistic, messages or warnings. This is merely one of the elements which prompts comparison with common incidents and features of a dream.

In a dream the off-stage voice, a not-uncommon characteristic of dreams, could symbolize the frustration of wish-fulfillment through the exercise of some censoring figure.

Throughout the fabric of the play, there is the movement of the male toward the female, Dushyanta toward Shakuntalā and vice-versa, and there is recurring frustration or interruption. An analysis of the play as a dream would reveal how this conflict and repression is resolved with satisfaction to the identifying members of the audience—those who enter into this as a collective dream.

We need to be aware, however, that as is characteristic of any dream, there is likely to be both complexity and the phenomenon of condensation. If we view the developing plot of the play *Shakuntalā* simply as a wish-fulfillment dream on the level of sexual gratification, we are very likely to miss the more subtle and interesting goal of the dream. (The terms "play" and "dream" are used interchangeably in this analysis.)

Ernest Jones says that, from the point of view of the unconscious, the movement of the individual toward the sexual opposite, seeking union, has symbolically a deeper unconscious meaning; the sexual act has within it on the unconscious level a seeking to dissipate the unconscious anxiety in respect to death.[6] He also says that sexual

[6] "It may be correlated with the astonishing fact mentioned previously, that in the unconscious the two ideas of sexual union (particularly incest) and of rebirth (i.e., return to the mother's womb) are regarded as equivalents . . . in this way it comes about that (re-)birth and coitus are equivalent ideas when the object is the mother,

union has the implication for the unconscious of the achievement of rebirth, and through rebirth, the achievement of Nirvāna.

At this point we look ahead and note both that King Dushyanta has by the end of the play achieved a reunion with his beloved, Shakuntalā, and also that the closing lines of the play indicate that the uppermost wish of King Dushyanta is the following: "And may the purple self-existent god, whose vital Energy pervades all space,/from future transmigration save my soul!" (p. 205).

The male audience for whom Kālidāsa wrote Shakuntalā— through identification with its sublime hero Dushyanta—experiences an energizing of both their repressed wishes and the attendant anxieties which have initially caused the repression of their wishes. According to Freud and others, two universal major goals of the human unconscious are: 1) to effect union with the parental sexual opposite (in the case of the male child, the mother; in the case of the female child, the father); and 2) in the wake of the unconscious driving for possession of the parent of the opposite sex comes anxiety and fear of castration; i.e., death at the hands of the parent whose role, in fantasy, has been usurped. These anxieties of the unconscious are resolved in a fantasy of rebirth, Nirvāna—that state of nonbirth; the circle comes full round with the unconscious symbolization of rebirth through sexual union.

This is predicated as being universally true for all men for all time in all cultures throughout the world. The extent to which this dilemma is resolved for the individual is dependent both upon the specific growing up and experiences of the individual and also upon the conditioning factors of a particular environment and culture. Thus an analysis of the play Shakuntalā can show that the play is grounded in the universal nature of man, but also it can reveal to us certain specific characteristics of the conditioning environment of the Indians for whom the play was written. The hidden fantasy at the heart of the play Shakuntalā then suggests that

and it is thus comprehensible that rituals symbolizing either of these acts have the power of restoring life." Jones, "Psycho-analysis and Anthropology," II, 140.

the Indian culture of the fifth century A.D. did not promote an easy resolution of the Oedipal conflict for the male Indian. As we return to a psychoanalytic analysis of the play *Shakuntalā* as if it were a dream, we would discover in symbols those characteristics of Indian culture which obstructed resolution of the Oedipal conflict. We would also discover that the ultimate resolution offered by this fantasy-play is the classic, universal resolution, namely, identification with the parent.

If for a moment we view Kālidāsa's play as a psychological sounding board for the feeling and thinking of the Indian audience for which it was written, we find ourselves tempted to speculate widely as to aspects and characteristics of the development of Indian culture. For example, in relating himself to authority figures, namely the father figures, the Indian male would have acute difficulties. We see in the character of the King Dushyanta, the Indian difficulty to take direct and immediate action, arising out of spontaneous feelings. Does this perhaps not throw some new light upon the dominant negative attitude of the Indian, both historic and modern, toward life? If in this most basic area of his life, the Indian tends to be immobilized, does this perhaps account for his difficulties at taking action in the solution of life's problems? Might this not result in elaborate rationalizations, dignified by the labels of religion and spirituality, for claiming that after all life is of no importance?

Complex and speculative as these questions are, there can be little doubt that from the level of feeling *Shakuntalā* as a fantasy reveals through psychoanalysis, that its satisfaction for the audience for which it was written was a resolution of a basic Oedipal conflict.

ROYAL W. WEILER

Comments

In appraising Kālidāsa's *Shakuntalā* as a world classic, I would attach much less significance than Dr. Mitchell does to what the play tells us of the social and cultural peculiarities of Indian life in the fifth century A.D. It seems to me, too, that his interpretation of the work as fundamentally a wish-fulfillment fantasy, arising from a basic Oedipal conflict, leaves the greater part of *Shakuntalā* unexplained and unappreciated. To me the great virtue of Kālidāsa lies in his mastery of language and his power to communicate the deepest and most varied human emotions—love, anger, tender sympathy, grief at separation, etc.—and to convey a sensitive awareness of nature. Relatively little of this is lost in a competent, unabridged translation like that of Arthur Ryder. The achievements of the playwright are there for anyone to observe and enjoy who has nothing more than the translation in front of him.

Some of Kālidāsa's unique ability becomes apparent if we consider what he was able to do with his story. The original theme of *Shakuntalā* appears in several sources, but it is the one in the *Mahābhārata* (summarized by Ryder in the Everyman's edition of the play) which Kālidāsa probably drew upon. Into this somewhat inanimate story Kālidāsa breathes life, making full use of his poetic skill and dramatic technique. In the epic story Shakuntalā welcomes the king himself; in Kālidāsa's version this indelicacy is eliminated by the creation of two delightful maidens who serve

Royal W. Weiler is Assistant Professor of Sanskrit at Columbia.

as Shakuntalā's companions. In the earlier version, the king refuses to recognize Shakuntalā because of fear of public scandal unbefitting the king; in Kālidāsa's rendering, the king is spared this indignity and loss of stature by being made the victim of a curse which blots Shakuntalā from his memory. Further, in Kālidāsa's play Shakuntalā appears before her husband, the king, before the delivery of their son, thus heightening the poignancy of Shakuntalā's dilemma and the king's failure to recognize her. Our sympathies for Shakuntalā *and* the king are thus aroused as they both appear in the grip of an almost unrelenting fate.

There are other factors which contribute substantially to *Shakuntalā's* importance as a world classic. In the first act of the play, Shakuntalā, with her personal charm and natural beauty, is the innocent child of nature. Later Shakuntalā's capacity for silent suffering in the face of adversity shows the girl emerging into the fullness of womanhood. The restraint with which she endures the pangs of separation, the curse of the irascible Durvāsas, and the subsequent rejection of her by her husband—without a word of complaint or reproach from her—does much to enhance Shakuntalā's character. As she develops from an innocent bride into an ideal wife, the exemplar of marital faith and devotion, we can follow the maturation of her love and appreciate Kālidāsa's insight into human nature as revealed through his depth of characterization. For variety and contrast, on the other hand, he draws characters from all walks of life: hermit girls, sages, kings, generals, policemen, fishermen, and celestial beings.

Kālidāsa's method of evolving his plot is also noteworthy. Though there is relatively little action, this apparent deficiency is more than compensated for by his poetic skill. Indeed, a somewhat static development of the plot is typical of the Indian theater, where far greater importance was placed on the recitation of appropriate verses at the appropriate time by the appropriate character. In this way the depth of characterization, as revealed by the inner thoughts of the characters, is related to the unfolding of the narrative. Scenic contrasts are provided in eloquent descriptions of the earthly beauties of nature, the formality of the king's domain, and the splendor of celestial realms. In many respects we have a paradise lost and a greater paradise regained. The story of Shakuntalā as developed by Kālidāsa is told in terms of love and the vicissitudes of life: joy and sorrow, love and rejection under the power of fate, and final emergence into a happiness and peace which is man's dream in life fulfilled.

As Professor S. N. Dasgupta has said, Kālidāsa succeeds as a dramatist "mainly by his poetic power in two respects: he is master of the poetic emotion which he can skillfully harmonize with character and action, and he has the poetic sense of balance and restraint which a dramatist must show if he would win success." [1] Thus, the status of Kālidāsa's *Shakuntalā* as a classic rests not so much on its dramatic power, as on the artistic balance of dramatic and poetic qualities. The excellence with which Kālidāsa communicates through dramatic and poetic imagery the most sublime elements in human life, his sympathetic understanding of human nature, and the beauty and significance of nature in general mark *Shakuntalā* as a world classic well deserving the attention of every educated person.

While these profound qualities of Kālidāsa's art may not have provided the immediate stimulus for Sir William Jones to publish the first translation of *Shakuntalā* in a European language in 1789 [2] —he wished rather "to show that the Bráhmans at least do not think polite literature incompatible with jurisprudence" [3]—it was, nevertheless, through him that the essential beauty of Kālidāsa's play came to animate nineteenth-century romanticism. Jones's influence on European literature, largely through G. Forster's trans-

---

[1] S. N. Dasgupta and S. K. De, *A History of Sanskrit Literature—Classical Period* (University of Calcutta, 1947), I, 135.

[2] The first printed text of *Shakuntalā* (though not necessarily that used by Jones) appeared in Calcutta in 1761. Sir William Jones's translation into English went through four editions: Calcutta, 1789; London, 1790, 1792; Edinburgh, 1796; and was reprinted at Calcutta in 1855, 1887, 1899; and in London in 1870.

[3] Quoted from Jones's preface to his edition of *Shakuntalā* (1789) by A. J. Arberry in *Asiatic Jones* (London, Longmans, Green 1946), p. 26.

lation of his *Shakuntalā* into German, was pervasive and indirectly exerted a profound influence on many writers, especially Goethe, who patterned his *Vorspiel* to *Faust* on Forster's translation of Jones's prologue to his translation of *Shakuntalā*. The qualities of "delicacy, freshness, and ripeness of sentiment" [4] in *Shakuntalā* were recognized by Goethe, who, reflecting Schopenhauer's enthusiasm for the Upanishads, immortalized Shakuntalā in European literature through his well-known lyric:

Willst du die Blüthe des frühen, die Früchte des späteren Jahres,
Willst du, was reizt und entzückt, willst du was sättigt und nährt,
Willst du den Himmel, die Erde, mit Einem Namen begreifen;
Nenn' ich, Sakuntalā, Dich, und so ist Alles gesagt.

Wouldst thou the young year's blossoms and the fruits of its decline,
And all by which the soul is charmed, enraptured, feasted, fed?
Wouldst thou the earth and heaven itself in one sole name combine?
I name thee, O Shakuntalā, and all at once is said.

[Eastwich's translation]

Rückert was similarly inspired by the beauties of Indian poetry. Forster's version of Jones's original translation formed the basis for many other translations into European languages. During the later half of the nineteenth century, however, new translations were made from the original Sanskrit and Prakrit texts into French, German, Dutch, Swedish, Danish, Italian, Spanish, Russian, Polish, Hungarian, Icelandic, and other languages. The most useful and scholarly translations into English are those of Monier-Williams in 1853, based on the Devanagari recension, and Ryder's translation (1912), based on the critically edited text of the somewhat longer Bengali recension as published by R. Pischel in the Harvard Oriental Series (volume 16). The superiority of the later text is indicated by Professor Ryder—with whom we must agree—that it would be "hard to believe that any lesser artist could pad such a masterpiece, and pad it all over, without making the fraud apparent on almost every page." [5]

[4] F. W. Thomas, "Language and Literature," in *The Legacy of India,* edited by G. T. Garratt (Oxford, Clarendon Press, 1937), p. 204.
[5] Arthur W. Ryder, *Kalidasa—The Translation of Shakuntala & Other Works* (Everyman's Library, 1912), p. 103.

Indian achievements in science and philosophy have often been rendered obsolete by modern developments in atomic theory, linguistic analysis, dialectics, and the like. Kālidāsa's *Shakuntalā*, however, remains the most enduring achievement of Indian drama and a work assured of permanent status among the world's literary classics. Whereas some other Indian works presume and require some degree of acquaintance with historical background and secondary sources, *Shakuntalā* stands out as a work of universal import readily apparent in a good translation. It is, nonetheless, true that matters of social, cultural, and dramaturgic relevance can be more readily grasped and appreciated if the reader can consult secondary materials which treat more fully the general framework and significance of Indian drama. Apart from Ryder's excellent introduction to his translation of *Shakuntalā* in the Everyman's Library and his summary of the story of Shakuntalā in the same volume, other works which are of some value in comprehending the framework of this drama are A. B. Keith's *The Sanskrit Drama* (Oxford, 1924), S. N. Dasgupta and S. K. De's *A History of Sanskrit Literature* (Calcutta, 1947), as well as the brief treatment in A. A. Macdonell's *India's Past* and *Sanskrit Literature* and G. T. Garratt's *Legacy of India*. A somewhat more detailed, but competent study of Kālidāsa and his works is that by G. C. Jhala, *Kalidasa, A Study* (Bombay, 1943).

In conclusion, I can do no better than offer Ryder's ultimate evaluation of Kālidāsa's *Shakuntalā*: "The best proof of a poet's greatness is the inability of men to live without him. . . . Analysis of Kalidasa's writing might easily be continued, but analysis can never explain life. The only real criticism is subjective. We know that Kalidasa is a very great poet, because the world has not been able to leave him alone." [6]

[6] Ryder, *Kalidasa*, pp. xvii and xxi.

Synopsis of Discussion: Second Session

Comment in the second session centered less upon the reasons why these books should be presented—their importance being taken for granted—than upon how to present them. At the outset of the discussion the chairman, W. Norman Brown, asked if it were possible to teach a book of, for example, Arabic literature, if the teacher was not somewhat familiar with Arabic or Islamic studies? What kind of teacher should a qualifying course be given to? Is it not better to give up the material than be content with an untrained teacher? Are there values in these works for undergraduates when the teacher cannot cope with the philology, history, and language? Enlarging the subject, he asked if it were only the larger schools that could be assured of adequate teaching? What chance does the small school have? What kind of guide books can be developed?

The members of the conference rose to these questions with vigor. Mr. Mahdi saw no reason why a man not a specialist in Islamic studies could not teach Islamic classics, so long as two conditions were met: that Islamicists produce objective, circumspect, and accurate translations for him to use, and that the problems in the texts be indicated to him. Thomas Aquinas and Averroes benefited from Aristotle and Socrates in translation, and neither was a specialist on Greece. Rather than being one of special knowledge, is not the problem one of the art of critical reading, he asked.

A second position was taken by Mr. Winder. In view of what it is possible to hope for, he thought, the best kind of teacher might be a mean between the specialist and the dilettante. Summer schools might produce such men, or the schools that now are conferring joint degrees.

This was an inadequate arrangement to the mind of Adelaide Hahn, whose position clearly favored the specialist. It is dishonest, she said, for a teacher to deal with a translation if he cannot read the original language. How can such a man judge whether a translation is reliable? How indicate the original style or the real greatness of the author? The first need, she said, is for a philologist trained in the language. If there is none, it is better not to try to deal with the literature.

The question of linguistic ability prompted Mr. Burch to propose other qualifications. Yes, he said, a teacher of the Qur'ān would be better off knowing Arabic, but by the same standards he ought also to have deep religious feeling, for example, or better yet, mystical experiences. To teach the Upanishads he ought to be trained in philosophy, and so forth. Yet in fact, St. Augustine, who lacked Hebrew and good Greek, was nevertheless a great teacher. The question, he maintained, was not well put. It should not be a matter of first deciding to teach classics and then finding a teacher; it should rather be to find good teachers and then let them teach what they wished. William S. Weedon seconded that and added that a teacher's desire to stimulate the students to ask questions was also important.

With regard to the technique of presenting the books, K. D. Irani suggested that the best approach was to find related concepts in numerous books. It was courting superficiality, he thought; to give students a book to read and then simply ask them what they thought of it. This only makes them think they have understood when they have not. In fact, there is no need to establish a course to read books; students who want to read are free to do so. Let those who have read a series of classics, he suggested, gather in a course and discuss the areas in the books that can be connected:

modes of expression, imagery, and the like. Then, he suggested, the student may acquire a range of concepts that will free him to think independently.

The way to that goal, he admitted, was not without obstacles. In regard to the Upanishads, for example, there were difficult questions. The works were huge, for one thing; too bulky to be read in full. There would have to be selection, and even then the subtlety of the philosophy might escape the student. The Qur'ān was another example. What would a teacher in practice do to teach the Qur'ān to undergraduates? To teach it adequately there should be some thought given to its historical development, its antecedents, its implications, and what came of it in Islam. If all that were shown, would the course not be one on the history of ideas rather than the study of the text? Still, he concluded, aside from such vexing questions, if the student could be brought to connect ideas at different times, the study of classics would have a purpose.

Mr. Burch disagreed with several of Mr. Irani's points. For one thing, the Upanishads are not so sizeable as Mr. Irani has suggested. What is long is Shankara's Commentary, and that is dull. The Upanishads themselves are well within the capacity of a student to read. Even the Indian epics, Mr. Burch argued, are not so long that at least the teacher cannot read them. Mr. Irani was mistaken, too, about the willingness of students to read books. The point is, students do not want to read those books. That is the problem of education: making them want to read. Finally, Mr. Burch said, Mr. Irani should not seek a purpose for reading the books. They are not read as a part of vocational training, they are read for and in themselves.

Environment, which some of Mr. Irani's comments had suggested to be useful, was for J. A. B. Van Buitenen the keystone of understanding. As a Sanskritist and philologist, Mr. Van Buitenen was strongly disposed to relate a book to its cultural environment. To take *Shakuntalā* as a point, while Mr. Mitchell had emphasized psychological values and Mr. Weiler universal values, Mr. Van

Buitenen would emphasize first Indian values. In this great piece of Sanskrit literature, fundamental Sanskritic values are expressed in superb poetry: the ideal of the hermitage, pangs of separation, the departure of a daughter from her home on marriage, and others. They are Indian values. In any attempt to show the book as great to an undergraduate, it must first be shown as a great Indian book. That means, he pointed out, a rather deep penetration of the cultural content around it.

He had noted, he added, Mr. Winder's remark about the difficulty of integrating great books in a continuum, and he had been somewhat puzzled by the independent existence at Columbia of one course in Oriental Civilization and another in Oriental Humanities. At Chicago, there was one integrated course on Indian civilization in which the great books were viewed as vehicles of cultural content. The books there, he said, were first understood in Indian terms and only after that in our own. The question that was central, he said, was whether we could neglect an entire civilization underlying a great work. Were we not obliged to put it into its tradition?

In reply to Mr. Van Buitenen's remarks, Mr. de Bary agreed that environment was important. The two courses at Columbia, he said, are complementary. Ideally he would like the students to take both, that in civilization first and the humanities second. He did not think that a work could or should be lifted entirely out of context; but there was a danger that the study of the context might become an end in itself, rather than a means to understanding what in these works is of a particular time and place, and what in them transcends the time and place of their creation. There are, moreover, advantages to concentrating on the books in a colloquium which permits teachers in different disciplines to join in the discussion and illuminate a work from different directions. Thus there can be present a specialist who controls both the text and context, and others who may be more alert to philosophical issues, literary values, etc.

Mr. Mahdi had observed the Chicago program described by Mr. Van Buitenen and thought that one of its characteristics ought to be mentioned. It was strictly a social science program, he said. He realized that the social sciences had progressed greatly in considering cultural problems. In his observation, however, if great books were introduced as auxiliaries within the social sciences, it was invariable that only those aspects expressing the cultural milieu were brought out. Other aspects, important, not in understanding another culture, but in training the mind to consider certain problems, were neglected. The function of the liberal arts in training the mind, he said, was completely lost.

Two final questions, raised at the conclusion of the discussion, should be mentioned among the many touched upon in the course of the afternoon. Yu-kuang Chu of Skidmore felt that since the majority of the delegates represented small schools, it behooved those from the larger schools to indicate what their experience might suggest as to the best course for the smaller schools to follow. This question anticipated the problems to be discussed in the fourth and final session, and was left pending. Also unanswered was the question raised by the chairman in closing the meeting: where were the teachers to come from who would be needed for the extension of this type of work, and what should be done to encourage and sponsor the training of such teachers?

JOHN T. MESKILL

HERMAN L. SINAIKO

The Analects of Confucius

The rapid growth of interest in the non-Western civilizations in recent years has raised a wide variety of problems for those concerned with general education. All of the old, familiar questions involving the aims and organization of courses, the selection of readings, and the teaching methods to be employed have to be reconsidered when non-Western materials are introduced into general education programs. In this paper I shall argue for the inclusion of the *Analects* of Confucius among the very limited number of non-Western works that undergraduates might read as a part of their general education and indicate some of the specific problems involved in teaching the *Analects* whether it be in the context of an introductory course on Chinese civilization or a general course on the "great books" of the non-Western world.

In his preface to volume one of *The Great Books of the Western World* Robert M. Hutchins describes the great books of the West as those "that have endured and that the common voice of mankind called the finest creations, in writing, of the Western mind." Applying this standard to China, the *Analects* might well head the list of the great books of Chinese civilization; everyone has heard of Confucius, of his immense importance in Chinese culture, and of the *Analects* as the work which contains his ideas. And if this is not sufficient, it can be pointed out that the *Analects* did not merely

Herman L. Sinaiko is Instructor in Humanities in the College and in the Department of Oriental Languages and Civilizations at the University of Chicago.

"endure" in Chinese literature for many centuries, it was raised to the status of an official Classic and for many generations was memorized by all educated Chinese as a part of their "general" education. In this limited sense, then, the *Analects* is unquestionably a great book.

Furthermore, the study of the *Analects* can provide an excellent introduction to Chinese thought and civilization and deserves to be read and pondered by all who wish to reach some understanding of China. Of course Confucius did not go unchallenged, nor Confucianism unchanged, during the past two millennia; there were always other competing religions, ideologies, and schools of thought. Nevertheless, Confucianism has played so large a role in the history of China that it has long been a cliché to characterize Chinese civilization as Confucian. And, notwithstanding the continuous developments and alterations in Confucianism, the *Analects* still stands as the best single statement of the basic principles and values of that tradition.

All this general testimony suggests that the *Analects* is a work admirably suited to the needs of a general education program. However, it is altogether likely that the initial response to the book by most students will be one of confusion and disappointment; for in the usual sense of the term the *Analects* is not a book at all, but a collection of fragments. It consists of about 500 sections arranged in twenty chapters. The sections range in length from short sentences of a few words to conversations and discussions a few pages long at most. There is no particular order, for the most part, in the arrangement of the chapters or in the sections within each chapter. The sections themselves deal with a wide variety of subjects; topical political issues, judgments of great men and important events of the past, the proper relations of rulers with their ministers and subjects, Confucius' attitude toward particular disciples, the nature of various virtues, etc. The students will in all probability be disturbed not only by the fragmentary character of the work but also by an apparent lack of coherence on the part of

Confucius with regard to his aims, his principles, and his primary interests. Many of Confucius' statements will strike them as trivial and more than a few will be so obscure and vague as to be unintelligible. In all likelihood Confucius will appear as a rather stern Chinese gentleman who taught etiquette and public administration to aspiring young civil servants and addressed homilies to rulers. It scarcely needs to be said that this view of Confucius is not confined to undergraduate students.

It seems necessary, if a fuller understanding of the *Analects* is to be achieved, to go beyond an examination of the work itself to some consideration of Confucius' life and the social and political context in which he lived, and in this respect the teaching of the *Analects* will differ considerably from that of most great books. The reasons for this difference in treatment lie in the disconnected, composite nature of the work itself. It was apparently put together long after Confucius' death, from a variety of sources; some of the passages are couched in the style of a period much later than Confucius and contain serious distortions of his ideas, while others seem to be completely spurious interpolations. These are minor difficulties which can be cleared up with a judicious footnote or comment. An even greater difficulty arises from the fact that the majority of Confucius' statements, as recorded in the *Analects,* were not intended as general truths with a universal applicability. In many cases these statements are answers to specific questions asked by particular disciples or rulers in a definite pedagogic or rhetorical situation. For the most part, Confucius appears in the *Analects* as a practicing teacher and a hopeful political reformer, not as a political theorist. In consequence extreme care must be exercised in generalizing from any one of his statements and wherever a specific context is supplied full weight must be given to it. This may involve providing students with biographical information (if it exists) on several of the important disciples, rulers, and other personages that figure prominently in the *Analects,* as well as some explanatory material on the complex political situations referred to.

There yet remains the general social and political context of Chinese civilization in Confucius' own day. This context is implicit throughout the *Analects,* but without any further information students may be unable to perceive it. It is unlikely, for example, that even a careful reading of the text of the *Analects* will reveal the feudal form of government or the degree of social and political anarchy in late Ch'un Ch'iu times. But whatever may be said of China in the late sixth and early fifth centuries B.C., this much is clear: Confucius did not live in a Confucian society. Of course, many of the basic institutions, ideas, and modes of behavior that were later shaped into traditional Chinese civilization as we generally conceive it already existed in Confucius' day, but many others did not. The very success of Confucianism in later centuries makes it difficult for us to realize the novelty and significance of many of Confucius' statements. What was a commonplace in the Sung and Ming periods may have been a striking, and perhaps dangerous, intellectual innovation at the time of Confucius. Confucianism, as it became the dominant political tradition in China, had to accommodate itself to changing conditions and to translate the principles and ideas of Confucius and the other early Confucian thinkers into viable political institutions and programs. In the process much that was alien, and even antithetical, to the ideas of Confucius was incorporated into the tradition. The history of Confucianism after Confucius is a fascinating one; its major figures were often philosophers and statesmen of the first order, but it would be a serious error to interpret Confucius in the light of their thought and behavior. Confucius can only be accurately understood in relation to his own times.

Placing the *Analects* in the context of its contemporary world should provide students with the opportunity to penetrate the apparent obscurity and triviality of the text and enable them to perceive the genuine ethical and political problems Confucius faced. What is the good life for man? How can a just society be established? What moral and intellectual qualities are required in a man for the just and effective exercise of political authority? In case of a conflict between a man's public and private responsibilities which should take priority? In the *Analects* these questions and others like them are raised in terms appropriate to ancient China, but their significance is scarcely limited to that time and place.

When a man is seen in his historical context there is always a tendency to interpret his thought as a product of his times. The ideas of Confucius, as represented in the *Analects,* are particularly susceptible to this kind of analysis and have often been dealt with in this fashion. There is no question that the thought of Confucius was, in very large measure, the product of his particular world. He was deeply concerned about the wretched condition of his society and his activities as a teacher and reformer were almost entirely, albeit unsuccessfully, directed toward alleviating and improving that condition. It is not simply that he neglected, through the pressure of contemporary events, to give a coherent, systematic expression to his ideas or that such an expression has failed to survive the centuries, but rather that he would have felt such an exposition to be of little or no value. The precise formulation of general ideas, which usually receives the closest attention in European philosophical reflections, was of interest to Confucius mainly in terms of its immediate relevance to crucial issues of his day and age. To say this, however, is not to imply that the validity of Confucius' thought is limited to those particular problems. The *Analects,* as I have suggested, cannot be adequately understood without reference to supplementary material not contained in the text. But this additional material should serve to illuminate Confucius, not to explain him.

The study of the *Analects* can be an important and meaningful part of a general education only if it begins from an awareness that the problems Confucius dealt with are no less relevant today than they were 2,500 years ago. Without this awareness students can have only an antiquarian interest in the *Analects* and are not likely to consider seriously Confucius' attitude toward those problems or the solutions he proposed. On the other hand, if students are conscious of the universal character of the questions he raised, and if they do reflect seriously on his answers to those questions, they will come into contact with a different and largely unfamiliar approach to many of the great issues that have always confronted mankind. I do not mean to prejudge the value of that approach. It may well be that Confucius' thought has value only within the context of his unique historical situation or, more generally, within the framework of traditional Chinese culture. It is quite possible that what he had to say has no immediate significance for us beyond the influence his opinions may still exercise in our contemporary world. This situation, however, is not peculiar to the *Analects;* it applies equally to all the great literature of the past, including our own Greek and Roman classics. And, as with the works of Plato and Aristotle, the true worth of the *Analects* can only be determined by a careful and sympathetic reading of the text itself.

In a paper of this length and character it is hardly possible to do justice to the full scope of Confucius' thought, and, therefore, I shall not even attempt to do so. Instead, in the remaining pages, I will briefly describe without any attempt at documentation two facets of his thought that might well engage the interest of students. The first of these, his humanism, is likely to attract students initially, and the second, his approach to political theory and reform, is likely to be rejected by them at first sight. I have chosen these two simply to indicate the kind of contribution a study of the *Analects* can make to a general education.

In our contemporary world the power of religious faith to support the moral and political order of society has long since been weakened by the continuous attacks of science. Classical philosophy, which traditionally supplied an alternative basis for ethics, has also been rendered suspect, and neither the natural nor the social sciences have been able to remedy the deficiency to date. Even the hope of the eighteenth and nineteenth centuries that science would some day do so is no longer widely held. The difficulty is not that common standards of public and private behavior no longer exist, but that there seem to be no certain grounds for those standards. Several modern philosophies such as utilitarianism, pragmatism, and, most recently, existentialism, have attempted in a variety of ways to provide a viable foundation for morality. In spite of their diversity these modern approaches tend to share one basic characteristic: they all are forms of humanism and they search for the grounds of morality in the human condition. Confucius, too, has often been called a humanist and, in its general sense of a man for whom the central object of interest in the world is humanity, the term seems quite appropriate. His humanism, however, did not lead him to deny the existence or importance of nonhuman forces in the world and he clearly had a definite sense of divinity. Nevertheless, overwhelming evidence in the *Analects* indicates that his chief concern was for the life of man in this world. He explicitly avoided speculation about spirits and death in favor of knowledge of men and life. And in all his discussions about virtue and morality he never appealed to anything beyond the natural condition of man to make his points. In this respect, then, Confucius appears to have a good deal in common with the philosophic temper of our modern world.

Because of its modernity and familiarity, students are likely to feel a greater initial sympathy for the general humanistic tenor of Confucius' thought than for many of his more particular views. For this reason the study of the *Analects* might well begin with a general consideration of Confucius' humanism and advance gradually to more detailed and precise formulations of its special qualities. A few brief examples of the kinds of ideas students will encounter in this procedure may be suggestive.

To begin with, Confucius' conception of man, so far as one can piece it together from his statements, is clearly quite different from those found in European thought. Students will not find in the *Analects* an abstract notion of man as a creature with one or more unique defining characteristics; Confucius was interested in man's concrete situation in the world, not in his formal attributes. Considered from this point of view many of the quite simple and obvious facts of human life take on a new significance. Thus, the family with all of its complex functions and relationships and their attending emotions, obligations, and claims is seen as both the foundation and the pattern of normal human existence. In the community of the family the infant is nurtured and protected as it is gradually equipped for adult life, so that, in the most immediate way, the very possibility of becoming a man presupposes a family group. The family also seems to be the original locus of all the primary human feelings, activities, and relationships, such as affection and love, fear, hope, shame, respect for authority, cooperation, and compromise. In this special sense, then, Confucius has a radically social conception of man.

Some Western commentators have described this aspect of his thought by saying that Confucius conceived of men primarily as members of a family or other social group and not as individuals. Unfortunately, this is often taken to mean that for Confucius the individual has no rights, duties, or value apart from his membership in a given community. No careful reading of the *Analects* can support such an interpretation. Confucius did recognize the enormous importance of the social context in which men live and he strongly emphasized the ethical and political obligations which a normal life in society entails, but in doing so he constantly stressed the need for dignity, integrity, and moral self-sufficiency in the individual. He rejected the notion of moral absolutes which exist or can be known aside from the actions and characters of individual men. The moral attitudes Confucius advocated and the virtues he sought to instill in his disciples were exclusively grounded in men. Hence the good man, for Confucius, does far more than merely exemplify the principles of morality in his conduct; for, since those principles have no reality or meaning apart from himself and his fellows, he is personally responsible for their maintenance and

growth in human society. In the face of this responsibility the necessity for a continual cultivation of one's character is apparent,
and Confucius frequently says as much in the *Analects*. The sobri-
ety and moderation of Confucius' ethics and his insistence on
man's social responsibilities should not obscure this fundamental
individualism which permeates his teachings and is an integral
part of his thoroughgoing humanism.

Starting with Plato's *Republic* the Western tradition of political
philosophy has largely centered its attention on topics relating to
the forms of political life, e.g., the relative merits of democracy in
contrast to aristocracy and monarchy, the advantages of a mixed
form of government, direct vs. representative democracy, the proper
separation of governmental powers necessary for an effective check-
and-balance system, etc. Concomitantly, Western revolutionary and
reform movements have commonly attempted to achieve their aims
by effecting changes in the existing formal structure of government.
In the *Analects* there are many passages dealing with general political questions as well as discussions of very specific contemporary
problems. However, in both cases Confucius never refers to any
other form of government than that existing in China in his own
day and he never so much as suggests any changes in the form or
structure of the governments he knew. It is easy to account for
this fact by pointing out that Confucius was unaware of other forms
of government and that the classical Greek thinkers were confronted with a multiplicity of them. This explanation may be true,
but it ignores the primary focus of Confucius' approach to politics
and there is no reason to believe that his notions of political reform
would have been essentially different if the China of his day had
had a diversity of types of government.

In their discussions of politics the Greek political theorists distinguished between a government of men and a government of law.
The law here referred to was neither criminal nor customary but
constitutional. They recognized the primacy of customary law in

every society, and on this point Confucius would have agreed with them, but, unlike Confucius, they devoted little attention to it. By constitutional law they meant those basic, general principles which give a form and a distinctive character to the political life of a society. A society governed by constitutional law was marked by the justice and impartiality of its political activities. The concept of a government of law was generally established by contrasting it with the notion of a government of men. The fact that individual men are swayed by their passions and self-interest, and therefore may employ political authority unjustly and arbitrarily, led these thinkers to assert the superiority, for practical politics, of the law. The distinction has long been a commonplace in the West and every schoolboy knows that "we have a government of law and not of men."

In Confucius students will meet, probably for the first time, a political thinker who argues seriously that good government depends on the moral and intellectual qualities of the men who actually exercise political authority. On this issue Confucius challenges the contention of the main stream of Western thought. Living in a world with more than its share of irresponsible, self-seeking rulers, he was fully conscious of the corrupting influences of power and the inability of most men to resist them. Thus the education of his disciples seems to have had one great aim: to produce men capable of wielding political power with justice and intelligence for the benefit of society as a whole. Only when such men were in positions of authority could government function as it should. In the *Analects,* therefore, political theory is discussed in terms of the political behavior of good men and political reform is sought through the education of gifted individuals.

The demands of this education were rigorous; Confucius tried to imbue his disciples with the highest ideals of dedicated public service and, at the same time, to prepare them for office in a world where treason, venality, and cruelty were the usual order of the day. The truly good man, according to Confucius, will accept personal hardship and poverty and even, if necessary, lay down his life for his principles. At the same time, if he has a genuine opportunity to put his principles into practice, he will be willing and able to accommodate himself to the, perhaps, immoral or dangerous realities of the situation. If this program for reform seems hopelessly idealistic, it should be remembered that the Confucian tradition, based in large part on these ideas, maintained a viable and stable political order in a great empire for two thousand years. The details of contemporary politics bear little resemblance to those of ancient China, but the difficulty of translating political ideals into practice is as real for us as it was for Confucius. For students the very unfamiliarity of Confucius' approach to political theory and reform can serve to highlight the great issues involved.

The *Analects,* despite its small bulk, is a rich and provocative work. In touching so briefly on two rather general aspects of Confucius' thought I have completely ignored many of its most interesting facets. The nature and interrelation of all the virtues, Confucius' attitude toward tradition and antiquity, the insistence that education be open to all regardless of birth (with all of its political implications); these are only typical of other topics which are treated by Confucius. The *Analects,* as I have tried to make clear, is not an easy book to understand, and it presents special difficulties from the point of view of teaching. They are not insurmountable, however, and the admittedly sketchy, inadequate remarks on Confucius' humanism and his approach to political philosophy are merely aimed at demonstrating that the effort will be fruitful and rewarding.

WING-TSIT CHAN

The Lotus Sūtra

No one can understand the Far East without some knowledge of the teachings of the *Lotus Sūtra,* because it is the most important scripture of Mahāyāna Buddhism, which cuts across the entire Far East. In a narrow sense it is a scripture of the T'ien-t'ai School in China and Tendai in Japan and the chief sūtra of the Nichiren School in Japan. But in a broad sense it is the most basic sūtra for all Mahāyāna. This is because it is used by practically all the different schools; because it was the first to preach revolutionary Mahāyāna doctrines and is as yet the most comprehensive statement of them; and most important of all, because it has been the source of inspiration for Buddhist practice in the Far East for the last 1,500 years. If out of several hundred Mahāyāna sūtras one is to choose only one as the most representative and most meaningful, most students will select the *Lotus.* No wonder that when Chang Jung, an ardent advocate of the harmony of Confucianism, Buddhism, and Taoism, died in 497 A.D., he held in his left hand a copy of the *Classic of Filial Piety* and the *Tao-te ching* and in his right hand the *Lotus.* Ever since its appearance in China in the third century, and especially after the fifth, the study of the *Lotus* has been pursued most vigorously and extensively. According to the *Biographies of Eminent Monks (Kao-seng chuan),* of twenty-one monks famous for reciting sūtras, sixteen recited the *Lotus.* More lectures have been given, more research conducted into its

Wing-tsit Chan is Professor of Chinese Culture and Philosophy at Dartmouth College.

subject matter and terminology, and more commentaries written on it than any other Buddhist scripture.

This scripture is written in the form of a drama in the loose sense of the word. It is a drama on the greatest scale ever conceived by man. Its stage is many Buddha-worlds. Its time is eternity. And its actors are the Lord Buddha Shākyamuni and innumerable beings. The scene opens with Shākyamuni sitting in a trance. Gathered before him are 12,000 arhats, 6,000 nuns headed by his mother and including his wife, 8,000 bodhisattvas, 60,000 gods, Brahma with his 12,000 dragon kings, and hundreds of thousands of heavenly beings, demons, and other beings. As the congregation fold their hands in homage to him, a ray of light issues forth from his forehead which illuminates the 18,000 Buddha-worlds in the East, in each of which a Buddha is preaching. The entire universe is shaking. Flowers rain all over and perfume fills all space. It is announced that the Lord is now going to give a discourse (ch. 1).

Out of trance, the Buddha begins to speak and says that only Buddhas have perfect knowledge and are qualified to preach and they are now preaching to all beings. At this the proud arhats, saints of Hīnayāna or Small Vehicle Buddhism, or rather Theravāda Buddhism, who consider themselves already perfectly enlightened, leave in silent protest. Shākyamuni teaches not the Three Vehicles —those of the Srāvakas who attain their salvation by hearing the Buddha's teaching, the Pratyeka-buddhas who attain to their personal enlightenment by their own exertions, and the bodhisattvas who postpone their own Buddhahood for the sake of helping all beings to be saved. Instead he teaches only the One Vehicle. He has taught the other vehicles merely as an expediency or as a convenient means to those who were not yet ready for the highest truth, the One Vehicle. In this vehicle, Nirvāna is not extinction of existence, as taught in Hīnayāna, but extinction of illusions and ignorance. Everyone will be saved. Anyone who practices charity, is patient, observes discipline, is diligent in spiritual cultivation, makes offerings to the Buddha, builds a stupa with gold, silver, crystal, amber, sandalwood, clay, or in the case of a child at play, sand, who carves a Buddha figure in copper, pewter, or lacquered cloth, or paints a Buddha figure with a brush or even a fingernail, makes music, recites a verse, offers a sound or a flower to the Buddha, or merely raises his head or folds his hands or utters a simple word of admiration, *namo,* will attain salvation (ch. 2).

The disciple Sāriputra is now full of joy and in ecstasy. He realizes that he is really a son of the Buddha, produced from the Buddha Law or Dharma and born out of the Buddha's mouth. He is assured by the Lord that he will be the Flower-Light Buddha in the Buddha-world whose ground is crystal with eight broad walks lined with golden ropes, and where a jewel flower will spring up wherever the feet of his disciples will tread. Anyone with devotion and faith will become a Buddha. He applies expedient and convenient means to save them all in accordance with the requirements of the circumstances, just as a father, whose house is on fire and whose sons still think of play, offers them a goat cart, a deer cart, and an ox cart to lure them out. Thus saved, they are given only the ox cart, the best of all carts; that is, not the Three Vehicles but the One Vehicle (ch. 3). Or like the father of the wandering son, who comes to work for hire without knowing their relationship, and who receives from the loving father not only wages but all his wealth (ch. 4).

Speaking to Mahākāsyapa and other disciples, the Lord tells the parable of rain. It falls on all plants, though they are ignorant of the fact that because their natures differ they respond to the rain in different ways. Only the Buddha knows the true character and reality of existence. He will care for all beings and enable them to become Buddhas provided they have faith, however simple (ch. 5).

Then Shākyamuni foretells many future Buddhas. So-and-so will become Buddha Radiance, in the Buddha-world of Brilliant Virtue, whose period will last for 32 kalpas or billions of years and will be called Great Splendor. So-and-so will become the Buddha of Sandalwood Fragrance in the Buddha-world called Happy Feeling, whose period, called Perfect Joy, will be 104 kalpas. And so on, (ch. 6).

Interrupting his predictions, he tells of an Ancient Buddha who, he remembers, has a life of 5,400,000 myriads of ten million cycles. After attaining enlightenment, he recited the *Lotus* for 8,000 cycles. All his sixteen sons have become Buddhas and continue to recite the sūtra. The last son, Shākyamuni, is the one repeating it now (ch. 7). Then he continues to foretell the future of all disciples, monks, and the multitude, that they will all be Buddhas and live in Buddha-worlds where there will be no evil ways or women (ch. 8). The surest way to become a Buddha is reverence for the *Lotus Sūtra,* whether by obeying its teachings, studying it, expounding it, copying it, distributing it, or offering it in temples. Reciting even one verse will lead to salvation. On the other hand, a single word of blasphemy is a great sin (ch. 9, 10).

Now a great seven-jeweled stupa arises from the ground and is suspended in the midair. As a voice emits from inside, Shākyamuni tells the congregation that inside is the Total Body of the Buddha, Prabhūtaratna, who has vowed to appear wherever the *Lotus Sūtra* is first proclaimed. As Shākyamuni issues a light from his forehead and lights up all Buddha-worlds, Buddhas as innumerable as sand in the Ganges River arrive before the shrine. He opens it with his finger. There the Ancient Buddha sits in a lion throne in meditation. He has come, he says, to hear the gospel as he has vowed to do. He invites Shākyamuni to sit beside him in the shrine (ch. 11). Following this, all present vow to proclaim the *Lotus.* A girl who wants to do the same has to change her sex in order to do so (ch. 12–13).

Now Shākyamuni turns to Manjusrī and other bodhisattvas and tells them how to preach the *Lotus.* The preaching, he says, is to be done in four ways, namely, with right actions and intimacy, with a serene, pure, honest, brave, and joyful heart, with uprightness and no depravity, and with great compassion (ch. 14). Some offer to continue to preach the *Lotus* after Shākyamuni departs, but he assures them that it is unnecessary, for the earth will always bring forth an infinite number of bodhisattvas to do the work. Asked how he could have taught so many followers in only forty years of teaching, he replies that in fact he is teaching throughout eternity (ch. 15). For the Buddha is really eternal. His true character knows neither being nor nonbeing, neither life nor death. Before restoring the stupa to its place, the two Buddhas, Shākyamuni and Prabhūtaratna, continue to preach for 100,000 years.

As the eternal preaching goes on, all believers receive immense rewards, such as happiness (ch. 17), freedom from ailments, being born among gods, fulfilling all wishes (ch. 18), and special abilities of the body such as the ability to hear the sound of the universe (ch. 19). The bodhisattvas are always ready to help them and bestow these blessings, and it is very important that bodhisattvas be revered (ch. 20). At this point, the Buddha reveals the miraculous power (ch. 21). Amazed and awed, all beings now come before the shrine (ch. 22). Touching the foreheads of an infinite number of bodhisattvas, he urges them to spread the gospel. All then depart rejoicing (ch. 22), and the drama ends.

The remaining chapters explain that the *Lotus* can heal the sick (ch. 23); tell about Buddha Wonder Sound who manifests himself to preach the sūtra and to save people even by transforming himself, if necessary, into a woman (ch. 24); and about bodhisattva Avalokiteshvara (Kuan-yin in Chinese and Kannon in Japanese), who will save people from fire, water, prison, and punishment, whether or not they are guilty, possess evil desires, or suffer from ignorance, delusions, etc; and who will bestow children, boys and girls, upon all (ch. 25). Other chapters describe certain spells (ch. 26), relate the conversion of King Wonderful Splendor (ch. 27), and tell about bodhisattva Universal Virtue's offer to protect the *Lotus* (ch. 28).

This drama is as fascinating as it is fantastic. It is full of light, color, sound, fragrance, and action. It has a great deal of suspense and anticipation. It contains verses and fables. And it is a beautiful blending of fact and imagination. As a literary piece it is too repetitious, for what is said in prose is virtually all repeated in verse form. It lacks unity and balance. The climax comes too early with the appearance of the stupa in chapter eleven. Buddhist scholars have tried their best to argue that the first fourteen chapters deal with manifestations or the "realm of traces" while the last fourteen deal with reality or "the realm of origin," [1] or that the first half deals with salvation of the world, or figuratively speaking, the lotus flower, while the second half deals with the nature and personality of the Buddha, or the lotus seed. This, however, is making the sūtra more systematic and more philosophical than it really is. The *Lotus* is neither a theological treatise nor a philosophical essay. There is only a very brief passage in chapter fourteen expressing the idea of the Void: that dharmas are neither born nor annihilated, neither begin nor end, neither rise nor fall. Rather it is a dramatic presentation of fresh and revolutionary ideas offered as a message to enable religious practice and enrich religious experience. As such it is personal, dynamic, warm, and inspiring. It is a message of faith, hope, and love.

These novel and appealing religious ideas are not presented in abstract terms but in concrete images and living symbols. More than any other scripture, the *Lotus* has been the source of motifs of Buddhist art. Its figures dominate such famous caves as Tunhuang and Yünkang. For several hundred years the twin figures of the two Buddhas in the shrine were most popular subjects in Buddhist painting and sculpture.[2]

Of all the symbols, the lotus flower itself is the central one. It has penetrated Far Eastern culture, both Buddhist and non-Buddhist. It has been the symbol for Buddhism in general. In a popular sense, it stands for purity, as it rises from mud but remains clean, and it is in this sense that most Chinese and Japanese understand it, especially women, who take it to symbolize their feminine purity.

[1] Junjirō Takakusu, *The Essentials of Buddhist Philosophy,* edited by Charles Moore and Wing-tsit Chan (Honolulu, University of Hawaii, 1947), p. 182.

[2] J. Leroy Davidson, *The Lotus Sutra in Chinese Art* (New Haven, Yale University Press, 1954), p. 24 ff.

The Neo-Confucian philosopher, Chou Tun-i (1017–1073), in his famous essay on the lotus, saw in it nobility of character. But in its original meaning, the symbol has a far more philosophical import. It means the source of life and the power to continue to give life.[3] When the *Lotus Sūtra* says that wherever the Buddha's disciples tread, flowers will spring up, it means that Buddhas will be born out of the lotus. Thus the springing up of a lotus means the beginning of a new life. When Chinese poets secularized the Buddhist symbol and described women's small feet as lotuses, saying that with every step a lotus would spring up, they were thinking only of feminine beauty and did not realize that unwittingly they hit upon the central idea of the lotus symbol, namely, that it is life-giving. This is the idea underlying all Mahāyāna concepts.

What are these concepts as expressed in the *Lotus Sūtra?* First and foremost is the new concept of the Buddha. He is no longer just an ascetic who preached for forty years in India. Instead he is an eternal being, omniscient, omnipotent, and omnipresent. He is neither one Buddha nor many, and therefore all Western terms like monotheism are meaningless for Buddhism. He is the father of all Buddhas. He is not only the hero of the drama, but also the organizer and proprietor. He not only acts but also leads all the dramatic personnel, including the most humble, who in time will play a role. In short, he is a living Buddha, whose voice of teaching continues for all time and is heard everywhere. The truth preached by him and all the Buddha-sons is living truth, continuously unfolding itself and continuously enlightening people, just as lotuses are continuously springing up. Without saying, this concept of the Supreme Being makes Mahāyāna radically different from Hīnayāna Buddhism, which insists that the Buddha was but a man in history. The concept also fulfills a dire need in the Far East which is not met by Confucian humanism or Taoist naturalism.

Equally revolutionary and important is the doctrine of universal

[3] A. K. Coomaraswamy, *Elements of Buddhist Iconography* (Cambridge, Harvard University Press, 1935), p. 18.

salvation. Instead of having each arhat work out his own salvation, as in Hīnayāna, the new message promises that all will be saved by bodhisattvas. No misfortune, ignorance, or even sin will condemn a being to eternal suffering. This is the Great Vehicle, salvation for all.

This Great Vehicle, or rather Great Career, is the career of the bodhisattva, who voluntarily postpones Buddhahood to help save all beings. An infinite number of bodhisattvas go through all sufferings in order to save them. Their whole personality and career can be characterized by one word, compassion. They inspire, console, protect, and lead all beings to ultimate Buddhahood. They have taken vows and dedicated themselves to this end, and they will not become Buddhas until all become so. What a magnificent concept! These Buddhas and bodhisattvas are willing to undertake tremendous toil, go anywhere, and use any means to bring about salvation. Like the father saving his sons from the burning house, they are resourceful and resort to many expedient and convenient ways. This is not only a benevolent concept but also a very liberal one, for the very narrow path of rigid discipline to salvation in the Hīnayāna is now widely broadened so that none will be prevented from entering Buddha Land.

This doctrine of convenient means has been misinterpreted in the West as the end justifying any means. Like any other religion, Buddhism has not been free from abuse. But the four ways required for teaching the *Lotus* already mentioned should leave no doubt about the moral and spiritual prerequisites for any action. In reality, the various convenient means are but different phases of the same thing. It is the One Vehicle. The other Vehicles are but expedients to meet the requirements of those who have not seen the highest truth but understand only the common truth. People with an either-or point of view will find this Buddhist doctrine of twofold truth difficult to understand. But there is nothing contradictory in viewing the lotus on the common level as flower, leaves, and stem, and on the higher level as the lotus itself, that is, the seed.

Similarly, viewed as common truth, the Buddha is Shākyamuni, a historical being, a Buddha of the "realm of traces"; but viewed on a higher level, he is Tathāgata, the eternal being, or Buddha of the "realm of origin." These two levels are not contradictory. They are harmonious.

The ever-readiness of bodhisattvas to save beings by all means does not suggest that people should be passive. On their part, they must show devotion and faith. Faith, even as expressed in so simple a form as reciting the name of the Buddha, will lead to salvation. This is another aspect of Mahāyāna Buddhism that satisfies a great need in the Far East, where Confucian and Taoist rationalism leave little room for such tender feelings as faith and devotion in religion. Whether or not the element of devotion was derived from Hinduism, it gives the great multitude hope for salvation through simple means.

This hope for salvation is beautifully and affectionately personified in the most popular bodhisattva, Kuan-yin. The embodiment of mercy and compassion, he goes through much suffering and assumes many forms, whether that of a Buddha or an animal, and goes everywhere and anywhere to save all beings. He has four, eight, eighteen, or a thousand hands, to save them in all possible ways under all possible circumstances. In Japan, Kannon retains his transcendental character as a Future Buddha. In China, however, he has been presented in feminine form, perhaps to satisfy the Chinese love of sensuous beauty, perhaps to represent more appropriately the quality of compassion, especially as a protector of women and bestower of children, or perhaps to give Buddhism a loving Mother, much as the Virgin Mary is in Christianity. At any rate, Kuan-yin has been for centuries an inexhaustible source of comfort and inspiration for the Chinese. The twenty-fifth chapter of the *Lotus Sūtra* is especially devoted to him and has been singled out as a separate sūtra. It has been studied, recited, copied, distributed, and offered in temples, all as expressions of devotion and faith, by millions and millions of followers century after century.

These basic Mahāyāna ideas—the eternal Buddha, universal salvation, the bodhisattva doctrine, the teaching of convenient means, the gospel of the One Vehicle, the message of salvation by faith and devotion, and the compassion of Kuan-yin—are all here presented in a single sūtra for the first time in Buddhism. It would be claiming too much for the *Lotus* to say that it contains all the important Mahāyāna doctrines. Those on the Void, Twofold Truth, Instantaneous Transformation, Meditation, etc., are not treated here. But as a single document, it contains more important ideas than any other Buddhist scripture.

All this is contained in a book of twenty-eight chapters totaling about 69,000 Chinese characters. This, of course, refers to the Chinese translation *Miao-fa lien-hua ching*[4] made by Kumārajīva (344–413). This is the version used and revered by the Chinese and Japanese, and the one rendered, with deletions, into English by W. E. Soothill, entitled *The Lotus of the Wonderful Law, or the Lotus Gospel.*[5] We have no idea who the author or authors of the sūtra were, when it was written, or in what language. All we know is that it must be older than 255 A.D. because the first Chinese translation, a partial one, was done by an unknown missionary in China in 255 or 256.[6] Of the three extant Chinese translations—by Dharmaraksha (Chu fa-hu), called *Cheng fa-hua ching,* in 286; by Kumārajīva in 406; and jointly by Jnānagupta and Dharmagupta, called *T'ien-p'in miao-fa lien-hua ching,* in 601—that of Kumārajīva has been accepted in the last fifteen centuries as the most authoritative. His original translation contained only twenty-seven chapters. The famous Chinese traveling monk, Fa-hsien (576–652), in quest of the twenty-eighth chapter, started for India in 475. He found in Khotan the chapter on Devadatta, a cousin and a traitor of the

---

[4] Sanskrit title, *Saddharma-pundarīka Sūtra.* For a good study of the sūtra, see Edward J. Thomas, *The History of Buddhistic Thought* (London, Kegan Paul, 1933), ch. 14.

[5] Oxford, Clarendon Press, 1930 (275 pp.).

[6] Another translation was done in 335 by Chih Tao-ken, now lost.

Buddha. He returned and requested Fa-i to translate it. This chapter has since been added to the Kumārajīva version.

Kumārajīva's version has surpassed others partly because it is the translation of the oldest text. Most probably the original came from Khotan. Jnānagupta said that it agreed with a manuscript in the Kuchean language, which he had seen. Since Mahāyāna Buddhism developed in Northern India or even further north in Central Asia, its early sūtras were in local dialects of these areas and only later put into Sanskrit. Kumārajīva's version also agrees with the Tibetan, and Tibetan translations are generally from the oldest texts. Takakusu believes Kumārajīva's original to be the oldest because it quotes from Nāgārjuna (c. 100–200), etc.[7] On the basis of textual criticism, scholars believe that the original was in twenty-one chapters, dated about 250 A.D., later expanded to twenty-eight.[8]

The more important reason for the supremacy of the Kumārajīva version is Kumārajīva himself. He was the one who opened up new studies in Buddhism in China, inaugurated a new era in translation, and trained as his pupils some of the most prominent Buddhist scholars, including the so-called Ten Philosophers of the Kumārajīva School, in Chinese history. Half Indian and half Kuchean, Kumārajīva became a monk at seven. He had such a great reputation in the Western regions that a Chinese king sent a general to bring him back to China. After the general had kept him in northwestern China for seventeen years, another Chinese king dispatched an army to bring him to the capital in 401. There he enjoyed the highest honors and had the highest title of National Teacher conferred on him. Over a thousand monks sat in his daily lectures. When he translated the *Lotus,* no less than 2,000 scholars from all parts of China gathered around him. His scholarship and Chinese literary ability matched the best of the time. All in all, he

[7] Takakusu, *Essentials of Buddhist Philosophy,* p. 178.
[8] Takakusu, *Essentials of Buddhist Philosophy,* p. 177; H. Kern, *The Saddharmapundarīka or the Lotus of the True Law,* vol. 21 of Sacred Books of the East (Oxford, Clarendon Press, 1884), p. xxii.

started a new epoch in Chinese Buddhism, and the *Lotus* is one of the monuments of that achievement.

Since the translation agrees with the Tibetan, its accuracy cannot be questioned. However, Kumārajīva did take liberties. For example, he translated both *tathāgatasharira,* literally "bone of the Tathāgata," and *tathāgatasya-ātmabhāva,* literally "the original nature of Tathāgata" as *ju-lai ch'uan-shen* or the Total Body of the Buddha (chs. 11 and 19).[9] Evidently he preferred to preserve the spirit of the work rather than translate literally. No wonder the lively Mahāyāna spirit prevails throughout the whole work.

Is this spirit preserved in Soothill's partial English translation? He purposely omitted many repetitious portions. One omission on page 183, the only statement on the Void referred to above, is unfortunate. And there are some inaccuracies. For example, on page 75, "of Nirvāna nature" should have been "always tranquil in themselves and devoid of appearance." However, no European translation is free from mistakes. As Suzuki has pointed out,[10] Burnouf in his French rendering, *Le lotus de la bonne loi,*[11] and Kern in his English translation, mistranslated *sarvadharmānām anutpādah,* literally "acceptance of the idea that all elements of existence are not created," as "une patience miraculeuse dans la loi" and "acquiescence in the eternal law," respectively. Kern's translation is complete, but it is a version of a Sanskrit manuscript dated 1039,[12] much later than the Kumārajīva text. At any rate, Kumārajīva's version is the one that gave Mahāyāna Buddhism its meaning and vitality. In spite of omissions and occasional mistakes, Soothill's version had preserved these qualities.

How shall we read it? We should not look in it for arguments or information. Since it was written and has been used for religious

[9] Fuse Kōgaku, "Hokkekyō no seishin to yakkai no mondai" ("The Spirit of the *Lotus* and Problems of its Translation and Interpretation"), *Journal of Indian and Buddhist Studies* (Tokyo), vol. 1, no. 1 (January, 1957), pp. 79–80.

[10] D. T. Suzuki, *Studies in the Lankāvatāra Sūtra* (London, Routledge, 1930), p. 125, note 2.

[11] Paris, 1852.   [12] Kern, *Saddharma-pundarīka,* p. xxxviii.

practice and experience, it is to be appreciated with good will and understanding. It does not matter whether one reads it in its entirety or in part, whether this or that section first, and whether in great seriousness or with a carefree spirit. One should approach it as he approaches a lotus flower. Look at its color now and then, and smell its fragrance here and there. If one is in the proper spirit, a new lotus may even spring up for him.

PETER A. BOODBERG

Comments

Speaking as a representative of the Pacific "backwaters" of America, I should like to call your attention to certain problems that appear to be of major importance to some of us at Berkeley, particularly in connection with the great task of incorporating the essence of the Chinese classics into the thesaurus of the Western tradition. My remarks will center around the theme of what I am inclined to call "linguistic imperialism." I feel that unless our Occidental societies accompany their all-in-all graceful retreat from attitudes of imperialistic arrogance in the political and economic fields by some effort in the direction of readjusting their linguistic sights and of cultivating a greater capacity for linguistic and philological resilience under the impact of the tremendous volume of cultural and literary information that is coming to us from Asia —the noble project of expanding our humanistic tradition to a truly global scale is doomed to failure. Assimilation of new information implies in-corpor-ation of new material into one's native structure and hence—as stated here by one delegate yesterday—that structure's transformation. No wonder that a task of such magnitude should evoke repeated expression of pessimism as regards our qualifications for such an undertaking.

All of the great languages of Asia have shown in the past few decades an amazing resourcefulness in successfully incorporating into the very fiber of their linguistic structure most of our scientific

Peter A. Boodberg is Professor of Oriental Languages at the University of California, Berkeley.

and technological notions. We of the West should be able to match this impressive achievement of the Asians by an equally creative, imaginative, and bold utilization of the vast riches of our own linguistic heritage in fashioning "new terms" for "new ideas" as we attempt to absorb some of Asia's humanistic thought.

The task is enormous, but not necessarily hopeless. Within the great Mediterranean family, the languages of Europe have for centuries lived in symbiosis. Ever since the Romans found it imperative to recast many of their linguistic conventions in the irradiating light of Greek experience, there has been constant interplay, interfriction, interborrowing, and crossfertilization among the linguistic members of the Western division of the Indo-European family. The cultural partnership of the European world and the Semitic civilization has also been of sufficient duration to permit the absorption of a considerable number of Semitic "logoi" into our system of thought. The most summary survey of the Western "international" vocabulary would reveal at least 3,000 viable Arabic words (from "algebra" and "alcohol" down to "zenith"), and innumerable felicitous phraseological creations of Hebrew poets have subtly transformed the diction—and even syntax—of every European tongue through the translation of the Bible. The Sanskrit language, a sister tongue of Latin and Greek, has contributed a not insignificant list of important technical terms, albeit not as viable as the Arabic ones, to our common vocabulary.

As for the two great civilizations east of India, we may observe with some satisfaction that Japanese loanwords begin to be increasingly noticeable in English, but the magnificent contributions of the Chinese mind to human thought remain locked to us—linguistically speaking. Chinese monosyllables are not easily incorporated into foreign idiom when kept encased in the sarcophagi of our transcriptions which are notoriously irregular, uncertain, and confusing. It is not an exaggeration to say that the richness of the Chinese vocabulary—vocabulary remarkably monolithic and homogeneous among the great vocabularies of mankind—remains entirely untapped and is at present practically inaccessible to the general humanist. The problem of translating classical Chinese involves, moreover, a larger issue transcending that of diction. Of all possible human grammars, the structure of classical Chinese appears quite incommensurable with that of the Indo-European tongues. Let us consider for a moment the glosso-philosophical idiosyncrasies of Indo-European. Our language builds up subtle distinctions by means of those elusive and ineffable little particles called prepositions (used not only syntactically, but as morphological formants, in such pregnant terms as "co-gnition," "perception," "pre-conception"). Our nominal categories are saturated with notions of number and gender (grammatical "sexualization" of inanimate things and abstract words has undoubtedly exercized great influence on the pronounced tendency toward excessive personification in Western tradition). Our verb is a complicated network of such categories as past, present, future (our tense system), perfect and imperfect (aspect of action), mood and voice, person, number, and gender (in conjugation), and the hybrid forms of the infinitive and participle. Finally, one may hazard the supposition that the Indo-European civilizations would never have developed their sophisticated ontological philosophies without the assistance of the mighty midget, the Indo-European ontological verb "to be."

Classical Chinese operates without all these paraphernalia. There are in classical Chinese no real prepositions; Chinese nouns and pronouns have no gender or number; the classical Chinese verb cannot be differentiated according to the twelve categories enumerated above and can hardly be distinguished in its monolithic structure from the Chinese noun. Classical Chinese lacks a verb covering the enormous territory encompassed by our "to be."

I must, therefore, in all frankness and honesty say—speaking as a philologist with long experience in studying classical Chinese texts and worrying over that problem of incompatibility of the two linguistic traditions—that while historical narrative, some technical and scientific texts, and novels have been with some measure of success transposed from the original Chinese into European languages, the more subtle kinds of writing, particularly poetry and what goes under the name of philosophy in China have never been translated, but only twisted and distorted in Western idiom through the imposition of our own linguistic idiosyncrasies, both in diction and syntax, upon the Chinese creation. Before we can translate Confucius or the writings of any other Chinese sage, we need to make a tremendous creative effort of devising out of the rich linguistic resources of our tradition a large number of calqued terms which would render in our idiom the contour of the Chinese etyma effectively and meaningfully, fully digesting and assimilating the underlying notions, and refraining from superimposing the so-called nearest, haphazardly chosen, and usually idiosyncratic, albeit elegant English equivalents. We need to work hard on simplifying our grammatical structure, cutting it to the bone, so as to approach as nearly as possible the austere simplicity of the original. And we should have enough faith in the wondrous flexibility of our linguistic heritage to deem such an experiment not only possible, but fruitful. It may take an entire generation even to begin the essential work and it will require a large cadre of workers. It may demand the enlistment of every one of us, the professional philologist, the creative teacher, the imaginative writer, the poet, the artist, and every devoted humanist.

May I, at this point, take issue with Professor Hahn's insistence on the prerequisite of technical linguistic competence in the original documents for teachers of foreign literatures. I have underlined in a preceding passage the abysmal failure of the representatives of competency in my own narrow field and, as a delegate from a monstrous academic institution that can afford to employ a linguistically competent interpreter in every major literary field, I should like to say a few words in defense of the small college where foreign literatures are often taught in translation by non-specialists, yet effectively and imaginatively. The great and rich centers of professionalism would do well to remember more generously the great educational and humanistic accomplishments of those often self-sacrificing workers and concentrate more—whenever criticism is the order of the day—on cases of professional negligence within their own ranks. Not that I would advocate closing our eyes to existing tensions in our field: tensions between professional and amateur, tensions between disciplines, and even within a given discipline. Our academic societies would often benefit from a more candid recognition of the existence of those inevitable tensions. The infinite loneliness of scholarship—of which Mr. Bokhári spoke last night—will always remain an individual problem for every one of us. But we can all join in one great task, that of humanist teachers trying to impart to our students our partial awareness of the lights shining in Asia. "He who can warm up the old and acknowledge the new, may be termed a teacher," said Confucius, and "teacher" in Chinese also means "musical leader"; a leader of a symphony or chorus, and one of many voices.

The Chinese Novel

As a medium for cultural exchange, the novel seems to
have several advantages over other forms of writing. A most obvious one is that it is the form which best survives translation. Compared with poetry and the drama, the novel's effects are less bound
to the particular "genius" of its original language. It is also relatively free from those formal conventions, which often appear arbitrary and incomprehensible to the uninitiated. The novel is more
immediately intelligible, more "accessible," than the monumental
religious or philosophical formulations, which are so rich in spiritual
insights derived from their unique historical past that special imaginative efforts may be required to fathom their meaning. There is the
prevalent feeling that even the most casual reader can almost always
get something out of a novel. On the crudest level there is the story,
the reader learns that this happened . . . and then . . . and then.
He may like or dislike it, but he feels that in following a tangible
story, he has not utterly wasted his time. He also forms some new
mental pictures of how a foreign people lives, he is told about the
look and feel of things, how things are done, and if he is reading
a Chinese novel, he learns a great deal about details of food and
dress. But even if an interesting story together with exotic information may help save a student from utter cultural provincialism,
there are clearly other reasons why certain novels outside his own

Yi-tse Mei Feuerwerker is completing a dissertation on the Chinese novel of manners for the Comparative Literature Department at Radcliffe.

traditions should merit his serious consideration in a "Great Books" course. Any novel really worth reading is like a mine: although much that is worthwhile may be found at the more easily accessible levels, it should be explored to the depths for its richest veins.

The special character of the novel enables it to contain within its structure both the "universal" and the culturally "particular" in an efficacious way. We shall probably never be able to give a more precise definition to the novel than to say that it is prose fiction of a certain length. But we may add that it is of all forms the most concerned with empirical reality and therefore the most closely connected with a people's social history. Novels are not the literal texts of social history itself; what they provide is a sort of running commentary on it. They indicate what has happened to religious and ethical ideals after they have been popularized and perhaps diluted, or as they are reflected through the novelist's individual mind; they reveal the imperfect ways in which social institutions operate in ambiguous and refractory human situations. The novel stands at the point where social history and the human soul intersect.

To illustrate this point I would like to take a simple example. In the *Hung lou meng,* or *Dream of the Red Chamber,* there occurs the unforgettable episode in which the hero Pao-yü, then a boy of thirteen or fourteen, is severely beaten by his father. Pao-yü is suspected of malfeasances characteristic of degenerate young aristocrats: intimacy with boy actors and attempted seduction of his mother's maid. A combination of circumstances happens to have worked his father up into a murderous rage, and he is apparently determined this time to flog his son to death. The servants, however, contrive to send a secret message into the inner apartments, and although half-unconscious, and horribly bruised and mangled, Pao-yü is saved by the intervention of his mother and grandmother. It is a marvelously constructed scene, full of drama and suspense, and of the vivid interplay of character, but I intend to examine it from only one point of view: the way in which the "human" or "universal" reality works through an apparently peculiar "cultural" situation.

Anyone who has heard anything about Confucianism has heard about filial piety, about the autocratic father, and his first reaction will be to regard this as a typically Chinese scene. But it is not a scene which can be dismissed by a reference to this cardinal virtue of the Confucian system, for what the scene tells us is that any moral code, when applied to a specific human situation, immediately becomes involved in multiple tensions, complexities, and ambiguities. No one in the book directly challenges the father's right to put to death a son who has thus disgraced his ancestors; in fact the father claims that it is unfilial of *himself* to have begotten such a worthless son. That which thwarts the father from exercising his—in terms of the Confucian family system—justified prerogative or, rather, from carrying out his rightful duty, is the completely irrational, perversely irrelevant, almost hysterical behavior of the women in the household. This behavior has its source in precisely the unreasoned, indulgent love which abetted Pao-yü in his effeminate and irresponsible way of life. One lesson that this novel teaches is the difficulty of moral judgment. For the scene is dealing with the crucial, perennial problem of the child-parent relationship, or, rather, with the broader problem of growth and maturity in its relation to discipline, to authority, and to the rightful expectations of the masculine adult world as represented by the father. Certainly the author, who is to a large extent Pao-yü himself, looks back on his own youth, as is evident from the book, with mixed feelings. He is full of self-reproach for his frivolous and wasted life, for his having failed to live up to his father's teachings, inimical to his nature as they were. On the other hand, he feels affectionate gratitude to his grandmother and mother who made possible for him all the happiness—he has discovered how rare a thing it is in this world—he knew when he was growing up. All these rich human meanings, not necessarily peculiar to the Chinese, are implied in the flogging scene. I shall return to the *Dream of the Red Chamber* later; enough has been said to suggest that the novel in offering such a candid and intimate view of Chinese society, transcends particular social conditions even while working through them.

It is almost ironical to make such extravagant claims for the Chinese novel's possible value in a "Great Books" course, in view of the ignominious position it occupied in the traditional Chinese view of literature. These works, which we are discussing here under the exalted label of Oriental Classics, were not honored in their own country as classics at all. Until recent times they were not even regarded as worthy of the name of literature; and this attitude goes a long way toward explaining both the character and the limitations of the Chinese novel as a form. This is not the place to discuss the historical development of the Chinese novel, but certain points should be made to enable us to place the novel in the perspective of Chinese literature.

A novel written in the colloquial language was a latecomer onto the Chinese literary scene. Its ancestry is rather obscure, and is confused rather than clarified by the history of its generic label *hsiao-shuo*. It seems to have developed from the merging of certain elemental and primitive narrative forms which had been appearing in handwritten copies and later in print after centuries in the chrysalis of oral tradition. These precursors, which have all left their mark on the novel, include popularized historical narratives, Buddhist apologues, and, most typical of the developing urban life and the "mass" public, short stories (stories that were short) combining realism and sensationalism. Thus the novel belongs, with the drama and various types of lyrical poetry, to the popular, colloquial sub-tradition of Chinese literature which developed independently of, but not without interaction with, the old classical literary tradition.

That novels were not written in the classical language was one important reason why they were never granted a recognized place in the established literary scene. Even more objectionable, from the point of view of the literary powers that be, was that despite

certain piously claimed didactic intentions, the novel defiantly refused to make itself thoroughly respectable. Schooled today in the
novels of D. H. Lawrence and James Joyce, the Western reader
of the Chinese novel need no longer be shocked as he once might
have been. The Chinese novel remained indecently subversive. It
retained to the end the rough, indifferent, coarse-grained features of
the low-born literary underling. It was by turns irreverent, satirical,
or rebellious, maintaining a critical attitude toward established
social and ethical codes and utterly disdainful of the rules of de-
corum and reticence, which incidentally accounts for the ellipses
or Latin passages in a good many translations of Chinese novels.
This lack of respectability gave these novels more freedom perhaps
to investigate the seamier side of life, the dark inner recesses of the
human heart, areas of experience which the classical literary tradition either glossed over or was unable to find a place for.

The outlook on the part of the novels is due in large measure to
the state of affairs in China when they made their appearance. It
was between the fourteenth and the sixteenth century that the
novels which had been evolving through a process of cumulative
authorship began to assume their final forms, and toward the end
of this period that novels by individual authors made their appearance. Long as the history of the Chinese novel is, its fully-developed
examples arrived, after all, at the tail-end of China's great civilization. During the Ming and Ch'ing dynasties classical learning was
increasingly strait-jacketed, classical writing often merely imitative,
society overlaid by formal ceremonies and fastidious etiquette—all
served only to veneer underlying tensions which the novels alone
were seeking to express. Hence the decadent *fin de siècle* moral
atmosphere of the *Chin p'ing mei,* written during the last decades
before the fall of the Ming dynasty; and the decline of the great
family through decay and corruption depicted in the *Hung lou
meng,* a microcosm of the Chinese empire in its last heyday of
glory and prosperity, but already poised over the gulf of ruin. The
Western novel has depicted the increasing maladjustment of the

individual to society; the Chinese novel, while placing less emphasis on the self-responsible individual, has been no less concerned with the collapse of traditional values in periods of cultural decline and social disintegration.

It was not until the Republican era, when the persistent dichotomy between a classical and a vernacular literature was broken down that the Chinese novels were studied as masterpieces of colloquial literature. With the establishment of the Communist regime the novels have reached the acme of exaltation, their merits perhaps exaggerated as if to make up for all these centuries of neglect and persecution. Their criticism of conditions under the old regime have now won them the honorable epithets of "anti-feudal" and "revolutionary."

The failure of the Chinese novel to become respectable or even legitimate until recent times meant that it never achieved the status of a serious and dominant literary form, as was the case of the European novel in the nineteenth century. In range, quantity, and achievement, it is hardly comparable to the other glories of Chinese literature, poetry or prose essays. There was no "art" of the novel in China, no "critical" theory. The Chinese novelists were indifferently conservative in their attitude toward the outer form of the novel: they simply used the forms as they found them, indulging little in technical experimentation. Even in the latest nineteenth-century examples of the old novel, vestiges of those precursory primitive genres are to be found: tag-phrases proper to oral narration, supernatural frameworks, interspersed verses, episodic structures. Moreover, a fact which was significant for the unfolding of plots, the format of chapter division and headings once evolved was never deviated from. These primitive features of the Chinese novel have multiplied by a hundred fold the headaches of translators, and often given rise to feelings of dissatisfaction or vexation on the part of the Western reader. It is all the more remarkable that there were certain individuals in traditional China who, perhaps alone in understanding the possibilities of this unappreciated and circumscribed form, entrusted their talents to it and conveyed through it their view of experience. Some of their works happen to be literary masterpieces. So even if in recommending them to the non-Chinese reader, we are giving them an emphasis which is actually out of proportion to their significance in Chinese literary history seen as a whole, we are recommending them as genuine and great novels which can impart insight not only into Chinese society, but also into the human situation.

What these novels may have to say to any educated man will become more apparent when we look at the novels themselves. The three which I am going to discuss briefly are by no means necessarily those which I consider to be the three greatest Chinese novels; for one thing, the quality of available translations has in large part dictated my choice.

It is in some measure due to its delightful translation that the first book is included here at all. It may seem like digressing to bring in the *Hsi yu chi* (translated by Arthur Waley as *Monkey*) which strictly speaking is not a novel at all. Although its story does not take place in the everyday social world but in a fantastic universe populated by bodhisattvas, deities, demons, and monsters, it does embody an attitude toward the social world. It is a mixture of history, legend, folk-lore, hagiography, and fantasy, the culmination of a story which had been retold and elaborated over centuries. Many long prose narratives in China were evolved in this way; they continue to be transmitted orally even today among the people, their scenes and episodes performed by opera troupes, narrated by teahouse story-tellers, or in our modern century, serialized over the radio. *Monkey,* however, is the tale in its authoritative, written form welded into continuous narrative, although its sixteenth-century author, Wu Ch'eng-en, did not feel free to deviate from certain formulas which by his time had already been incorporated into the story. His narrative proceeds at a leisurely fashion, its episodes multiplied at times to the point of repetition and tediousness.

The book is a sort of *Pilgrim's Progress* as written by Jonathan Swift or, rather, by Rabelais, if one can imagine such a combination. Critics have often erred in taking the novel too seriously. Traditionally there were the Buddhist and Taoist commentaries, and now we have the Marxist interpretation. There can be no question about the book's anti-bureaucratic satire, as Monkey's pranks turn heaven inside out; what has confounded the Marxist critics is the difficulty of deciding whether the monsters are on the side of the feudal landowners or of the people. The pilgrimage of Tripitaka and his three disciples to India in search of the scriptures is allegorical in the sense that through their behavior and their adventures the author is making certain statements about human nature and experience. Tripitaka may be regarded as Everyman; Monkey, the mind or intelligence; Pigsy, the physical appetites; and Sandy, well —Sandy is just Sandy. The dangers encountered on the journey are the inordinate desires and evil impulses that assault man's soul, but I doubt if it is very rewarding to work out the allegorical interpretations beyond this in any very detailed or systematic way.

What gives the book its underlying unity, and constitutes its abiding charm is rather a state of mind, a way of regarding the world and its doings. It is thought that Wu Ch'eng-en wrote the book in his old age, after a lifetime of failure, disappointment, and deprivation. He had seen through the world and its pretentions, and refused to be taken in by its political and religious institutions, the two great objects of man's blind idolatry. Yet the book is without a trace of bitterness. The accreted legend of Tripitaka's quest for the scriptures probably appealed to Wu Ch'eng-en mainly because of the fun he would get out of romping through the universe, of mixing nonsense and trivialities with high seriousness. It also gave him a chance to set forth his view of human nature. Man in his quest for salvation, encountering innumerable obstacles and unknown dangers, bewildered, blundering, rash, absurd, unable perhaps to understand fully the serious implications of his journey, or to be worthy of salvation when he finally attains it, is nevertheless pretty tough, resourceful, and above all, likable. *Monkey* is a very funny and irreverent book, but I think, a very wise one too, because it does not condemn. It is to be read not for serious analysis, but for enjoyment and for contact with a state of mind. Waley's translation is considerably abridged, but it captures quite miraculously, on the whole, the spirit and tone of the original.

The second book is completely different in spirit from *Monkey;* as in *Monkey* it contains social criticism, but in the *Chin p'ing mei* (translated by Clement Egerton as *The Golden Lotus*) social evils and man's weaknesses are no longer laughing matters. Both *The Golden Lotus* and *Dream of the Red Chamber,* which I shall discuss later, are typical novels, in that they are primarily concerned with individual beings as they perform in actual social situations. For the same reason we consider Jane Austen and Henry James as more typical, though not necessarily greater, novelists than Emily Brontë and Herman Melville.

The social world of *The Golden Lotus* is that of a big household —a medicine merchant and his wives, relatives, and slaves—and the medium-size city beyond its walls. The book teems with hundreds of characters who jostle one another in crowded rooms, where partitions seem to be far from sound-proof and full of crevices. Indeed eavesdropping and spying are important activities in this novel, which does not hesitate to expose the most clandestine aspects of a man's life. Privacy, solitude, introspection, discursive analysis of feelings, all seem impossible in such surroundings. When not in the bedchamber (but there are no solitary activities there) the characters are busily engaged in business transactions, political maneuverings, social visits, and above all, group entertainments. They feast and drink, listen to singing girls or tell lewd stories. The novel's chief method is the objective, close-up presentation of these innumerable social scenes. It is through the rendering of the characters' speech and outward behavior that their inner moral life and their mutual relationships are revealed. Egerton's translation, the most complete available, reproduces quite faithfully the direct, matter-of-fact style of the narrative passages and also manages to catch the coarse and lively flavor of the dialogue.

In spite of the whirl of social ceremonies and gatherings, the inward meaning of man's social doings no longer exists. The novel was written by an anonymous author during the last decades of the Ming dynasty, and it reflects the collapse of all moral values which tradition and political stability had served to support. There is no getting away from people, but there are no real personal relationships; there are only the ties that enable people to use and exploit one another for the sake of sex or money. Money brings with it power and sex provides the opportunity for license; both are the only real and solid things in the novel. Those who do not understand the use of these two are the "good" characters, they are also the stupid and ineffectual. There is a tone of deep pessimism, even of fatalism or cynicism in the novel; evil seems to have tainted all relationships, permeated all institutions. Only in death is the transitoriness of the pleasure and power-grasping life revealed with terrible finality.

Golden Lotus, the fifth wife, is the most energetic and vital representative of this immoral world. She is more calculating, more ruthless than the rest, although she is not above miscalculating and bringing upon herself her own gruesome end. She belongs to that group of women in Chinese history and fiction who symbolize the irresistible temptations but fatal consequences of sexual indulgence, the *femmes fatales* whose deadly charms bring ruin to men. She becomes intensely alive through her earthy speech, and through her ability to project her feelings by means of telling acts and gestures. One remembers Golden Lotus best in a series of striking scenes: her bewitching beauty as she comes smiling through the doorway, her hair full of flowers; her angry frustration as she scratches her stepdaughter's face while waiting in vain for a faithless lover; her violent jealousy as she curses and cuts up, under her husband's eyes the tiny, embroidered shoes of her dead rival, his former mistress. It is through the building up of such scenes that the novel reveals its terrifying power.

The novel is not an easy one to handle in the classroom not only because of its passages of pornography, which are actually just as organic to the structure of the book as are its money-counting passages, but because of the problem of knowing how to take its moral theme. The author begins with pious statements of his moral intentions, but in view of the actual content of the novel, one may perhaps wonder whether hypocrisy or self-delusion is at work. An analogy may be supplied by Pepys who recorded in his diary that he bought a pornographic work and read it in his office on Sundays, commenting "a mighty lewd book, but not amiss for a sober man to read once over to inform himself in the villainy of the world." The problem in the case of *The Golden Lotus,* however, is not whether a convincing excuse can be offered for the pornography, but whether a book which is the product of so negative a view of life can ultimately be regarded as great. In spite of its vitality and force, the book is an oppressive one. Its devastating picture of a rotten world provides no glimpse, no hint of better possibilities; there is too utterly a lack of poise and breadth, an absence of hope.

The third and last novel is the *Hung lou meng* (translated by Wang Chi-chen as *Dream of the Red Chamber*). Written in the middle of the eighteenth century, it is often regarded as the culmination of China's novelistic tradition. It is also a study of the decline of a family through decay and corruption, but in contrast to *The Golden Lotus,* the book is filled with a tender and nostalgic beauty. This is no doubt due to the fact that the author, having fallen upon evil days in his later years, was recalling in this partly autobiographical work the happier bygone days of his youth. *Dream of the Red Chamber* is the only major Chinese novel which deals with the perennial theme of European novels, the initiation of youth into life. The conflicting pressures exerted on the hero Pao-yü as he is growing up come out into the open in the flogging scene which I discussed above.

The main part of the first eighty chapters of the book, which is all Ts'ao Hsüeh-ch'in lived to complete, covers roughly the hero's life between twelve and fifteen. But even then the shadow of tragedy is beginning to loom large in the background. The prophetic verses in the fifth chapter, foreshadowing the sad fate that is to overtake almost all of the young girls in whose company the hero grew up are placed there to add poignancy to the depiction of the seemingly carefree earlier scenes. These verses are admittedly almost impossible to translate, but when omitted entirely, as is done in all English versions of the novel, one of the main themes of the book—that with the passing of youth and innocence come sorrow, misfortune, and death—becomes somewhat obscured. In chapters 70 to 80, the novel's plot has already taken its tragic turn, and the dark premonitions multiply, foretelling the ultimate ruin of the family.

The *Dream of the Red Chamber* is unique among Chinese novels for its penetrating analysis of the psychology of young love. To find anything remotely like it we have to look, not in the novels, but among the lyrical dramas, such as *Hsi hsiang chi* or *Mu tan t'ing;* yet the *Dream of the Red Chamber* surpasses them both in subtlety and complexity. From the point of view of the adult reader, Pao-yü is an effeminate weakling and his beloved Tai-yü a hypersensitive neurotic, but we should remember that they are adolescents awakening to the ecstasies and torments of first love. One reason why the *Hung lou meng* has maintained its position as China's most popular novel is that it enables its readers, in a way which no other work in Chinese literature has done, to relive, in a more heightened and wonderful way, the sentimental, sad, and comic experience of their own first loves.

Yet this poem of youth also contains one of the most vivid characterizations of old age—the grand matriarch. In fact the book is a gallery of marvellous portraits, each intensely individualized, each contributing surely to the unfolding of events. Perhaps too much ingenuity has been exercised by traditional commentators on the contrasting or pairing of characters (for example, A is B's opposite, C is D's shadow), but their grouping and balancing is subtly done. One of the primary problems of all these different people living in the intimacy of a single, large, aristocratic household is the achievement of personal relationships that are meaningful, that go beyond satisfying the superficial demands of social etiquette. It is a problem beset with difficulties and possible only among those who are morally sensitive. In a society which fastidiously insists on the proper modes of deportment one simply does not call a spade a spade. Perhaps the spade lacks a name. Conversational exchange in the novel, so full of polite circumlocutions, rhetorical euphemisms, and witty banterings, must nevertheless be used to reveal the unarticulated conflicts and compromises that may ultimately lead to genuine understanding and love. This dialogue written in the living language of present-day Peking, in which new nuances, hidden ironies are revealed with each re-reading of the book, is the superb achievement of the novel. It is unusual to meet an educated Chinese who has read the novel once; he has read it over and over again many times. If its fascinating dialogue is the reason why this novel is the one that most bears re-reading, it is also the reason why one must insist on a perfect translation, more so than in the case of the other two books, and the reason why all translations are inevitably found wanting in varying degrees.

While the youthful cousins are preoccupied with the delicate problem of adjusting their relationships, other members of the great household around them are busily engaged in more material pursuits. Under the façade of social splendor the family is rotting from within. The young rakes indulge in nightly carousals, and the women secretly plot against each other for their private gain. Under the protection of the family's power and wealth, members do not scruple, in their dealings with the outside world, to tamper with the courts of justice, to bribe, or even to murder. But the family is already overreaching itself and living beyond its means.

We do not know what final disaster later hit the household, since we do not have the complete novel. E. M. Forster has made the observation that most novels show a falling off toward the end, they become feeble when the plot has to be wound up. In a sense, then, it may have been Ts'ao Hsüeh-ch'in's good fortune to die in illness and poverty when he was about forty, leaving behind his unfinished manuscript. For the readers dissatisfied with the last part of the novel can now heap all their abuses on poor Kao E instead who audaciously undertook to add the last forty chapters. He has been celebrated for his rendering of the lonely scene of Tai-yü's death which coincides with the festivities of her lover's marriage to another. This scene may well account for some of the novel's popularity among those who enjoy shedding tears over their reading; but for others the scene is too contrived, too melodramatic, and unworthy of the earlier parts of the novel. At any rate, whatever claims one might wish to make for the *Dream of the Red Chamber* as one of the great novels in world literature must be tempered by the fact that one is dealing with a fragment that can never be seen at its full length or judged as an integral whole.

Obviously one could go on talking indefinitely about these inexhaustible novels. One could also mention others. A significant omission from this paper is the *Shui hu chuan* (translated by Pearl S. Buck as *All Men Are Brothers*), a novel no less read and appreciated by generations of Chinese readers. It is regretfully omitted, because, in my opinion, the available English translations, although in some cases conscientiously done, are not only inadequate, but actually falsify the spirit of the book. I have tried to place the novels I have mentioned in the context of Chinese literature and to suggest a few ways of approaching them, to suggest what kind of books they are, what, to me, is the special quality of each. But one of the marks of a great book is that it is susceptible to a wide variety of readings; each student, each reader, must read the book closely, and discover it personally for himself.

How should one read these Chinese novels? In his book *The Craft of Fiction* Percy Lubbock has written about the difficulties of retaining in one's mind the form of any novel "as a whole, complete and perfect. . . . As quickly as we read, it melts and shifts in the memory . . . we cannot retain the image of the book, it escapes and evades us like a cloud." These difficulties are magnified tenfold in the case of Chinese novels, with their multiple episodes and their plethora of unfamiliar names. The best way to grasp a Chinese novel in its entirety is to read it over as many times as possible, but life may be too short for most of us to do this adequately. The second best thing would be to take a segment of a novel, some crucial scene or passage, some dominant aspect or recurrent theme, and examine it closely to see what it really means, how it functions in the context of the book. What does it reveal? What makes it tick? This procedure will help organize in one's mind the myriad impressions obtained from the book, and no matter where one starts, it ideally should lead towards the central meaning of the work.

Although the Western reader who has some acquaintance with Chinese history, society, and language may get more out of a Chinese novel, this type of background knowledge, essential though it is for the teacher, is not as essential for the reader in respect to novels as it is in respect to poetry, drama, or religious and philosophical classics. A more useful preparation on the part of the Western reader would be his experience of great novels in his own culture, his tested ability to relate their meaning to his own life.

DONALD KEENE

The Tale of Genji

The greatest glory of Japanese literature is unquestionably *The Tale of Genji*. It has been recognized as such ever since the early eleventh century when first it circulated in manuscript, and no one has ever suggested that it might be the second-best Japanese classic, or one of several equally great masterpieces. Scholars of both ancient and modern times have devoted the major part of their lives to commenting on and elucidating the text; its themes and incidents have furnished the material for innumerable novels and plays; it has inspired some of the loveliest works of Japanese art. In our day Junichirō Tanizaki, the outstanding modern novelist, has sacrificed years of his own career in order to make two complete translations of *The Tale of Genji*. Arthur Waley's English version, over which he labored ten years, is considered by many to be the finest translation of this century, and ranks by the beauty of its expression as a classic of English. It is a work of inexhaustible riches, to which we may return again and again with pleasure and enlightenment.

It might seem only too obvious that such a work deserves to be known not only by the small number of students of Oriental (or, more specifically, Japanese) culture, but by every educated person. Yet the teacher who would introduce *The Tale of Genji* to American undergraduates must be prepared to encounter difficulties. It is not that the book is baffling, that it reeks of what has unhappily

Donald Keene is Associate Professor of Japanese at Columbia.

been termed "the Mysterious East," or that an appreciation of it lies beyond the powers of a person untrained in the history and philosophy of Japan. Far from it—read in the Waley translation it is as immediately intelligible and moving as, say, *The Remembrance of Things Past* by Marcel Proust, a work to which it has often been compared. The comparison is naturally not an exact one, but it suggests what will probably be the real difficulty in the adoption of *The Tale of Genji* in programs of general education: it is a delicate and subtle work which is memorable not for the stirring deeds performed by its characters nor for ingeniously worked out plots and sub-plots, but for its portrayal of the aesthetic and emotional life of a society. There will undoubtedly be some sensitive students in any class who respond to such a book, but the chances are that many—even among those who can read with appreciation a work of Oriental philosophy—may find *The Tale of Genji* effete, immoral, or inconsequential.

If, however, for fear of such comments we fail to include *The Tale of Genji* in our teaching programs, we can only present a most distorted picture of Japanese literature. We cannot bypass it as we might *The Remembrance of Things Past* by dismissing it as a late or peripheral work; it is, as I have suggested, the central pillar of all Japanese literature, and indeed, in the opinion of many the finest product of Japanese culture. By a strange paradox this oldest of Japanese novels—it is in fact the oldest true novel written anywhere in the world—is too "modern" for some tastes. This "modernity" rather than any mysterious Oriental unfamiliarities is most likely to puzzle students; thus, they are seldom disturbed when they read that a man has several wives, for they take this for granted as a custom of a distant country, but many are shocked when Genji, a good man, is portrayed as being simultaneously in love with several women. Again, the students quickly accept the fact that the Japanese of a thousand years ago considered certain directions unlucky and would not travel in such directions on a given day, but they are indignant that the leading figures are too absorbed with aesthetic matters to bother about affairs of state. One is tempted to say that what the student needs for an appreciation of *The Tale of Genji* is less a familiarity with Japanese institutions than the kind of sophistication which a reading of modern Western literature might give him. If he can enjoy modern Western writing, *The Tale of Genji* may actually give him more immediate pleasure than, say, the novels of Dickens or Thackeray. Just as the traditional Japanese architecture, essentially unchanged for centuries, is more congenial to many people today than the baroque and rococo triumphs of their own ancestors, so this great novel, written almost a thousand years ago, may move us more directly than works composed far more recently in the European past.

The Tale of Genji is an extremely Japanese book, unmistakably so, and to read it is to learn much about the Japan of its time and today, but it would be a terrible mistake to read it for information or, in the current phrase, to gain a better understanding of Asia. It is one of those rare books which can heighten our enjoyment of life by revealing new possibilities of beauty. It chronicles the triumphs of the aesthetic ideals of what was probably the most exquisitely cultivated society ever realized on earth, and though it suggests that ultimately these ideals were not enough, they can add an extra dimension to our experience of life. Who can ever forget after reading *The Tale of Genji* the love letters folded carelessly but elegantly, the page-boy in bewitchingly baggy trousers, the pine-tree, so jealous of the attentions paid to an orange-tree that it shook billows of snow from its heavily laden branches? The loving detail given to the descriptions of nature, to the appearance, manners and clothes of the characters, to the delicate hesitations expressed in the countless exchanges of poems, may at first irritate the undergraduate more accustomed to the stronger stuff of European novels, but it may also, to paraphrase Flaubert, give him an education in sentiment and beauty.

The Tale of Genji, however, is certainly not merely a series of charming vignettes. It tells a story which, if wanting in the scenes of physical violence and bloodshed which commonly merit the adjective "exciting," has its own unflagging interest, whether read as the love adventures of a handsome and supremely accomplished prince, or as one of the most subtle and penetrating expositions of the varieties of love. It is hard to think of any other novel which has in particular so many female characters who remain unique and unforgettable. *The Tale of Genji* can and should be read like any other novel, but it carries with it also the personality of a whole culture.

It is noteworthy that a novel should be considered the glory of Japanese literature. In most other parts of Asia the writing of novels was unknown before the arrival of the influence of European literature. Even in such countries as China and Korea, where the novel has had a long history, it was considered to be an idle pastime, the amusement of women and semiliterates, and not a form of serious writing. The excellence of *The Tale of Genji* was partly responsible for the novel being considered to be a dignified literary medium by the Japanese, but it was chiefly the Japanese belief in the importance of the emotions—even of physical passion, so deplored by the Confucian scholars—which gave this sanctity to the novel. The author of *The Tale of Genji,* Murasaki Shikibu, in a famous passage described her theory of the origin and importance of the novel:

To begin with, it does not simply consist in the author's telling a story about the adventures of some other person. On the contrary, it happens because the storyteller's own experience of men and things, whether for good or ill . . . has moved him to an emotion so passionate that he can no longer keep it shut up in his heart. Again and again something in his own life or in that around him will seem to the writer so important that he cannot bear to let it pass into oblivion.[1]

This view of the novel may not seem so startling to us after all the modern developments in our literature, but it is extraordinary that in the year 1010 or so there should have been so cogent an ex-

[1] Arthur Waley (tr.), *A Wreath of Cloud; Being the Third Part of "The Tale of Genji."* (London, Allen and Unwin, 1927), p. 255.

planation of why people write novels. In the insistence on the importance of preserving and transmitting the author's most deeply felt emotions, we may be reminded of Proust's discovery of his life's work in the search for and recollection of time past. Despite Murasaki Shikibu's clear statement, however, later men preferred to find in *The Tale of Genji* a didactic intent of Buddhist or Confucian nature, depending on the commentator. It was declared variously to be a lesson in the vanity of the things of this world, an account of the workings of retribution, or a series of biographies of model women. Even today such views retain a surprising currency. Many well-educated Japanese think of *The Tale of Genji* as a novel which demonstrates how Genji because of his affair with Fujitsubo, his step-mother, is punished when his own wife is unfaithful to him. The novel has also been interpreted by Marxist critics, who insist that it is an exposé of the corrupt aristocratic society of Murasaki Shikibu's day, and that she was a disgruntled member of the lesser nobility anxious to assert the claims of her class. Certainly none of these interpretations accords with what Murasaki Shikibu herself wrote, and as early as the eighteenth century the great scholar Motoori Norinaga declared that such interpretations were based not on a consideration of the nature of the novel itself, "but rather on the novel as seen from the point of view of Confucian and Buddhist works. . . . To seize upon an occasional similarity in sentiment or a chance correspondence in ideas with Confucian and Buddhist works, and proceed to generalize about the nature of the tale as a whole, is unwarranted." Motoori's comment still stands today as a model of good sense.

Motoori declared that *The Tale of Genji* was a novel of *mono no aware,* a term which is difficult to translate, but means something like "a sensitivity to things" or, to translate one untranslatable phrase by another, *lacrimae rerum.* It is a novel in which people who are sensitive to the innate sadness of things, their brevity, the passage of beauty, the impossibility of love meaning everything in life, are treated sympathetically despite their lapses from moral standards. Their punishment is in their own hearts, in their growing old, and is not marked by the arrival of a chastising lightning bolt or by the flames of a burning hell. There is certainly no attempt to indict the society for the failings of the individual. The characters of *The Tale of Genji* are people who devoted themselves entirely to the cultivation of the senses, who created a world of marvelous grace and beauty, and who were often extremely unhappy. This unhappiness—or perhaps "melancholy" would be a better word—comes from their awareness of the sorrow of things, from their appreciation of the implications of the moment of parting or of the fall of a leaf. The novel darkens in tone as it goes on, and pessimistic Buddhist doctrines, often enough in the mouths of the characters earlier in the book, begin to acquire conviction, but there is no attempt made in Buddhist fashion to describe the world as a place of dust and ugliness. The world is lovely, the people in it are lovely, and though this is not sufficient for lasting happiness, the world is worth remembering and chronicling in the details which Murasaki Shikibu has summoned up. Its sorrows as reflected in the novel may lead to a Buddhist awakening, but the novelist's purpose was to depict *mono no aware,* and not to preach a sermon. It is up to the reader to supply the rest.

The emphasis on aesthetic matters in *The Tale of Genji* is a notable characteristic of Japanese culture. There is hardly an aspect of Japanese life untouched by a love of beauty. In religion, for example, the complex Buddhist doctrines taught in India and China tended to be simplified in Japan to artistic formulae. The Zen Buddhist insistence on sudden intuition—so congenial to the Japanese—rather than on intellectual attainment, shares the same aesthetic bias. A belief in intuitive experience, in the preferability of the emotions to cold logic, in the necessity of presenting thought and experience in an elegant and pleasing form, avoiding the harsh edges of more direct expression, has accounted for many of the finest things in Japanese arts and letters as well as some of their shortcomings. The exquisite poetry in thirty-one syllables (the *tanka*), for example, is one pure lyrical impulse, devoid of intellectual content and prevented by its brevity from becoming explicative, perfect of its kind but lacking the vitality and content of less polished forms. One of the supreme triumphs of Japanese aestheticism, of course, is *The Tale of Genji,* and the sign of its triumph is our willingness to accept as a whole world, the only possible world, what we objectively know to be only a very small part of the world. Within its bounds ugliness is the greatest crime, and ignorance of a poetic allusion or a mediocre penmanship cause enough for derision and even ostracism. There is no place here for starving farmers, sweating laborers, corrupt officials, and the other people of eleventh-century Japan whose numbers, we know, must have far exceeded those of the court society Murasaki Shikibu described. The element of coarseness, which Western writers have consciously injected into their works so as to give the illusion of a complete world, is virtually absent. There is bound to be some hostility on the part of American undergraduates to a book which places so much emphasis on the aesthetic and emotional life of a society, and they will not hesitate to voice it. Though *The Tale of Genji* is outside our traditions, it is unlike the writings of, say, Shingon Buddhism in that the student feels no obligation to be respectful to it as toward another people's religion. The teacher must be prepared for such questions as: "What did Genji do at court?" "Why didn't he concern himself more with the improvement of the condition of the poorer classes?" "Why couldn't he be satisfied with only Murasaki if he loved her so much?" Even the student who asserts that after finishing *The Tale of Genji* he felt like eating a raw steak to reestablish his contact with a cruder, more virile society, is merely expressing the common belief in the necessity of a leavening vulgarity.

It is as futile to expect to convince all the students of the greatness of *The Tale of Genji* as it is to hope that a reading of the *Divine Comedy* will take the place of television in their lives, but *The Tale of Genji* deserves to be a part of the general education of American students if only because it is the most perfect expression of the universal sensitivity to and love of beauty. It depicts a world one stage beyond the level of Utopias; here there are no wars, the state runs itself without need for political activities, everyone has everything he wants without the necessity to work. The people of this society turn not unnaturally to the cultivation of beauty in their appearance, behavior, and surroundings, and for them the supreme delights of love are not a one-time experience, but an art to be perfected. That it is an incomplete picture must be readily admitted, but the student should be encouraged to consider what is in *The Tale of Genji* and nowhere else, rather than what Balzac or Zola might have found in Murasaki's society.

The fact that *The Tale of Genji* is a novel and not a diary or court chronicle is too obvious to require explanation, but because of the remoteness of the world it treats, there is a tendency on the part of some to forget that it is fiction, that Genji never existed, and that the author had to devise and control a plot and characters, just like any other novelist. Its techniques are not those of the Western novel, but they are consciously employed. For example, the first chapter states most of the principal themes of the work in a seemingly casual manner. The death of Genji's mother, brought about mainly on account of the jealousy of the other court ladies, is a foreshadowing of the famous death scenes of Yugao and Aoi. The emperor's love for Fujitsubo, for the resemblance she bears the dead lady, is echoed again and again in the novel in Genji's search for new loves, and has its final tragic statement in Kaoru's love for Ukifune. Again Genji's love even as a child for Fujitsubo, and his coldness toward Aoi, though briefly stated, here prepare us for their fuller exposition later on. The general mood of the opening chapter, the sensitivity to things of the emperor, sets the tone of the entire novel, and with the second chapter, the famous discussion of the different categories of women, tells us as clearly as the overture to *Don Giovanni* the kind of work which is to follow.

Like any great novel, *The Tale of Genji* is interesting from page to page. We want to know what will happen to Yugao or to the princess with the red nose or to the girl Murasaki. But it is the character of Genji himself which properly claims our greatest attention. He is not only described as being peerless but convinces us of his attributes in a manner rare in literature, and though seemingly perfect from the very outset, he develops as he tastes sorrow and as he becomes "sensitive to things." His capacity to love, his beauty, wit, and talent mark him as a hero, though he performs no heroic deeds. Such a hero stands apart from our traditions, and even from later Japanese ones, as is witnessed by the fact that in the recent Japanese film version of *The Tale of Genji* it was felt essential to enhance Genji's qualities by having him overcome bare-handed three sworded adversaries. The imagination boggles at this "improvement" of the original, as much as it would at a scene inserted in *Macbeth* in which Macbeth debates the proper choice of stationery before penning a letter to Lady Macbeth. Genji has no need of his fists to prove his status as a hero; he moves a whole world as surely as the most powerful men of fiction. He is a superman who breathes no fire. I am reminded by him of the music of Mozart, perfect in the details as in the whole, growing always a little faster than we ourselves grow; and as a taste for Mozart's music is likely to follow rather than precede one for Wagner's, Genji may continue to claim us when we find ourselves exhausted by more strenuous heroes.

I have dwelt at some length on the difficulties of presenting *The Tale of Genji* to undergraduates, but what I have said is of course true of many great works of our own tradition. That all students will not appreciate *The Tale of Genji* must be a foregone conclusion, but it is worthwhile to teach it for the sake of those who can appreciate the work, in the hope also that others will some day enjoy what now escapes them. By reading of the society which it depicts we can understand our own better, and parts of our experience which we may tend to take for granted will suddenly be thrown into relief. It is a book which tells us as much about ourselves as about eleventh-century Japan.

One other problem which may face teachers is how much of the book to attempt to include in their courses. Ideally, of course, the whole novel should be read, but it runs to over a thousand pages, and there may not be time for the students to read the whole. The first sixth has appeared in paper covers and is readily available. It not only serves as a good introduction to the entire book, but can be read with pleasure by itself. The last two volumes of Waley's six-volume translation, though they relate events after Genji's death, are particularly moving, and offer another good choice for those unable to read more. As I have already had occasion to mention, Arthur Waley's translation is one of the marvels of our time, and fully does justice to this unique work.

KENNETH REXROTH

The Poetry of the Far East
in a General Education

It is curious that the whole program of humanistic education popular in our own time should ignore Oriental literature generally and lyric poetry in particular. The only poetry that our self-
styled humanistic revival seems to recognize at all is dramatic and
epic poetry. Nothing could less resemble the situation in Far Eastern countries where traditionally poetry was of almost primary
importance in the curriculum of an educated man. It shared importance with the philosophical, ethical and sociological treatises
which form the basis of classical Far Eastern education. This, of
course, is no longer true of Far Eastern education, but the tradition
is still very influential even in "modernist" Japan and in Red China,
although the old ways are supposed to have been discarded. Anyone who reads the newspapers must have read many times about
the great poetry contests held in Japan in which the royal family,
and the generals, and bankers, and all sorts of other people take
part. Not only that, but as I always tell people when I read Chinese
and Japanese poetry, the greatest generals, diplomats and statesmen, and members of the royal family have been numbered
amongst the major poets of both countries. The modern sensibility
in Chinese poetry might almost be said to begin with a Han em-

Kenneth Rexroth, poet and critic, who was prevented from attending the conference by his absence in France, submitted these remarks through the medium of a
tape-recording.

peror. All the major Chinese poets prior to the Sung dynasty were not merely gentlemen farmers or from that class, but high-ranking courtiers and officials. This does not mean that they had sinecures. Most of them were very practical administrators and some of them —like the poet Wang Wei—were almost universal men—poets and painters, amateur scientists, all sorts of things—reminiscent of Leonardo da Vinci.

We recognize in American society that our whole program of education—the kind of man we turn out—is open to serious criticism. We do not produce well-rounded men. The value of poetry in education is just this: that it produces a deeper and wider and more intense response to life. The presumption is not that we will be better men—that's up to us—but that deeply familiar with poetry, we will respond to life, its problems, and its people, its things, objects, everything, in a much more universal way, and that we will use much more of ourselves. As you know, one lobe of the brain is relatively inactive, and poetry is just like one of those phony ads we read in the newspapers about various kinds of new thought: "Do you realize that half of your brain doesn't work?" Well, much more of the the whole man presumably is involved in the appreciation of poetry than almost anything else, and this is supposed to condition you so that you respond to life generally in a much more whole way. Chinese poetry, which is a product of a culture acutely aware of this fact or hypothesis, is especially, I would say, suited to produce these results. Then, of course, Chinese and Japanese poetry, Chinese poetry certainly, is probably the best —on objective evaluation, empirically let us say—the best non-epic, non-dramatic poetry ever written. There are very few early Greek poets, Sappho, for instance, who can compare with the poet Tu Fu. He is almost certainly the greatest non-epic, non-dramatic poet who ever lived, and a man of immense breadth and sympathy and insight. As I said in the notes to the translations I did of him, he has certainly made me a better man—although that is *not* the function of a poet.

Of course, the place for Chinese poetry, Oriental poetry, Japanese poetry in American education is also determined by the fact that as we move on into a more interrelated world every day, it is essential that we know more and more about other cultures. I think there is very little doubt that the way we get closest to the minds of other people is through their greatest artistic expression and particularly their poetry. If we want to know about the Roman mind in an idealized form, we read Virgil. If we want to know about the ordinary common man of the Roman upper classes with all his prejudices and self-indulgences and wisdom and so forth, we read Horace. So that appreciation of Japanese poetry—Far Eastern poetry generally—helps us to identify with other people who are relatively strange to us.

In reading the poetry of the Orient we discover, of course, that most of these people are very much like us. Japanese poetry particularly represents the spontaneous and yet stereotyped responses to so many of the basic situations of life summed up in little poems —almost, in my point of view, epigrams, although they are not epigrams in the modern, but in the Greek, sense. They might be called epigrams of the sensibility. I think that the educational level at which this sort of thing could begin is the beginning. Children, very small children, love Japanese poems. The first thing my little girl ever learned to write or read was the Japanese poem: "The Deer on pine mountain where there are no falling leaves knows the coming of autumn only by the sound of his own voice," and it's still one of her favorite poems. Of course, she spent a good deal of time in the mountains as a little child. Otherwise it would not have made any sense to her. But there are various other poems on all sorts of subjects which particularly lend themselves to elementary education.

Even though in Japanese poetry you have an unbelievably high level or degree of formalization both in subject and in style, I don't think that this formality of Far Eastern verse matters very much. Because, of course, in translation it all disappears. Japanese poetry depends for its effectiveness on very subtle things: on vowel music, on the relative pitch of the vowels (by which I don't mean it's a tonic language, but on assonance, and similar effects) and on consonant changes like the changes that take place in the evolution of a language—of p's and b's and v's and f's, of r's and l's and m's and n's, and so on. The kind of consonantal music which is much more subtle than anything like our alliteration. All this, of course, immediately vanishes in translation. The only thing that remains of the form is the shortness, the epigram of the sensibility rather than an epigram of wit. So that Japanese poetry, which is the most formal, ceases to be so as it comes over to us in our language, and its formalism is not a block or a difficulty. The prosody of Chinese poetry is very complex indeed. There are a large number of rules governing it, almost all of which have to do with the specific nature of the language itself. For instance, the music of Chinese poetry depends to a large degree on patterns of the Chinese tones. As you know, the Chinese language is a tonic language like Irish or Swedish and goes up and down, and this is built into the poet—this is his language. It is the most natural thing for the Chinese poet to use this outstanding peculiarity of his language this way. Since there is nothing at all like it in English, it disappears in translation. So that what happens is that in the translations of Arthur Waley or Ezra Pound or Amy Lowell or Florence Ayscough or Witter Bynner or any of the major translators from the Chinese into English, you get a simple objective, extremely objective—objectivist—unrhetorical kind of verse where the accent is upon various responses of a deep humane wisdom.

How much is lost in translation? Well, of course, in one sense everything is lost; in another sense, no. The job of translating Chinese and Japanese poetry, since there is so much you can't translate, makes you do certain things as an Occidental poet. It purges so many of the vices of Occidental poetry. It accomplishes in one blow the various programs of the twentieth-century revolutions in poetry—all the manifestoes of the imagists and objectivists and so forth have to be fulfilled if you are going to write decent translations of Chinese verse.

In conclusion what I want to say is that what the job of translating Japanese and Chinese poetry has done for the translators, the effective worth it has had on the translators, is an indication of the role which Far Eastern poetry would play in a general world-wide humane education. You cannot translate Japanese poetry carelessly because as a poetry of sensibility, if handled carelessly, it immediately degenerates into the most mawkish sentimentality. Therefore it behooves the translator to pay attention always to his spiritual bookkeeping. You may know a famous telegram of James Joyce's with the message: "A sentimentalist is he who would enjoy without incurring a tremendous debt for the thing done." In other words, any spurious or faked or stolen emotional and spiritual satisfactions show up immediately. And the deep insights into human motivation and the identification of man in his mental and moral and social and spiritual problems with the life of the living universe is the fundamental message of the whole Far Eastern life, let alone poetry. This again forces the translator, if he would not write simply dull pseudo-imagistic verse, to draw close to his own roots, to gather himself down against his own roots as a human being and to approach other people on the most fundamental terms, and all men as part of the universal life. We think so often in the West of ourselves over against an inanimate and insensate and "value-neuter"—as the academic philosophers call it—universe. This leads in existentialism to the picture of the individual soul as a created lonely individual over against his creator (amongst religious existentialists) or over against nothing (in Jean Paul Sartre and his followers). The existentialist dilemma does not exist in the poetry of Tu Fu anymore than it exists in the poetry of Francis Jammes. Man is at home in the world. Well, since we are very busy in some of our activities making the planet less and less like a home, any propaedeutic which "homifies" things, which makes us more at home with one another and with the world in which we live, is of inestimable value; and that alone, that moral attitude, that kind of aesthetics seems to me very badly needed in the world today. I can think of few things more readily assimilated, more immediately liked and likable by students and more far-reaching in their effects. I can think of few subjects more suited for wide and immediate introduction into our general curriculum, not, of course, as subjects in themselves—but as part of general courses in literature or civilization, and, since the translations of Ezra Pound, Amy Lowell and Witter Bynner are incomparably the best work of those poets and amongst the best American poems of the twentieth century—as readings in our own literature.

HELLMUT WILHELM

Comments

Speaking of the methods for bringing Oriental classics close to the student or to the general reader, it is perhaps useful to take up again some of the remarks that have been made as to the general purpose of such an endeavor. To reduce to a minimum the many well-put ideas of yesterday and today, there are two main reasons mentioned why the classics of the Oriental tradition should be brought to the attention of the Western student. One is to get him acquainted with a foreign culture, and one is to contribute to the molding of his character. Actually, these two purposes can hardly be separated. They are two aspects of the same thing. You can mold the character of the student in a humanistic course only by making him acquainted with a wide range of expressions of human existence and of human experience. Only in this way can he live up to the great pride and the great responsibility of the humanist: *nil humani mihi alienum.* So these two purposes are actually one. There is, of course, a difference in emphasis, and I would say both of these aspects have to be emphasized at one time or the other.

Let us take the "get-acquainted" aspect first: I think this is very important to make the student acquainted with the fact that human life goes on in different forms in other cultures, and to make him acquainted with the great books which are the best instruments at our disposal to bring home this fact. Only then will he realize that in cultures which are basically different from ours in their institutional

Hellmut Wilhelm is Professor of Chinese History in the Far Eastern and Russian Institute, University of Washington, Seattle.

set-up, it is still the human being who is the main agent of development and of things that go on there. That would not exclude going into some of the particulars under which these works have been written and of the topics they deal with. Of course, there is much to be said in favor of Mr. Keene's approach of letting these works speak for themselves to us as Westerners—to accept in a way the falsified version of the translations—but I think the real impact of a piece of art can be grasped only if it is known what this piece of art meant to the people for which it was written at the time it was written. Then only I would suggest one might come to grips with the problem of a piece of art and of the complexity of human life that is caught in this particular piece of art. This, then, will bring to us the conviction that in certain situations which we institutionally would consider to be despotic or authoritarian, there is still a vast range of human expression that escapes the whip of the despot. This is true for the great philosophical and religious writings, but it is particularly true for writings in the field of "belles lettres." Because here we have authors at work who are artists, who are poets, and who as such have a perception that transcends the perception of the normal human being. These artists live within a given set of institutions, a given set of social mores and well-accepted values, but their creative sensitivity sees deeper and goes beyond the particulars into the universals, to use a phrase of Mrs. Feuerwerker. This does not mean that the particulars can be neglected. The way to the universals is always through the particulars; universals cannot be grasped except through the particulars; otherwise we end up in generalities which are commonplace and trite. But in the mind of the poet, the author of a novel, and perhaps even more so the author of a poem or a drama, these particulars are made to speak and to gain a meaning that goes beyond the specific institutional, historical, cultural situation in which they were created. And that is, I think, the reason why works of art can bring us into much closer contact with a specific culture, because through the particulars they lead us into a field that then becomes basically human.

These were some of the ideas that occurred to me when I read Mrs.

Feuerwerker's paper, and which also emerged in some of the teaching I have done in Chinese literature. This task, of course, involves a lot of work as yet undone, much of which has been mentioned yesterday and today. We who are not the amateurs but the specialists still have to do a lot in this field to provide sensitive translations which will not just make good reading for a Western student or for a Western general public, but which try to trace the mind of the artist and the artistic impact of a literary creation. When working at this task we shall have to keep our minds open to the general human situations which appear here in a specific cultural garb. We shall do well to avail ourselves for this task of the help of our own artists and poets whose ears might be keener than ours in discovering the basic human sound within a particular artistic form.

As a last point, I want to mention that no student can get into a fruitful relationship with any great book, Occidental or Oriental, if he has to read it under a two-hours reserve rule. Fortunately the recent trend towards paperback editions has brought books again within the reach of many students. An appeal should be made to our publishers to include in their paperback editions still more of the great books of the Oriental traditions than are available now. Only in this way can the student be given the conviction that these works are not just "classics" but are something that they want to own both mentally and physically, that they should keep on their shelves.

Comments

The point I would like to make is comprised in the word *tempo*. If there is one thing we Westerners can learn from Oriental classics, it is to slow down, to savor experiences in leisurely fashion, to ponder on philosophical intuitions. The great contrast in tempo has been dramatized for me during this visit to New York. Thursday evening I saw the musical, *West Side Story,* all vigor and speed. Friday evening we saw a film of a Nō play, all controlled pose and movement so slow as to be almost imperceptible. I suppose nobody who is impatient of Nō tempo can understand or enjoy Nō. Similarly, it seems to me, most of the classics that we are concerned with call for quiet meditation rather than reading. For full appreciation of novels like the *Red Chamber* and *Genji* we must share with the characters their feeling of unlimited time for poetic pursuits and trivial pastimes with no thought of wasted hours.

The Chinese in particular have a lordly command of space and time. It appears in their painting where often much of the paper is bare, in the philosophers where the reader must supply the connecting links between anecdote and anecdote and between dark saying and dark saying, in the poetry where four lines may give a precise notation of an experience that leads the mind on to infinity, where "The words have an end but the meaning is inexhaustible."

This means, I think, that the study of Oriental classics must be unhurried, that it is more valuable to help the student to read himself

Harold Shadick is Professor of Chinese Literature at Cornell University.

into intimacy with select passages than to attempt to "cover" a large range of works. Imposing reading lists to be "covered" in a semester or a year frighten me. To chase from one text to another, just because it is on the reading list is a strenuous and self-defeating operation. Confucius spoke of raising one corner and expecting the student to come back with the other three. The Zen masters gave their disciples conundrums to chew on. I think that in the teaching of Oriental philosophy and literature we should emulate them. A possible compromise in our academic context is to spend most of the class hours in a close study of short samples from the philosophers and poets and, parallel with this, have the students read extensively in novels and plays as a basis for summarizing discussion and the writing of essays.

Several persuasive voices have argued that we should accept the limitations of translated material and frankly treat a translated Oriental classic as a sort of mongrel in between an English book and an Oriental book. This may be all right for novels, but with poetry and philosophy it will hardly do. A readable translation is forced to offer facile solutions for the puzzles and ambiguities which are the very substance of the original. I have found it rewarding to provide students with the original text of a few poems and parallel with it three English versions, one strictly word-for-word, one a very close translation in intelligible but clumsy English (which may contain alternative renderings), and the third a smoother free translation, sometimes from an existing publication. I believe this method could profitably be extended to philosophical selections and to prose essays to reveal something of the rhythm and tension of thought and style. I think that such material could be used by teachers who know no Chinese or have a very limited knowledge of it.

Synopsis of Discussion: Third Session

In commenting on the *Analects,* Yi-pao Mei thought that its value had been well set forth in Mr. Sinaiko's paper, and he agreed with the latter especially regarding the humanism that gives Confucius' message a special timeliness to the modern West. There were, nevertheless, three questions that Mr. Mei thought should be dealt with in presenting Confucius to modern students. Chinese society and culture, he said, have often been described as stagnant and Confucius or Confucianism blamed for it. A responsible Chinese philosopher has said that ever since Confucius, Chinese philosophy has spent 2,000 years in mere exegesis, "Bible study." If that is true, how much of it is due to Confucius himself? Secondly, the mainland Chinese themselves are denouncing Confucius nowadays. Instead they are going in for sciences and industry in the Western manner. Why should foreigners take up a Chinese the Chinese have discarded? Finally, it has been asserted recently that the Chinese Communist government is merely another face for traditional Confucian government, that government in China has always been authoritarian, by an elite, and so forth. Since, as Americans, we dislike Communism, he asked, why study Confucianism?

As regards the *Lotus Sūtra,* Mr. Mei confessed that he himself, like many other Asians, was not actually too familiar with the *Lotus.* In his opinion the *Lotus Sūtra* was not to be ranked as great because of its popularity so much as because it gave expression to ideas prevalent throughout East Asia. In his estimation, the *Tao-te ching* would rank even higher on the list of great books, a judgment in which Mr.

Chan concurred, saying that the *Lao Tzu* or *Tao-te ching* has exerted more influence per word than any other Chinese book.

The Chairman thought it was clear that the books on the program were meant as no more than examples of great books. There was no intention of representing them as the greatest works of the Orient. If choices were to be expressed, he himself, for example, would prefer to see the *Mencius* before the *Analects* on a list of great Chinese books. For that matter, he would welcome less emphasis on Confucianism in general.

On the subject of the choice of works, James I. Crump, Jr., wondered whether many Chinese novels deserved a place among great books. Aside from Mrs. Feuerwerker's three, he could think of few others that he would include without hesitation, even if there were good translations of them. He agreed with the Chairman that the *Mencius* was to be preferred to the *Analects* among great books. The importance of the *Analects,* he said, rests on a Taoist principle. As a jug is useful for its emptiness inside, so with the *Analects*. It is a meager book with big holes into which much can be interpreted. The *Mencius,* however, is longer, better put together, and with more information about its times.

To know what Oriental works to include in a course on great books, it would be well to decide what direction education should take, according to Angelo P. Bertocci. Which is more valuable, he asked, to show the Chinese as similar to us or as different from us? One of the greatest values may lie in letting the student realize humanity and its complexity in contrast to merely knowing about other civilizations. Selection rather than quantity is important. The question is, how are we to select? Mr. Bertocci also noted the importance of a grounding in Platonic philosophy for teachers of Western classics. Were teachers of Eastern classics to receive any similar training? Mr. Reischauer assured Mr. Bertocci that Orientalists were aware of that problem and that, although it put a heavy burden on students to give them adequate training in both language and discipline, work was underway toward a solution.

The value of great books as a means of cultural comparison received further comment in this session. Charles MacSherry considered the *Lotus Sūtra* capable, through its dazzling imagery, of illuminating general education. That brilliance of the *Sūtra,* he said, may at first suggest Revelation, as its drama may suggest Job. Ultimately, however, the *Lotus* would not afford enough in the way of a philosophy to serve for purposes of comparative study. What it can tell us something about, he said, is the history of ideas, especially in terms of art. Remains of Greco-Roman humanistic ideas entered both Christian and Buddhist sculpture. In both traditions, however, realistic sculpture, which had been the humanist legacy, was rejected in favor of styles that concentrated on inner spirit. The evidence of that is visible in works, for example, of southern France on one hand and of the Northern Wei dynasty on the other. Here the *Lotus* is helpful, he said. The *Lotus* was known to those who could not read or write, for whom ideas had to be expressed in other ways, such as art. Since we can see an analogous development in Western art, he concluded, there may have been an analogous development of ideas. By examining the *Lotus* we can, without falling prey to easy generalization, consider the analogy.

Mr. Crump seemed to feel that the *Lotus Sūtra,* since it came to the popular mind much altered from the original, was a very difficult work to handle. Many of the simplest acts of superstition described in fiction were descended from the *Lotus.* One of its best uses, he suggested, might be in a comparative study of watered-down religions.

Translation struck him and others as a central issue. Mr. Crump did not look at literature as Mr. Keene did. Not that disagreement was intolerable; there was comfort in knowing that one hundred flowers can blossom here even though not in China. His heart, however, was with Mr. Boodberg, whose sophisticated neology would be beneficial to translations from Chinese.

Even if Mr. Boodberg's approach were accepted, however, Mr. Mei observed, a tremendous task would remain to be accomplished. What should we do in the meantime? Mr. Mei visualized a composite volume of translations. Let a committee select the four or five best translations of a major work, he proposed, and join them in succession, chapter by chapter, to the Chinese text. Not only would such a book be a great boon to study, it might also be useful to those who do not read Chinese, he said.

Howard Hibbett, who sympathized with Mr. Keene's position concerning the *Tale of Genji,* wished to comment on one problem of teaching. A translation such as Arthur Waley has made is a work of art in its own right, he observed, and may tempt the teacher to discuss the original less than others. Whatever the translation, however, it is better to discuss it, since that is what the student has read, rather than the original. The specialist's interpretation is only one more reading of a classic, he said, and it should not be allowed to distract the student.

Chi-chen Wang was skeptical of bringing too much learning apparatus to Chinese literature. People read translations for a number of reasons, he supposed, but as for himself, he read to be transformed. He wished to offer his own experience as a case in point. As a boy, he said, he had read much Western literature before he ever knew English, and he had been transformed by those books. How had they been translated? Most of them had been done by Lin Shu, a man who knew not a word of any European language. Working with collaborators, he put over 150 works into classical Chinese. This showed, Mr. Wang said, that the important thing is to be able to translate into good, readable English. For that good translators rather than scholars are necessary. The best translator of Chinese verse he had found was Gerald Bullitt, a writer of English verse who, though knowing no Chinese, collaborated with Chinese scholars and produced excellent work. A welcome guest at the conference, Dr. Hu Shih, strongly endorsed Mr. Wang's position regarding idiomatic translations and also suggested that the Chinese short tale, an important form of fiction, deserved a place among great literature.

Claiming his right as chairman to have the last word, Mr. Reischauer pointed out, as he had before, that not all the disagreements expressed in the session were irreconcilable. In regard to the sharp disagreements about translations, he observed that different kinds of works—novels, poetry, or philosophy—present different problems of translation and demand different solutions. Each kind of translation has its value.

JOHN T. MESKILL

PART THREE

Practical Problems in the
Teaching of the Oriental Humanities

G. L. ANDERSON

Asian Literature in Comparative Courses: Some Practical Problems

The transition from the enthusiastic recommendation of certain types of courses (usually courses to be taught by other people) to the creation of such courses and their classroom debuts is always an instructive experience, at least to the faculty member involved. I propose to present to you in this paper a rather detailed account of a course I recently taught, emphasizing my treatment of the Asian materials. My justification for this limited and personal subject is that I hope I will touch on—though in many cases lightly—a number of problems involved in the use of Asian materials in general literature courses.

These problems include the relationship of the course to the department in which it is taught, the availability of materials both for the teacher and the students, the nature of the student group to which the course is supposed to appeal, and the relationship of the Orientalist to such academic experiments. My account may merely demonstrate the impossibility of such courses, but I shall assume nevertheless that the comparative type of course is possible—that is to say, that the students can profit from some material in translation and (more important) that the teacher can teach some material which he cannot read in the original language.

The problem of the nonspecialist—and I use the term to mean the

G. L. Anderson is Assistant Professor of English and Assistant to the Graduate Chairman at New York University. He is also editor of "Literature East and West."

person not trained in the language of the literary work—is an acute one, but it will not be wholly solved by an increase in the number of Orientalists on our faculties because there will always be the need for studies and courses across a large enough number of language barriers that the teacher will be forced to use materials he does not know in the original. Erich Auerbach once mentioned to me that the approach of his book *Mimesis* could be extended with great profit into Far Eastern literature, but he said, "I am too old to learn Chinese." If you remember *Mimesis,* you will recall that Auerbach's competence in ancient and modern European languages was sufficient for a one-man university department.

This summer I was asked to teach a course in comparative literature at Indiana University by my friend Horst Frenz, the chairman of the program. The only stipulation was that the course contain some Asian material, and what finally emerged was an investigation of comparative drama and dramatic theory. We read Euripides' *Bacchae* in conjunction with the *Poetics,* the *Shakuntalā* and the *Dasharūpa,* five of Seami's Nō plays and some of his theoretical treatises, Chikamatsu's *Shinjū Ten no Amijima* (*The Love Suicide at Amijima*) and the brief statement of his theories in Donald Keene's anthology, works by Yeats and Brecht with their theatrical criticism, Wagner's *Tristan,* and Shakespeare's *Othello.* The *Tristan* I used as a point of departure for a discussion of theories of synthesizing the arts into a super-drama, and *Othello* as an excuse for briefly surveying dramatic theory from Dryden to the present as focused on a single, critically difficult play. All of these works I have been interested in and familiar with for some time. (A point I might make here about the relationship of the teacher to the department is that my level of competence was certainly increased by my having been given carte blanche to select the material—and I would urge that in using Asian literature the enthusiasms of the person who will teach the course ought to be reckoned with.)

The only political concession I made in preparing a prospectus of the course for the faculty committee was to include the *Hui Lan Chi*

(*Circle of Chalk*) to represent China, which, once the committee had registered its delight with the proposed course, I abandoned, first telling the class we would get to it later, then announcing that we did not have enough time for it. Despite the valiant efforts of James I. Crump and some others there is not sufficient modern scholarship on the Chinese drama, and particularly on specific plays—except for the *Chao-Shih Ku-Erh* (*The Orphan of Chao*) and this is devoted to its vogue in translation rather than to the original. The *Orphan* might be used, of course, as an example of "East-West relations" in such a course. I would note that there is little or no "influence" between Asian and Western literature in the selections above. When we get it, in the plays of Yeats and Brecht influenced by the Nō and in Brecht's case by Chinese theatrical techniques, it is not important purely as "influence," and Earl Miner has wisely entitled his new study *The Japanese Tradition*—not "influence"—*in British and American Literature*.

There is an amazingly simple principle of selection to employ in choosing the Asian materials for such a course. One should only use writings which are competently translated and for which a body of competent scholarship is available. The problem is not general material on Chinese or Japanese or Sanskrit literature but specific and intensive studies of authors and works. This principle immediately eliminates many works and even some major ones, but this is unavoidable. On the other hand, it seems to me now that a teacher in a remote college might easily prepare some of these works using books available only on loan without undue strain on his librarian.

To be specific, Kālidāsa's *Shakuntalā* is available in two translations. I would have preferred Ryder's in Everyman's Library, but it is out of print; Monier-Williams', in a paperback anthology, is adequate. Out of some fifty books and articles on Kālidāsa and Sanskrit dramatic theory only a dozen seemed minimum essentials, Keith's *Sanskrit Drama* being absolutely necessary. Yet perspectives emerge from the others: Kālidāsa's orthodoxy treated by a modern Indian "liberal," or to use a good eighteenth-century word, "dissenter," or a discussion of the *vidūsaka*, the clown, in a treatise on comic characters in Sanskrit drama, give the teacher defense in depth, as it were. Dhananjaya's *Dasharūpa* is available in Haas's edition and translation of 1912. This must be put on library reserve or the translation mimeographed. The teacher must also have Lévi's *Le Théâtre indien* to elucidate Haas's notes, and he should have a translation of the *Nātyashāstra*. The Japanese Nō plays have been well translated, of course, by Waley and others. Only with Seami, however, do we have translations, theoretical texts, and background material. I used the half-dozen plays definitely attributed to Seami in Waley's *Nō Plays of Japan*, including *Haku Rakuten*, which is atypical and may not be desirable. The *Kwadensho* I had mimeographed from *Monumenta Nipponica;* other theoretical selections can be found in Keene's anthology. Excellent studies of Seami are available in Richard McKinnon's articles and Oscar Benl's book and Professor McKinnon let me use his Ph.D. thesis on Seami, which includes a translation of *Yūgaku shūdō Fūken*. There are also two books by Nogami, one on Seami and another on the Nō and Greek tragedy. Finally, with Chikamatsu we have, besides a number of semipopular or antiquated articles and prefaces, two excellent translations, Donald Shively's of the *Ten no Amijima* and Professor Keene's of the *Kokusen'ya Kassen (Battle of Coxinga)*. Both of these have introductions and notes, and elaborate literary analyses. The domestic tragedy seemed pedogogically a better choice than the historical romance. I have mentioned that there is a brief account of Chikamatsu's theoretical ideas in translation. Few other selections of drama from India and Japan or elsewhere in Asia are available with this kind of scholarly material. I also made use of a literal, line-by-line translation of Act I of *Shakuntalā* done by Brewster Horwitz as a master's thesis some years ago at New York University under the direction of my colleague Robert A. Fowkes, and the notes to Monier-Williams' edition. Some editions published in India with notes in English were less useful. There exists, needless to say, considerable scholarship on the historical, sociological, and philosophical backgrounds of these works.

In such a course what types of investigations by the students are likely to be fruitful? The first would be a simple, noncomparative study of, say, Greek dramatic practice (in one play) with Greek dramatic theory (in one theoretical text): Euripides criticized by Aristotle, Seami's plays by his theories, Yeats and Brecht brought to the bar of their own systems. Critical comparisons of plays immediately occur to the student mind as potentially exciting topics, but the principle that there isn't much sense in comparing two things which have no basis of comparison needs to be asserted. Thus, love is not such a monotonous subject that it provides a sound basis for comparing *Shakuntalā, Romeo and Juliet, Ten no Amijima,* and *Tristan.* A more profitable line of investigation is the application of a dramatic theory to a work produced in an alien culture: the theory of rasa applied to *Othello,* for example. This happens to be a topic adopted by one of my students at Indiana for an M.A. thesis. The student, however, has had Sanskrit and is as qualified for such a project as one could hope.

The application of rasa theory to a non-Sanskrit work is the kind of project which I think has great potentialities in comparative criticism, and I should like to use this as my one detailed example. In the first place, this project strikes hard at the vague area between the linguistically dominated elements of a literary work in which principles conceived for an alien language presumably do not function, and certain logical and semantic elements for which principles that cross linguistic boundaries can be established. Also, rasa theory puts a new calculus into the hands of the critic which he can place beside the "plot" or "fable" orientation of Aristotle, the "action" criticism of Kenneth Burke (so well demonstrated by Francis Fergusson in *The Idea of a Theater*), and "image" analysis, of which an extensive recent example is R. B. Heilman's *Magic in the Web,* a study of *Othello.*

To use image analysis as an example to contrast with rasa theory (and to simplify very greatly), we can say that Heilman conceives of the dominant aesthetic structure of *Othello* as a series of images or clusters of images. This theory has been attacked on the grounds that the selection of images is, and must be, subjective, since all of the images cannot be discussed and though some invariably carry more weight than others, the doctors frequently disagree on which images are the dominant ones. Nevertheless, the unsatisfactory nature of both the plot and the superficial psychological structure of *Othello* (I base this dogmatic statement on the simple fact that no one has agreed on these things at least since Stoll's essay of 1915) leads me to think that it must be something else, and certainly to a large extent imagery, that makes me think *Othello* worth reading. I would note also that the *Bacchae* poses the same problem: its plot is not wholly satisfactory and its chief character has little grandeur and commands little sympathy, but it is an intensely lyrical and image-ridden play.

Now, how does rasa theory come into this picture? Unlike the aesthetic effect of imagery, the emotion of rasa is generated by the theatrical as well as the verbal elements in the dramatic complex. One rasa dominates a play—in the case of *Shakuntalā* it is the erotic rasa—but the individual acts and scenes generate subsidiary emotions, all of them, needless to say, elaborately classified by the Indian critics. To chart a plot development, one would use the conventional rising and falling line of a two-axis graph. To record images, one would have several series of points to represent a number of recurring images, and one might ask for a three-axis graph. But rasa in a play could only be depicted by a series of colored washes representing emotions sometimes created by imagery and sometimes by theatrical devices and not as easy to pinpoint as images. What this suggests, then, is that if the same effect is created by an image in one instance and a gesture by an actor in another, rasa theory catches the connection between the two, whereas image study ignores it. This notion can be a revelation to students who accept wholeheartedly the exclusively verbal orientation of some modern critics. It applies, of course, only to the drama, and while I have described it in terms of effect on the audience, the organization of a Sanskrit play is sufficiently formal that we do not have to leave ourselves open to the charge of indulging in the affective fallacy to the extent of analyzing audience psychology. That is to say, the gestures and stage business could also be codified and written into our text and be regarded as purely formal elements, though the particular emotion that suffuses itself over a given scene would still not be either exclusively verbal or theatrical but a mixture of the two. This type of comparative study, whatever objections may be made to my reduction of rasa theory as it is presented here, is valuable discipline for students, not to mention their teachers.

Some more obvious types of investigations and their problems for the teacher might be mentioned. I did not realize as clearly as I might have how much of the material in my course involved dance and the use of mask and chorus. Students who embark on investigations of these theatrical matters may be involving themselves in more than they know. One student, starting on a comparative study of Greek and Japanese masks, was still furiously hacking away at the Japanese material when I departed from Bloomington. His time to complete the course paper has been legally extended, and when it appears, I may need a leave to prepare to read it. But the student who has had practical training in the theater is a constant menace to the academic teacher of drama and must be dealt with boldly.

Finally, there is a whole category of potential research areas which ought to be declared "off limits": these have to do with the philosophical and religious backgrounds of Asian drama. To study the philosophical background of the Nō play, the student should begin by learning Japanese.

Before I pass to the role of the Orientalist in making the path to enlightenment safer for comparativists, let me say a word about the student's knowledge of Asian culture. He may not be as ignorant as you think—or even as you might wish.

Several of my students had had a course in Far Eastern civilization given by S. Y. Teng. They came to me with a good outline of what might be roughly called "orthodox" Buddhism. They were therefore prepared, as the rest of the class was not, to express astonishment at the Buddhism of the Nō plays and of *Ten no Amijima*. If a weak and vacillating man deserts his wife and children and runs off with a prostitute and they both commit suicide, does this guarantee the guilty parties immediate transformation to the Buddhist paradise to be born again as twins on the same lotus leaf? If this is the case, Buddhism might well become popular in the United States. One has to have an answer for this kind of question.

There is also the cult of Zen, with which the students may be familiar in odd ways, manifesting itself in the literature of the "beat" generation. This must be contended with. I have no plans to read Mr. Jack Kerouac's novel, *The Dharma Bums,* after my experience with his last one, but I note that Suzuki's *Zen Buddhism* has sold over 40,000 copies in the Anchor Books edition in just two years. One must be ready to discuss any paperback book that is applicable to the course is one of the principles here. But, also, one must be prepared beyond the narrow limits of the background of the text.

The problem of what the specialist in Asian studies can do to assist the comparatist and perhaps more importantly to help guarantee some level of competence in what the comparatist teaches can be simply stated. He must continue to produce scholarly works, critically oriented if possible, and he should produce some elaborately annotated versions of some texts as teacher's aids. I have said this before and, while it sounds simple, there are practical problems which make it more complex than one would think at first glance, or than I thought when I attacked my course.

In the first place, countless minor problems arise in the close reading of a text which could be solved instantly could the teacher employ— no doubt with foundation aid—Norman Brown or James R. Hightower or Howard Hibbett to walk around with him on the campus as he meditates the day's lesson. This would, however, be self-defeating, in that the Asian specialist then might as well be teaching the course. But if he did, of course, he would not be teaching it at his own university. In short, the training of more Orientalists and the retooling of them for comparative literature courses is the ultimate answer to most of the problems, and it is probably a better solution than retooling Western literature specialists in Asian civilization. Any literary scholar not obviously a crackpot can get a good deal of valuable data and save himself hours of time by stealing an interval here and there from the workday of an Asian specialist. What is the best translation of the *Bhagavad Gītā?* What is the nature of the Japanese belief in ghosts and apparitions in the *Genji* or the Nō plays? Would Professor ——— be a good person to speak on Sanskrit poetry?

The answers to these questions are available to the comparatist who approaches the Orientalist in his den or who catches him in the hall at a convention. Also, the wise scholar frequently says things in his office that he would not include in correspondence, let alone in print, and this kind of academic lore can be tapped. But there are limits to how much of a scholar's time can be taken up simply because he is courteous to a fellow teacher and his problems.

On the other hand it is a traumatic experience to look something up for the first time in a Sanskrit dictionary if you don't know the language. But it is a tactical blunder of the first magnitude to go to class with a quotation in the original language not translated. If you do, the worst student in the class will suddenly decide that this is the nexus of the play. Also, it takes more than a footnote in Monier-Williams to prepare you to explain what it means to a Hindu audience when Duhshanta announces he is of "Puru's race." And the time spent in seeking answers to minor questions can run into overtime, since one is likely to lack confidence in one's choice of books in philosophy or history if one has used only reference works in literature.

I suspect we are going to have to find a way for the specialist in Asian literature to take some time off with *adequate financial compensation* (my italics) to do some preparing of texts for the classroom. He will be taking time from his own research to do this, and he will be honored for it not in his own academic country. Probably he should do it in collaboration with the comparatist who has been teaching the material. I know of two works in Japanese, for instance, which I suspect would be valuable for my purposes. One is an analysis of Seami's plays; the other identifies the quotations in the plays and puts them in their proper historical, literary, and philosophical contexts.

In conclusion, I should like to mention briefly other types of courses which are possible. Comparative epic comes to mind mostly because it has received much critical attention at some periods in the West. Even if confined to "classical" epic and not allowed to expand as far as Tillyard uses the term in his recent work, assigning a class the Homeric epics, the *Aeneid,* the *Rāmāyana,* the *Mahābhārata* and the *Shahnamah* would have a sobering effect. The *Rāmacaritamānasa* might be thrown in also. I am at least partly serious about this. A class which has plowed its way through the entire *Mahābhārata* would have a true immersion in the East and the members would immediately adopt a lofty attitude toward their unlettered coevals.

Comparative poetic theory is a subject closer to my own interests. This I seriously considered for my Indiana course. I finally discarded the idea because I felt that I could not handle it, let alone the students. We do have available some good translations of texts: the *Wen Fu* of Lu Chi, various Sanskrit texts, some Japanese ones, and the Arabic *I'jāz al-Qu'rān* of al-Bāqillāni, translated by von Grunebaum in 1950.

Finally, comparative fiction is a subject of interest to many students and it could be used as the material for an investigation of fiction theory. We have several Chinese fiction classics in good translation, Irwin's book on the *Shui-hu chuan* (*All Men Are Brothers*) and Bishop's on the *Colloquial Short Story,* as well as Bishop's article "The Limitations of Chinese Fiction" in *Far Eastern Quarterly.* For the *Genji* we have a variety of good materials—as much as is available on Seami—when we include Lady Murasaki's *Diary,* the *Pillow-Book* of her contemporary Sei Shōnagon, and the study of Beaujard, to give us the literary background.

Modern fiction is also a rich field, and probably more interesting for an undergraduate course, but Japan is likely to overshadow both China and India on the reading list and the material may be only superficially easier to prepare—we have poorer background materials for it and may approach it with overconfidence. Needless to say, a single novel or play might be introduced into a conventional genre or "Great Books" course. Concerning this, another point must be made about the relationship of the Asian material to the administration of the course. If we are to use Asian material in sophomore-level required courses, we must have adequate aids available for the teacher, because some of the teachers will be reluctant to use it and many of the students in required courses are reluctant to read anything. But only through such introductions to Asian literature can we hope to feed elective courses.

In the University of Utopia there will be one Department of Languages and Literature and the Japanologist will be officed side by side with colleagues in French, Classics, and English. He will be briefed by his colleagues in the German Department as to what to do with *Faust* and the sophomore mind, and he will prepare the *Genji* for them. But even at this institution there will be courses like Archibald MacLeish's at Harvard: this treats just four poets, three Western ones and Li Po. While it is true that Mr. MacLeish operates at what may be described as the T'ang dynasty poetry center of the world, his interest in Li Po is certainly not narrowly comparative, and perhaps not comparative in any orthodox sense of the term. His course has in common with my own just one thing: we are teaching what we want to teach without direct regard for filling gaps in the program, or giving the students material which will increase their marketability in the academic world, or preparing them for a well-adjusted career in business. But here the comparison must end, for Mr. MacLeish is a creative writer and an original critic.

When I left Indiana I allowed to the powers there that my course, in theory at least, was a very good one, but that this kind of course ought occasionally to be taught by a critic with original ideas like Kenneth Burke. So far as I know, this view has not yet reached Mr. Burke, who may well have other plans, but it is a consummation devoutly to be wished. More courses need to be taught by all of us, but also we must persuade our best critics to look East by the range of our scholarship and by pressure from other courses including especially the lower division ones. Examples from Asian literature must occur readily to the literary critic if we are ever to have a truly unprovincial criticism.

ARTHUR DANTO

Oriental Humanities
and the Non-Orientalist

The demand for general education courses dealing with the
Orient is certain to exceed the supply of trained Orientalists available
to service them; and increasing numbers of non-Orientalists must accordingly be recruited to assist in this work. What I wish to discuss
in this paper are some of the difficulties the non-Orientalist must encounter when he undertakes to teach an Oriental Humanities course.
In part, what I have to say derives from my own experience as a
member of a staff offering such a course, but I mean to state these
difficulties with sufficient generality to avoid speaking in the mode of
autobiography.[1] So I shall first try to approach these problems in the
context in which they apparently arise, namely the system of specialization which prevails in a university, and the certainly well-founded
belief that mastery of a learned discipline is at least a necessary condition for effective teaching in that discipline. I shall then seek to show
that what I regard as the chief difficulties are not exclusively a func-

Arthur Danto is Assistant Professor of Philosophy, at Columbia University.

[1] Strictly speaking, I have done this course in cooperation with at least one specialist each time. Typically, I have worked with a Sanskritist on Indian material,
a Sinologist on Chinese material, etc. And this tandem conduct of the course goes
a long way towards mitigating a number of the difficulties I mention in this paper.
But since not every school which desires a course of this sort will have the benefit
of an Orientalist's service, I have sought to make my remarks general enough to
cover all cases. One thing which struck me very forcibly at the conference was the
variety of problems which different institutions are obliged to face, so that neither
the syllabus nor the system of staffing used at Columbia can be expected to suit every
need.

tion of that system and belief. For the difficulties I have in mind arise out of this system and belief in conjunction with another less tangible factor. Now, if this "extra factor" does in fact give rise to these difficulties, then, I shall argue, they cannot be resolved. But, if this "extra factor" does not give rise to them in conjunction with this system and belief, then, I shall argue, such difficulties as this system and belief alone give rise to are neither very important nor very damaging.

There is an item in the unwritten code of academic ethics which disapproves of an individual working outside the boundaries of his own field of special research. But this negative injunction is both understandable and sound. The amount of skill and information which must be achieved in order to know what are the problems in a given field, and more important, to know what sorts of answers are to count as solutions to these problems, makes it effectively unlikely that any person, however otherwise competent, will be better than a dilettante in any field save his own. Dilettantism, however, runs very much counter to the standards of professionalism it is essential for the academic man to uphold. Allegiance to the same professional standards more or less guarantees a uniform and high level of capacity and performance in each department of learning. And this, in turn, more or less guarantees that the general academic goal of discovering truth is being everywhere maximally pursued. To be sure, each of us realizes that the cellular structure of modern inquiry is not without its disadvantages, social and otherwise. But in the end, I think, too much can be said in favor of the system to countenance its abrogation, even in individual cases.

I refer to the ethics of professional sovereignty because our work as teachers is often at variance with it. If the system of instruction were altogether consistent with the system of specialized research, we would, as teachers, transmit the equipment of our respective disciplines to just those who have elected to serve the disciplines we profess. This is at best the ideal of the graduate school: at lower levels we not merely teach those who have no intention of entering our specialty, but often we find ourselves teaching subjects we have no *professional* license to consider at all. Though not everyone can accept this latter fact with equanimity, it at least suggests that there are competing obligations, and that assenting to the proposition "Training in a discipline is a necessary condition for working in it" need not entail assent to "Training in a discipline is a necessary condition for teaching in it."

But this would seem absurd, given the very conditions which make specialization so crucial in the first place. If it is not in fact absurd, this is because there is a special sense of "teaching" in terms of which it is allowable to discuss with students subjects which fall outside the range of one's special competence, and a special sort of course in which this can be done. The predominance of the general education course indicates, then, that we subscribe to rather a wider ideal of education than the ethics of specialization would appear to sanction.

Even so, there are bound to be tensions between the two orders of enterprise. Since no one could hope to have mastery over all the material which even the least ambitious of such courses must contain, anyone with professional standards must sometimes be haunted by an uneasy conscience, for there is something very nearly irresponsible in this sort of teaching, particularly in view of the wide range and rapid pace exacted by the syllabus. And lacking the kind of control over the material which we would minimally demand of a co-professional, we cannot but feel that we may be prey to the apparent truth and liable only to perpetuate our own confusion and misinformation.

Moreover, the student who takes these courses is exposed to the risk of not being able to discriminate between a superficial familiarity with, and a critical understanding of the very works—the Great Books—which require the most arduous intellectual application. These problems happen to be epidemic, so discussion of them is hardly called for here. I allude to them only to frame the context in which the question before us arises: is there any special incompetence which uniquely disqualifies the non-Orientalist from teaching in these courses? Most of the disqualifications I can think of fall into two main classes.

1. *Invincible provincialism.* Sometimes the problem of getting to know traditions (cultures) other than our own is conceived of as on a logical footing with the philosophical problem of Other Minds. One may set up either problem in such a way that solution of it is logically impossible, but presumably a milder version of the issue is intended. Analogously with the way protracted familiarity with behavior of an individual person gives one a special authority to pronounce on his feelings, motives, and intentions, prolonged exposure to another tradition allows one to comprehend its vagaries in a way normally closed off to the alien. One can, so to speak, become vicariously *chez soi.* But this is just what the non-Orientalist is unable to do. And this makes all the difference between teaching in a humanities course, every work in which stems from one's own tradition, and teaching in a similar course where all the books are from another tradition. There may indeed be differences between, say, the plays of Sophocles, Shakespeare, and Shaw. Still, all of them belong to one large tradition, the major lines and elements of which would automatically be accessible to those who natively dwell in the tradition they collectively exemplify. So, the argument runs, the difficulties of passing into a wholly alien tradition are different in kind from those encountered in passing from segment to segment within a single tradition. The non-Orientalist is provincial, and owing to the professional commitments which prevent his doing further professional work in a different discipline, he is invincibly so.

To this a number of small rejoinders might be made. First, it widens the gap between East and West by unrealistically narrowing the spiritual distance between the near and remote phases of the latter. But secondly, it imposes a specious unity on both. For in fact, the distances between China, India, and Islam are scarcely easier to compass than the distance between any one of them and Christendom. Surely it is only by dint of geographical nomenclature that the Eastern cultures are lumped together; and the argument, if carried through, would make the Sanskritist as invincibly provincial with respect to Japan, say, as the Westerner is with respect to India. Yet, the very same factors of supply-and-demand which might drive a Sanskritist to discuss the *Pillow Book of Sei Shonagon* and pre-Islamic Arabic poetry are responsible for bringing the non-Orientalist into the course to begin with. But the chief objection to this manner of argument is that it seriously raises the question whether courses of this sort ought to be given at all. For unless the works in question in some sense transcend their native context, and qualify by some standard criteria as universal literature, study of them had better be left to the specialist, and courses in them given only to those who seriously propose to make orientalism a career.

To put the matter briefly, I submit that in these courses we are not interested in the immediate historical causes of these works, save to the extent that in the absence of such information the meaning of a work would be opaque. A case in point might be the Sufi poets, whose strangely erotic imagery acquires an unexpected dimension in the light of a special historical explanation. But I would insist, first, that works so illuminated must afterwards count as universal literature by virtue of some inherent merit or some transcendent message; and secondly, that unless the required information is easily acquired and applied, and the works are then discussed on their own terms, they ought to be excluded from the course.

This much of a concession seems to reintroduce the argument, however. For am I not now saying that with regard to at least certain works, only the historically informed can illuminate their meanings? To this I can only reply that the non-Orientalist would normally be expected to do some preparation beyond just reading the books. And though there is always the danger that he might grossly misinterpret certain works, this danger can be lessened by diminishing the number of works the historical understanding of which is essential to the apprehension of their meaning. It could be further lessened, if not altogether eliminated, if there were some reliable *ancilla* to the Great

Books of the East. The compilation of such a book is presently anticipated by the Columbia staff. Let me add, however, that the purpose
of the course is only incidentally to transmit reliable information
about the East. But this brings up again that special sense of "teaching" in terms of which nonspecialist participation in general education courses is licit. And since this is a general feature of *all* such
courses, it need not be justified here.

2. *Linguistic ineptitude.* Suppose it be granted that the meaning,
rather than the immediate historical causes of a work, is what is central in this kind of course. Then, it might be argued, the non-Orientalist is still in a peculiarly ill-favored position to have access to what, by
his own claim, are the most important features of the works.

For the meaning of a book is in major part a function of the language in which it is cast. Of course, a true (or false) proposition is true
(or false) independently of the fact that it is expressed by this or that
sentence of this or that natural language. And the rules of valid
inference, whether explicitly articulated by the logicians of a culture
or not, are independently binding. But the only access the non-
Orientalist has either to the propositions or arguments of an Eastern
book is through the medium of translated sentences. And, lacking
control over translation, he is necessarily insecure in his assessments.
Worse, as a piece of writing departs from simple assertion and argument, and depends instead for its force and meaning upon those
connotations to which only the linguistically apt can be sensitive, the
message which comes through to the linguistically inept is increasingly dim. Indeed, a work which is moving and even profound in its
native idiom might, for that reason alone, be too fragile to endure
transplanting into an alien speech and cadence. But the fact is, a great
many works which we must include because of the high esteem in
which their culture holds them, come dangerously close to this. The
Qur'ān, to take one example, is a book the power and beauty of which
seem destined to remain locked up with the language in which it was
delivered. How then is the non-Orientalist to overcome this barrier?

I regard this argument as very much more forceful than the one from cultural solipsism. Obviously it admits of qualification. The identical argument precludes the Sanskritist from appreciating properly the fragile essence of works written in any different Oriental language. Furthermore, unless a certain amount of the essence comes through in translation it will clearly be lost on the students, and must, whatever its merits, therefore be excluded from the course. Finally, we do have some truly superb translations, such as those made by Arthur Waley or Donald Keene. But having said so much, it seems to me both pointless and silly not to recognize the force of this argument. So I shall assume that here is a genuine obstacle to that re-creation of the spirit of the work which advocates of Great Book courses so strongly enjoin on teachers of them. Even if linguistic mastery doesn't actually guarantee that he who has it will teach these courses properly, still, lack of this mastery may go a long way toward preventing even the most sensitive of minds from doing what the logic of the course requires. The question then is to determine in what degree this argument is finally damaging. I shall try now to discuss this, but I shall do so in a somewhat perverse way. For what I want to bring out is that "extra factor" I mentioned in my opening paragraph.

Suppose the non-Orientalist concedes the force of the argument from linguistic ineptitude, and decides it is time to stop being defensive. After all, the law of supply and demand has thrust him into a position where his services are wanted, and he may reasonably ask what reward there could be for his teaching the course if the books are as inaccessible to him as all that. He is going to have to make *some* sacrifice to teach the course. Is there, in view of the argument, any point in his making it?

Consider, for the purposes of contrast, the sort of gain which the specialist might plausibly derive from giving the course. First, he has an annual opportunity to reconsider the writings which are the best and most important exemplars of the cultures he is professionally committed to understand. But he does this in the light of everything he has learned about these cultures in a year's interim, so the works are almost necessarily fresh to him each time round. At the same time, reconsideration of the works enriches his subsequent researches, partly by forcing upon him a more synoptic vision than detailed scholarship affords, partly by suggesting new ways of interpreting these details. These are genuine benefits the nonspecialist cannot hope for, inasmuch as there must, by definition, be a discontinuity between his normal researches and the reading he must do for this course. If, in addition, there is this ineradicable opacity, given his linguistic disadvantages, can there be any profit for him at all?

Well, perhaps this argument is too harsh. Even a poor translation affords a partial insight. So imagine that the non-Orientalist is reassured in the following way. Here is an opportunity for him to read some really great books he might never otherwise get to know. He can regard the whole enterprise as a lark, as an occasion for self-improvement, as a subsidy which allows him a term's immersion in *exotica*. He may then return to his wonted labors refreshed by his delinquency, and by virtue of his now being able to spice his lectures with citations from Confucius and the Upanishads, he may pass for a remarkably learned man with broad humane interests.

I think these inducements count for very little. After all, any book deserves to be read once. The question has to arise in connection with reading them at least twice, for it is here that the argument strikes me as possibly damaging. Can there be any point in his reading these books *again,* as he must do, if only for the sake of the students with whom he intends to discuss them? As the non-Orientalist goes through these works for the nth time, without enjoying the sort of internal relation which the specialist has with the work and its context, and without the linguistic wherewithal to deepen his appreciation, the reading itself stands in peril of degenerating into a ritual and a chore, and his vitality as a teacher evaporates in proportion. Obviously one can expect him each time to approach the work through the perspective of what he has meanwhile learned in his own alien field. But this sort of illumination is at best incidental, and operates by weak analogues. The work remains external to him. So where's the gain?

This picture is as bleak as the argument which stimulated it was harsh. But I mean to dramatize the fact that if one construes the problem in these terms, the answer must be: there can be no gain. And I think none of the typical inducements one might think of for reading these books once mitigate the problem of a second reading. It is true, for example, that some understanding of the traditions of the Eastern countries will afford some insight into their current outlooks and actions. But it is doubtful that periodic perusal of the sources of these traditions will enhance the insights: one had better read some economics. Again, it is true that someone might discover some novel philosophical insights. But this is hardly an incentive to read the same books over again: one had better read some philosophy, and learn how to exploit the insight. Or finally, since the books of the East are often invidiously contrasted with those of the West, roughly as wisdom is contrasted with knowledge, one might encounter, say in the *Bhagavad Gītā,* some piece of superior wisdom. But this at best stimulates a re-reading of *that* book, not all the books in the course.

One could continue in this carping vein, but the point is clear enough. If the argument from linguistic ineptitude is wholly damaging, no countervailing practical advantages will suffice to overcome it. If it seems unduly calculating to speak of the Great Books in terms of practical advantages, my only excuse is that with *these* Great Books at least, none of the normal arguments in favor of dwelling in them will do if the argument from linguistic ineptitude is finally compelling. The alternatives thus are clear. Either the argument is in fact coercive, in which case the best to be expected is a single reading of the books, or else, if there can be multiple readings without exhausting the human resources of these books, the purported disadvantages of linguistic ineptitude are not wholly damaging. Now this is not a matter to be arbitrated in a wholesale fashion. It is to be decided case by case, providing one further difficulty is recognized. And to this I shall now turn.

Let us for a moment consider the criteria which govern inclusion of books in the course. First, there are books in connection with which the question of greatness does not arise, but which have to be included come what may. If we are to discuss Islam at all, we simply have to read the Qur'ān, whatever its literary or philosophical merits. Similar reasons apply to certain of the Upanishads, the Vedas, the *Bhagavad Gītā,* the *Lotus Sūtra,* the *Analects,* and a handful of others. These books would be uneliminable even if their intrinsic merit were null. Secondly, there are books which are perhaps not so overwhelmingly central in the structure and development of an Eastern culture, but which the culture itself happens to regard as possessing intrinsic merit. These contain, so to speak, the self-image of a culture, and exhibit what it thinks important and meaningful. I suppose the *Rāmāyana* and the plays of Kālidāsa would fall in this class, together with the *Forty-Seven Ronin,* the *Assemblies of Al-Hariri,* and a great deal of poetry. Even though no one would be tempted to honor Shakespeare by recommending him as the Kālidāsa of England, these books too are indispensable. Thirdly, there is a class of writings which are included because we have a prior schema regarding what different *kinds* of books represent any culture whatsoever.

Suppose, for instance, that a culture is to be represented by the following kinds of books: poetry, drama, fiction, philosophy, and sacred writings; and we decide there must be some of each kind of book for every culture we study. Then we might include works of negligible intrinsic merit, merely because they are the best or most representative work which a given culture has produced of a required kind. *The Romance of the Western Chamber* is a good example of a work which may be included by default, on the grounds that we want a Chinese drama. Finally, there are works we would include no matter what their culture thought of them, no matter if their historical importance were null, simply because they are great. The *Tale of Genji* and the *Dream of the Red Chamber* are examples of this.

A partition along these lines of the collection of books we read in the course would be neither exhaustive nor exclusive. Some works will be included for other reasons than these, and some works will be included for all the reasons I have mentioned. But I think the course will compensate the non-Orientalist for his efforts in proportion to the number of works there are of the last kind—Great Books in the truest sense. And I shall flatly declare that on this score the course is rewarding.

But now let us look at the matter in terms of the context of professionalism within which I began to set the problem. The non-Orientalist is not, after all, sheerly a dabbler in *allerlei wissenschaft*. He is a professional in his own right, has his own problems, tries to contribute to their solution, etc. In the common course of things he is obliged to read a great deal in connection with this. Because he is an educated person, he doubtless reads many things beyond what is professionally required. And amongst this extracurricular reading are apt to be some of the Great Books, so-called. These are read, of course, for no ulterior reasons, but only to satisfy the spirit's appetite. Yet there are so many Great Books, for all their statistical rarity, that one has hardly the time in a lifetime of reading to get through all of them once, much less read many of them twice. A Great Book is one of which it is categorically true that it can sustain and repay multiple readings. But what kind of an argument can we give for re-reading a special sub-set of the Great Books, particularly in view of the linguistic obstacles which block complete penetration into them? Or, even if the notion of complete penetration is meaningless with books of this order, even if the obstacle is set far enough back so that one might still enter them to a considerable depth, why these books rather than others? The arguments in favor of choosing a Great Book over books of other kinds break down when it is a question of choosing among the Great Books themselves. The man who re-reads such a sub-set annually is then making a sacrifice in terms not merely of time he might devote to his professional interests, but of time he might devote to reading or re-reading other Great Books. And this I regard as the chief difficulty.

There is no general way of meeting this difficulty, no convincing argument which can be given. And certainly none of the arguments which might lead a man to read these books just once, to teach this course just once. It finally becomes a matter of a man's private preference scale, the way he thinks to draw his own indifference curve. And this is the intangible factor to which I first referred. Providing one has, for whatever reason, a certain sympathy for these books and for the ideas they embody, a certain affection for the way of life and thought one finds in them, then they will be repeatedly rewarding, and such other difficulties as might arise are of no great import. That is what I have tried to show. I cannot claim to have *proved* it. But I have meant to suggest that this is not a matter which admits of proof.

GEORGE K. BRADY

Comments

This conference has been an inspiring experience, I am sure, for many of us who come from schools where a knowledge of Oriental matters has only recently been introduced. We have listened with due humility while the specialists told us what we should offer our students from the multitude of masterpieces from Oriental literature, and why and how they should be presented. As one of the humblest of the listeners, I am impressed with the high level, almost idealistic, discussion of the speakers. But certain practical considerations constantly encroach on my thinking.

It seems to me that little consideration has been given to the type of student who might take such Oriental courses as could be offered. It makes a great deal of difference whether the masterpieces are taught in the sophomore, junior, or senior year, or even in graduate courses. And in addition, much depends on the general cultural background of the students at any level. Some schools draw the bulk of their students from homes where culture, in the form of an interest in literature, art, and music, is commonplace. Many of these students have been abroad before going to college and have more cosmopolitan interests. But this is not a universal situation, and many of us are not blessed with such inspiring students.

As an illustration of this point, I take my own course, "Aspects of Oriental Culture" offered in our Humanities general education work at Kentucky. It is a two-hour, strictly elective course for one semester.

George K. Brady is Professor of English at the University of Kentucky.

The time limit was forced upon it by the general setup of our Humanities schedule, and the fact that the students have very limited free hours to expend on electives. It is offered at a popular hour to attract students who resist being inconvenienced. Some of the students are quite Midwest provincials and have no keen interest in the world at large. But they have a schedule to fill out and these two hours are almost manna from heaven for that purpose. If the word ever got around that the course demanded some heavy reading, I feel sure that whatever pull this schedule-filling convenience might have would disappear, and the course might die on the vine. As it is, the maximum registration for any term has been twenty-five, and this fall it has dropped to eight, the lowest in the three years since the work was introduced.

The answer to this situation is quite simple. Make the course a requirement for graduation. But even if this were desirable, it is certainly not feasible. The established vested interests would defeat the move as an encroachment on their preserves. They can point to the fact that the student already has an over-crowded required schedule for graduation, and too few electives as a result. The faculty even resisted allowing this course to serve as a substitute for any of the other required humanities courses. When we instituted the general education humanities program, we agreed on a minimum of Western cultural material necessary for a balanced college education, and to substitute anything else now would be to deprive the student of part of his heritage. Thus did the sages reason. Getting these Oriental courses accepted by the faculty and established among the students is not achieved by any waving of a magic wand.

The second reflection which troubled me during the course of the conference was the idealistic conception that no aspect of Oriental culture should be taught except by an Oriental specialist. This supersonic idealism has received some rather rough treatment during the conference, and I was not too much disturbed by the extreme view delivered so eloquently early in the conference. The whole concept was in general unrealistic. These new developments in general education cost money. In many schools you will be fortunate, indeed, if you have a dean or other administrator with vision enough to see the value of this Oriental development. They are beset by demands on limited funds, and there is little chance they will import an Oriental specialist where the demand is largely experimental. If he does not draw more than eight students from a body of 8,000, he might have to neglect his specialty for more general duties. But in all probability he will never be employed until local talent (good, bad, or indifferent) has established a field for him. This is the simplest of economic considerations.

A third reflection has developed in my mind as the conference progressed, and this has to do with the content of such courses as a smaller school could offer in the field. Since the conference was limited by its call to a consideration of literary masterpieces, and since the chairmen of the sessions (quite commendably) did not encourage extensive digressions, the problem as to whether such a course should be organized on lines other than the Great Books approach never arose.

During the past ten years I have read either the whole or large parts of most of the great works discussed at the meeting. Many of these works seem to me to be too difficult for the majority of our undergraduates. Furthermore, in a semester or a year course they still spread the student too thin to give him any useable understanding of the Oriental mind or the culture of the Oriental gentleman. When I faced the practical decision of what to include, I decided to concentrate student attention on a restricted area. Professor Anderson would quickly point out that this was due originally to my own limited contacts with the Orient, and in part this is true. But during the three years of teaching, my readings have rapidly expanded my own vision and grasp, and yet today I would still concentrate the attention of the student pretty much as I have in the past.

I do this on the theory that he knows so little to begin with about Orientalism that he cannot understand or grasp Asian forces in the lump or literature as a cultural achievement unless he knows something of the religious, philosophic, artistic, and social background of the work. He will read the *haiku* with very little appreciation unless he knows something of Buddhism and the whole Oriental attitude toward nature. Or the story of the Forty-Seven Ronin with its wholesale suicide at the end will strike the Bible Belt Baptist as an arrogant defiance of Divine law if he has not been informed about the Oriental concept of harakiri, and even then he is liable to think of the tale as something worse than melodrama. Professor Moore, of the University of Hawaii, insists that the only way to grasp the Oriental mind is by studying its philosophy. Professor Anderson is equally and eloquently determined that it can only be done by the literary approach. As the least of the voices crying in the wilderness, I would insist that the great landscape painters of China and Japan will help to open the doors for the sensitive and perceptive mind. But then none of us is or can be talking about the average American Midwestern undergraduate.

And one final reflection I am moved to record. The term "workshop" is pretty well worn, but the idea is still sound. Would it not be helpful if some school qualified to do so could organize an extensive summer workshop to help those who may be forced to rush in where angels fear to tread? If this movement to introduce Oriental courses is actually "spreading like wildfire across the land" the demand for teachers should be far outstripping the supply. Only a school which could obtain the backing of some big foundation could afford to undertake such a program. My guess is that it would have to be one of the larger Eastern schools, although I believe both Michigan and North Carolina have recently attempted this in the past few years. The idea might be worth consideration. At least two other people at the conference expressed very much this idea in my presence, and for this reason I am encouraged to pass it along.

CLARK S. MARLOR

Comments

Many teachers are not as fortunate as Professor Anderson, of New York University, who was given carte blanche in the selection and organization of the material in the comparative literature course which he taught this summer. There are occasions when the nonspecialist must deal with Oriental literature because of the particular circumstances in which he is placed.

The college where I teach does not have a department of Oriental specialists and yet I, for one, believe that as a teacher I am responsible "to lift the corner," as one of the previous speakers said, in order that students may glimpse Oriental literature. In a course entitled Advanced Oral Interpretation (oral interpretation is a fancy name for training in reading aloud effectively to others) I encourage students to bring Oriental literature to class and to read it before the others. As a result, we have heard Japanese and Chinese folk tales, Japanese *haiku* and Chinese poetry. The class has found this contact rewarding.

The predominant use of Chinese and Japanese literature was due to the fact that a great deal of material was available in comparatively inexpensive editions which students could easily obtain. Students would use other Oriental literature if it were available in inexpensive editions such as paperback books. Our library funds are limited and I do not think these funds can be spent on building a small collection of Oriental literature. It seems to me that a group of the type that is

Clark S. Marlor is Assistant Professor of Speech and Drama at Adelphi College.

meeting here might give serious consideration to authoritative translations in anthology form which could be purchased by students in comparatively inexpensive editions. Thus it is conceivable that a cross section of one type of literature, such as Oriental drama, or folk tales or lyric poetry, or a cross section of the literature of one country, such as Indian drama, Indian folk tales, and Indian poetry, could be anthologized. The work of introducing students to Oriental literature, by the teachers who are convinced of the importance of this work, could be greatly expanded if such anthologies were available.

As a further example of the circumstances in which the nonspecialists must deal with Oriental literature, I cite my own particular area of specialization in drama. It is inconceivable that a course in world drama would not treat the classic plays in India, China, and Japan. To omit some coverage of the drama from these three Eastern countries would certainly negate the very title of the course.

There is another occasion when the drama specialist must treat Oriental literature. This occasion arises in any college drama department which produces a number of plays during an academic year. If the department does not wish to be a mere copy of Broadway, and offer only repeats of Broadway plays, the inevitable decision involves the selection and production of plays from many countries and covering a variety of historical periods as well as styles of production. Oriental plays would therefore be included.

The drama-faculty person who directs an Oriental play accepts the responsibility of directing the play with the thought that here is a play to which he responds sympathetically and for which he will do his utmost to assure a sensitive projection. He therefore approaches the play with a great deal of humility and sets about the task of reading and consulting with authoritative sources to steep himself in the very essence of the play.

There would be more productions of Oriental plays if they were readily available. For years I have wanted to direct a production of *The Little Clay Cart.* Unfortunately I have not been able to find a good translation that has present-day production possibilities. The translation by Ryder, which was produced in the 1920s, seems dated and too precious with its jog-trot rhymes. What is needed is more up-to-date translation with production possibilities. Here is an area where the drama and Oriental specialists could work together.

Since much of the Oriental literature is part of that vast area of "oral-aural literature" the teacher must be able to read aloud effectively in English. This requires an ability to project the thought as well as the emotion of the particular selection; otherwise several very important aspects, involving idea, emotion, and beauty of sound, will be lost. Many teachers are not equipped to do an effective job on these aspects because of lack of experience and training. Although the speech teacher is a nonspecialist in Oriental literature, nevertheless, because of his training in oral reading, he is well equipped to handle at least these aspects of the literature better even than some specialists.

Synopsis of Discussion: Final Session

Yu-kuang Chu, speaking of general education in a small college, agreed at the outset that there is no standard course. Each school must shape its course according to the enthusiasm and competence of the instructor, the resources of the school, the level of the students, and other factors. The small colleges, though they have, of course, a great debt to Columbia, Harvard, and other big universities for the materials and help they provide, must make their own choices and decisions.

Secondly, Mr. Chu said, a number of apparently opposing views that have been stated in the conference are really complementary. Many of them have had to do with the question of the historical versus the contemporary approach. He had met, he said, two different attitudes among his students which required these different approaches. The first he called the attitude of "under-expectation." The student, considering Asia backward, expected its books to be backward too. By emphasizing the contemporary relevance of the books, Mr. Chu said, he could sometimes surprise and interest such students. The other attitude was the over-expectation attitude, in which the student expected the wise men of the East to offer everything that modern writers did, and then, for example, criticized Confucius for not having thought of government by the people. The antidote for that, Mr. Chu found, was the historical and cultural approach.

The technical and cultural approaches were, in a broad sense, also reconcilable. Mr. Anderson mentioned critical scholarship and a technical, literary viewpoint. That, Mr. Chu suggested, would be excellent for graduate students of literature. For the undergraduate, however, it might be less useful than the cultural approach. At Skidmore, for example, he taught a course on Asia through art, in which objects of art introduced cultural background. Bronzes served as a window for ancestor worship, nature worship, and so forth. Why not approach literature, he asked, in the same way, as an excellent vehicle for the life and thought of a people?

Consideration of the small college evoked comments on the difficulties of introducing Oriental subjects into the curriculum. The Chairman thought that Mr. Anderson may have underestimated the number of available Orientalists who are willing to teach standard undergraduate courses, offering their own specialties as extras. Mr. de Bary knew of such specialists, too, who had not found jobs. He said that the problem was not only one of bringing good men into the schools, but also of finding jobs for available men. Mr. Anderson explained that his point had been not that the specialist was reluctant to teach, but that the administration was often reluctant to hire him. The budget was the problem.

Another obstacle, John E. Blewett observed, is the already heavy program required of some students. So much concentration on education courses is required of prospective public school teachers, in particular, that there is little room in such a program for a new substantive course. The Chairman said that several professional associations have been formed to look into the imbalance of the education curriculum. The references to public education suggested to Mr. Winder that the possibility of introducing Oriental material into high school curricula should not be overlooked. On that, too, the Chairman said, a little work, at least in a negative sense, was done three years ago when an effort was made to correct mistakes about the Orient in textbooks. He reminded those interested in finding aids for the teaching of Oriental subjects in small colleges of UNESCO's activities in the field. When it was suggested that foreign visitors might be of help, he mentioned that information of that sort might be had from the China Institute, Asia Society, Japan Society, and the Department of State.

There is good reason to believe, Walter G. Langlois felt, that the amateur has a role in the program. A non-Orientalist himself, he was introducing into the curriculum at Boston College an honors course that he would describe as an example of what he meant. The enrollment in the course would be limited, he said, to a small number of sophomores of high I.Q. In the second semester, which is the one to deal with Eastern civilizations, the class will meet for two hours a week for fourteen weeks. Japan, China, India, and the Islamic world are to be the regions considered. Believing that philosophy, literature, and art are three of the great disciplines for seeking truth, he intends to introduce the students to a selection of works in those fields, his choice to depend on his own interests and training. In the sessions on Japan, for example, he will assign the *Tale of Genji,* Langdon Warner's *The Enduring Art of Japan,* and one of Suzuki's books on Zen Buddhism. He realizes that these books will not give his students a well-balanced view of Japan; that is not his aim. He wants to form their critical apparatus, not merely to give them knowledge; and to implant in them his own interest and enthusiasm. The success of a television series he recently did, discussing some of the same books, reinforces his belief that the course can be enjoyable and informative.

What he is doing is an example, Langlois felt, of the service amateurs can perform. They can reach people the professionals have not the time, or even perhaps the language, to reach. The amateurs, needless to say, depend heavily on the professionals, yet in the long run, he concluded, the amateurs may determine how well the professionals perpetuate their race.

Miss Hahn suspected that the specialist could be as enthusiastic as Mr. Langlois implied the amateur was. If, however, she said, the amateurs are so enthusiastic, she would offer a compromise. Let them put their energy, if only for a year, into a study of the rudiments of the language their books were written in. That would help. Not really, Mr. Danto felt. In the first place, studying Chinese or Sanskrit for only a year is not useful. Secondly, there would be too many languages to study. Mr. Anderson observed that doing the kind of work in question, the amateur inevitably develops some interest in the language, at least in its structure and other characteristics.

The matter of a year's special training having come up, Allan B. Cole pointed out that a year's course of study of Asian subjects for nonspecialists is offered at Harvard. The Chairman suggested that anyone planning to take such a course acquire beforehand a written agreement from his superiors that he will not, from then on, be considered a specialist. Otherwise, he said, the man is likely to be made responsible for courses he feels incompetent to teach, and the hiring of a qualified man might be delayed. It should also be noted, Mr. Langlois said, that such study by amateurs is in the nature of a gift on their part, since it does not further their careers.

Listening to the discussion of nonspecialists and their roles, Mr. de Bary said, it had occurred to him that there are two types of nonspecialist. One, like Mr. Langlois, has little preparation himself and hopes to prepare the way for Oriental studies by his enthusiasm. The serious interest so aroused in students may create a need for a specialist, and progress may come about that way. The other is like Mr. Danto. Working alongside Mr. Danto, a professional philosopher, he had learned much from him. Were Mr. Danto to stay with the course, he might want to learn Chinese, as Miss Hahn proposed, but would that be desirable? The non-Orientalist tends to bring to the subject a fresh approach and to see things from the viewpoint of the students, as the specialist sometimes fails to do. Even with a specialist at hand, therefore, a non-Orientalist has a function. In other words, the non-Orientalist need not be thought of as a complete nonspecialist—he has his own special equipment to offer, though he may also have certain limitations which it is his duty to make clear to the students.

In a final comment on the question of the specialist and nonspecialist, Mr. Borton said the dichotomy so made was more superficial than real. The problem was one: to understand humanity in Asia. Everyone approached the problem in his own way. What delighted the specialist was that so many people were doing so.

JOHN T. MESKILL

Appendix

George L. Abernethy, Department of Philosophy, Davidson College; George L. Anderson, Department of Comparative Literature, New York University; Robert Antoine, S.J., Xavier College, Calcutta; Sister Mary Aquinas, Department of English, Rosary College; George Artola, Baltimore, Maryland; George N. Atiyeh, Department of Humanities, University of Puerto Rico; Victor F. Ayoub, Department of Anthropology, Antioch College.

Charles C. Bagg, Department of History, Reed College; Samuel H. Baron, Department of History, Grinnell College; Russell H. Barrett, Department of Political Science, University of Mississippi; Harry J. Benda, Department of History, University of Rochester; Thomas Berry, C.P., Far Eastern Institute, Seton Hall University; Angelo P. Bertocci, Professor of Comparative Literature, Boston University; John E. Blewett, S.J., Sophia Univ., Tokyo; Isabel St. John Bliss, Chairman, Department of English, Western College for Women; Ahmed Bokhári, Under-Secretary of the United Nations, New York; Peter A. Boodberg, Department of Oriental Languages, University of California (Berkeley); Hugh Borton, President, Haverford College; Richard S. Bowman, Professor of Comparative Literature, Cooper Union; George K. Brady, Department of English, University of Kentucky; Sister Mary Brian, Department of English, Rosary College; W. Norman Brown, Department of Oriental Studies, University of Pennsylvania; Burr C. Brundage, Chairman, Department of History, Cedar Crest College; Harry M. Buck, Jr., Department of Biblical History, Wellesley College; George B. Burch, Department of Philosophy, Tufts University.

Elsie A. Carrillo, Department of History, Marymount College; Wing-tsit Chan, Professor of Chinese Culture and Philosophy, Dartmouth College; John W. Chandler, Department of Religion, Williams College; Shih-chuan Chen, Georgian Court College; Sister Mary Chrysostom, Department of English, College of Mount Saint Vincent; Samuel C. Chu, Department of History, Bucknell University; Yu-kuang Chu, Department of Oriental Studies, Skidmore College; W. Norris Clarke, S.J., Department of Philosophy, Fordham University; Allan B. Cole, Curator, Fellowships in East Asian Studies, Harvard University; Paul F. Cressey, Department of Economics and Sociology, Wheaton College; James I. Crump, Jr., Asian Studies Committee, University of Michigan.

Taraknath Das, Taraknath Das Foundation, New York City; Charles E. Diviney, Chairman, Department of Theology, St. Joseph's College for Women.

A. Roy Eckardt, Head, Department of Religion, Lehigh University.

Walter R. Fee, Head, Department of History, Michigan State University; Louis Feldman, Department of Classical Languages, Yeshiva University; Yi-tse Mei Feuerwerker, Cambridge, Massachusetts; Murray Fowler, Department of Linguistics, University of Wisconsin; Sister Mary Francis, Department of English, College of Mount Saint Vincent.

Edwin N. Garlan, Department of Philosophy, Reed College; William J. Gedney, Professor of Literature, State University Teachers College, New Paltz, N.Y.; William C. Green, Department of Humanities, Massachusetts Institute of Technology; Charles C. Griffin, Department of History, Vassar College.

Roger F. Hackett, Department of History, Northwestern University; George G. Hackman, Department of Religion, Wagner College; E. Adelaide Hahn, Chairman, Department of Classics, Hunter College; Lucien M. Hanks, Jr., Bennington College; Harry Harootunian, Department of History, Pennsylvania State University; Howard Hibbett, Department of Oriental Languages, University of California (L.A.); Knox Hill, Editor, Journal of General Education, University of Chicago; Robert E. Hosack, Head, Department of Social Sciences, University of Idaho; Charles M. Hudson, Chairman, Department of English, University of Missouri; Shirley D. Hudson, American Council of Learned Societies, New York City; Hu Shih, Academia Sinica, Taipei, Taiwan.

K. D. Irani, City College of New York.

Lt. Col. James L. Jackson, USAF, Department of English, United States Air Force Academy; Irmgard Johnson, Department of Humanities, University of Florida; Norman B. Johnson, Department of Religion, Union College.

Melville T. Kennedy, Jr., Department of Political Science, Bryn Mawr College; Ben Kimpel, Department of English, University of Arkansas; Charles Kirby, Department of English, Saint Peter's College; Jonathan H. Kistler, Department of English, Colgate University; Hyman Kublin, Department of History, Brooklyn College.

Walter G. Langlois, Department of Romance Languages, Boston College; Edward E. LeClair, Jr., Department of Psychology and Anthropology, Rensselaer Polytechnic Institute; Edwin B. Lee, Department of History, Hamilton College; Harold O. Lewis, Department of History, Howard University; C. J. Liu, Department of Humanities, University of Florida; James T. C. Liu, Department of History, University of Pittsburgh; Jessie Lutz, Department of History and Political Science, Douglass College.

Charles MacSherry, Hillyer Art Gallery, Smith College; Muhsin Mahdi, The Oriental Institute, University of Chicago; Margaret Mahoney, Carnegie Corporation of New York, New York City; Sister Loyola Maria, Chestnut Hill College; Clark S. Marlor, Speech Department, Adelphi College; James A. Martin, Jr., Department of Philosophy and Religion, Amherst College; Yi-pao Mei, Department of Oriental Studies, State University of Iowa; John D. Mitchell, New York City; Poon-Kan Mok, Department of History, Occidental College; Ward Morehouse, Educational Director, The Asia Society, New York City; Frederick S. Mote, Department of Oriental Studies, Princeton University; Ernest P. Muller, Division of the Social Sciences—History, Bates College.

Richard H. Nolte, The Rockefeller Foundation, New York City; Patricia Nonnenmacher, Department of Foreign Languages, Montana State University.

Douglas Overton, The Japan Society, New York City.

Bernard Phillips, Chairman, Department of Philosophy, University of Delaware; F. W. Poos, Department of History and Languages, United States Merchant Marine Academy.

Peter M. Reed, Asian Studies, Sarah Lawrence College; Edwin O. Reischauer, Department of Far Eastern Languages, Harvard University; Kenneth Rexroth, San Francisco, California; John F. Richardson, Humanities Department, Stevens Institute of Technology; Richard C. Rowland, Department of English, Sweet Briar College.

Harold Shadick, Department of Far Eastern Studies, Cornell University; Otis H. Shao, Department of Political Science, Moravian College; Herman L. Sinaiko, Department of Oriental Languages and Literature, University of Chicago; C. Jay Smith, Jr., Department of History, University of Georgia; H. Daniel Smith, Department of Bible and Religion, Syracuse University; Harold B. Smith, Department of Religion, The College of Wooster; Robert G. Smith, Department of Political Science, Drew University; William H. Stahl, Department of Classics and World Literature, Brooklyn College; Capt. Joseph R. Stauffer, Department of History, United States Military Academy; Wendell C. Stone, Department of Philosophy, Rollins College; James E. Swain, Chairman, Department of History, Muhlenberg College; David E. Swift, Wesleyan University; Boleslaw Szczesniak, Department of History, University of Notre Dame.

Ssu-yü Teng, Department of History, Indiana University; Mary F. Thelen, Department of Religion, Randolph-Macon Woman's College; Ronald B. Thompson, Department of History, George Washington University; Henry J. Tobias, Department of History, Elmira College.

J. A. B. Van Buitenen, Department of Linguistics, University of Chicago; Charles F. Virtue, Department of Philosophy, University of Maine.

Sister Maria Walburg, Department of Classics, Chestnut Hill College; William S. Weedon, Corcoran Department of Philosophy, University of Virginia; Hellmut Wilhelm, Far Eastern and Russian Institute, University of Washington; Lea E. Williams, Department of Political Science, Brown University; R. Bayly Winder, Department of Oriental Studies, Princeton University.

A. E. Zucker, Chairman, Department of Foreign Languages, University of Maryland.

COLUMBIA UNIVERSITY

Jacques Barzun, Dean of the Faculties and Provost of Columbia University
Lyman Bryson, Professor Emeritus of Education, Teachers College
Arthur Danto, Assistant Professor of Philosophy
Wm. Theodore de Bary, Associate Professor of Chinese and Japanese
A. T. Embree, Instructor in Indian History
Horace L. Friess, Professor of Philosophy
L. Carrington Goodrich, Dean Lung Professor of Chinese
James Gutmann, Executive Officer, Department of Philosophy
Moses Hadas, Jay Professor of Greek
John A. Hutchison, Professor of Religion
Arthur Jeffery, Professor of Semitic Languages
Donald Keene, Associate Professor of Japanese
Howard Linton, Librarian, East Asiatic Collections
Maan Madina, Assistant Professor of Modern Arabic
John Meskill, Assistant Professor of Chinese and Japanese
John G. Palfrey, Dean of Columbia College
Ichiro Shirato, Lecturer in Japanese
Ryusaku Tsunoda, Curator, Japanese Collection, Retired
Barry Ulanov, Assistant Professor of English, Barnard College
Mark Van Doren, Professor of English
Chi-chen Wang, Professor of Chinese
Herschel Webb, Instructor in Chinese and Japanese
Royal W. Weiler, Assistant Professor of Sanskrit
C. Martin Wilbur, Professor of Chinese History

COLUMBIA COLLEGE COMMITTEE ON ORIENTAL STUDIES (*Conference Committee*)

Arthur Danto
Wm. Theodore de Bary, Chairman
A. T. Embree
Donald Keene
Maan Madina
John Meskill
Royal W. Weiler
Eileen J. Boecklen, Administrative Assistant

TRANSLATIONS FROM THE ORIENTAL CLASSICS
PREPARED FOR THE COLUMBIA COLLEGE PROGRAM

WM. THEODORE DE BARY, EDITOR

Major Plays of Chikamatsu, tr. Donald Keene	1961
Records of the Grand Historian of China, translated from the Shih chi *of Ssu-ma Ch'ien*, tr. Burton Watson 2 vols.	1961
Instructions for Practical Living and Other Neo-Confucian Writings by Wang Yang-ming, tr. Wing-tsit Chan	1963
The Mahābhārata, tr. Chakravarthi V. Narasimhan	1965
The Manyōshū, Nippon Gakujutsu Shinkōkai edition	1965
Su Tung-p'o: Selections from a Sung Dynasty Poet, tr. Burton Watson	1965
Reflections on Things at Hand: The Neo-Confucian Anthology, compiled by Chu Hsi and Lü Tsu-ch'ien, tr. Wing-tsit Chan	1966

IN PAPERBACK EDITIONS ONLY

Hsün Tzu: Basic Writings, tr. Burton Watson	1963
Mo Tzu: Basic Writings, tr. Burton Watson	1963
Han Fei Tzu: Basic Writings, tr. Burton Watson	1964
Chuang Tzu: Basic Writings, tr. Burton Watson	1964
Four Major Plays of Chikamatsu, tr. Donald Keene	1964

RELATED PUBLICATIONS OF THE COMMITTEE ON ORIENTAL STUDIES

Introduction to Oriental Civilizations, ed. Wm. Theodore de Bary		
Sources of Japanese Tradition 1958	Paperback ed., 2 vols.	1964
Sources of Indian Tradition 1958	Paperback ed., 2 vols.	1964
Sources of Chinese Tradition 1960	Paperback ed., 2 vols.	1964
Approaches to the Oriental Classics, ed. Wm. Theodore de Bary		1959
Early Chinese Literature, by Burton Watson		1962
Approaches to Asian Civilizations, ed. Wm. Theodore de Bary and Ainslie T. Embree		1964
A Guide to Oriental Classics, ed. Wm. Theodore de Bary and Ainslie T. Embree		1964